A Token of My Affection

Popular Cultures, Everyday Lives

Robin D.G. Kelly and Janice Radway, Editors

A Token of My Affection

BUSINESS CULTURE

Barry Shank

Columbia University Press   New York

Columbia University Press
Publishers Since 1893
New York   Chichester, West Sussex

Copyright © 2004 Columbia University Press
All rights reserved

Library of Congress Cataloging-in-Publication Data
Shank, Barry.
A token of my affection : greeting cards and American business culture / Barry Shank.
p.   cm.—(Popular cultures, everyday lives)
Includes bibliographical references and index.
ISBN 0-231-11878-3 (cloth : alk. paper)—ISBN 0-231-11879-1 (pbk. : alk. paper)
1. Greeting cards industry—United States—History.   2. Business etiquette—United
States.   3. United States—Social life and customs.   4. Consumption (Economics)—
United States.   I. Title.   II. Series.
HD9839.G73U573 2004
338.4'77455941'0973—dc22
2004041311

Columbia University Press books are printed on permanent and
durable acid-free paper.
Printed in the United States of America
c 10 9 8 7 6 5 4 3 2 1
p 10 9 8 7 6 5 4 3 2 1

To Claire, her Nana, and her Grandma

Contents

Illustrations

Figures

Acknowledgments

*T*he original set of ideas for this book came to me when I was interviewing for my first job in the American Studies program at the University of Kansas. Someone told me that it would be wise to have an idea for my second book, even though I had yet to finish my first one. But, as is my unfortunate wont, I ignored this good advice and went to Lawrence in late March 1992 completely unprepared for this standard question. It was Angel Kwolek-Folland who asked it of me during a lovely reception at the home of Beth Schultz. I don't believe that I froze for too long before answering that I was thinking of studying Hallmark. I'll never forget Angel's response: she smiled, nodded her head quickly, and immediately asked me questions about the importance and difficulties of "studying up." I had no idea at the time, however, what gentle luck had embraced me when I landed in the incredibly supportive and intellectually vibrant world of American Studies at the University of Kansas.

From before I could be even slightly articulate about this project, David Katzman and Norman Yetman were convinced of its value. They taught me how to describe it, how to identify the key ideas, how to write a book proposal, and how to link my research with my teaching. To paraphrase many of my favorite greeting cards, words could never fully express my gratitude or balance the debt I owe them for their unflinching material support and extraordinary intellectual encouragement of what has become this book. Intense conversations about ideas and feelings and ideas about feelings were the norm in and around Wescoe Hall. I am grateful for the passionate ideas of Cheryl Lester, Philip Barnard, Ann Schofield, Angel Kwolek-Folland, Iris Smith, Janet Sharistanian, Jim Carothers, Joane Nagel, Bob Antonio, Bill Tuttle,

Natalie Dykstra, Cotten Seiler, Robert Vodicka, Elizabeth Duffy, Nadine Requardt, Joel Morton, Deborah Whaley, Mary King, and Ingerlene Voosen Embry. In Mary and Ingerlene, I benefited from the most ideal research assistants this project could have. Mary had worked for American Greetings in a past life, and Ingerlene left Kansas after her master's degree in American Studies to work for Hallmark. Both turned up invaluable documents that contributed significantly to the arguments in this book. The Hall Center for the Humanities, expertly administered by Janet Crow, was an interdisciplinary home where many of the ideas in this book first received public airing. The contribution of this organization to the intellectual community at Kansas is priceless.

Luck again appeared when I moved to my new home in Comparative Studies at Ohio State University. Here I learned to swim in radical interdisciplinary waters, where fierce discussions of Deleuze or Bourdieu could shift rapidly to interrogations of the meaning of zero or the organizing strategies of the Zapatistas. I could never have predicted the amount of sheer intellectual joy that I now take for granted as a regular part of working life. I am grateful to our former chair, Chris Zacher, for allowing me time from teaching to complete early chapter drafts. Our current chair, David Horn, regularly employs his remarkably deft ability to prod us back to work without depriving us of our moments of fun. Hugh Urban not only possesses the determination of the truly driven and productive academic, but is a fabulous bandmate. Jill Lane, Smriti Srinivas, Jennifer Terry, Tom Kasulis, Rick Livingston, and Hugh Urban challenged my ideas in important ways during a departmental colloquium, helping me to see ways in which I could bring together what I had previously seen as divergent interests. Smriti Srinivas and Jill Lane insisted that I consider an alternate interpretation of several of Louis Prang's Christmas cards that resulted in a significant rethinking of chapter 2. Brian Rotman and Gene Holland inspire me to aspire still to the life of the mind, although they would probably disavow any interest in that project.

This book has benefited from the financial support of several institutions. The Hall Center for the Humanities at the University of Kansas provided an early travel grant that funded my first trip to the Bowling Green Popular Culture Library. A Humanities Research Fellowship from the same institution enabled release-time from teaching for a semester, allowing me to draft the valentine chapter. The Graduate Research Fund at the University of Kansas provided summer support for this project for three years, ensuring that regular progress in research and writing could go forward. A Research Fellowship from the Winterthur Museum, Garden, and Library allowed me a month of concentrated effort in the Joseph Downs Collection of Manuscripts and Printed Ephemera, out of which came many of the most important documents supporting my claims. Rich McKinstry and Neville Thompson made that work possible.

Finally, but actually first, there was a semester-long postdoctoral fellowship at the National Museum of American History of the Smithsonian Institution. Housing the complete production lines of two of the top five American greeting card companies of the twentieth century as well as various business documents and historical materials, the Norcross Greeting Card Collection at NMAH became the most important archive for this project. The staff in the Archives Center, at the Silver Hill, Maryland, research site, and throughout the museum went out of their way to facilitate the research for this book. I want to thank especially John Fleckner, Fath Ruffins, Craig Orr, Kay Peterson, Vanessa Simmons, Stacey Kluck, and my dear friend Charlie McGovern, who is in all ways one heckuva fella. Sharman Robertson of the Hallmark Archives helped as much as she could within the constraints imposed by the corporate hierarchy at Hallmark. Deborah Daindridge helped me locate important materials at the Kenneth Spencer Research Library at the University of Kansas. Tammy Lawson ensured that two days at the Schomburg Center for Research in Black Culture were among the most efficient and productive research experiences I have ever enjoyed. Lee Stallsworth expertly photographed many of the cards reproduced here. Grateful acknowledgment is extended to the Boston Public Library, the New York Public Library, the Library of Congress, the National Museum of American History, the Hallmark Historical Collection, and the Winterthur Museum, Garden, and Library for their gracious permission to reproduce images from their archives. Portions of chapters 1 and 2 were presented to the Gender Seminar at the Hall Center for the Humanities; various meetings of the American Studies Association; the Cultural Studies Symposium in Manhattan, Kansas; the Kansas State Historical Society; the American Studies Program at the University of Wyoming; and the Futures of American Studies Institute at Dartmouth College. Parts of chapters 3, 4, and 5 were presented to the American Studies Program at Dickinson College and the "Mass Culture: Beyond Good and Evil" conference organized by Kathy Newman and David Shumway at Carnegie Mellon University. Ann Miller accepted this book for publication by Columbia University Press. Anne Routon and Irene Pavitt saw it through to publication with professional aplomb. Paul Schlotthauer's expert copyediting saved me from errors large and small.

Friends across the country have contributed material support, sustained thought, and spirited criticism as this book developed. From the beginning, Charlie McGovern twisted the tuning pegs of this instrument, helping it to become more musical. Eliza Jane Reilly refused to listen to me whine and relentlessly prosecuted the charge of explicating the argument. Kathy Newman understood immediately the outlines of this project, even though she would have liked more evidence in support of it. Sarah Wayland and Alan Thompson provided me with a room, some coffee, and some damn fine wine during several research trips to the Washington, D.C., area. Barbara and Dan Hart patiently sat through many abstract sketches of points not fully formed. I am so happy that my old friends Steve Brock and Eileen Hammar, who moved to my neighborhood last year, were able to witness the final steps in this project. Bill Andrews, Jonathan Arac, Casey Blake, Susan Douglas, Natalie Dykstra, Van Gosse, June Howard, Frieda Knobloch, James Livingston, Sharon O'Brien, Eric Sandeen, Ann Schofield, Cotten Seiler, and Robyn Wiegman provided thoughtful responses to various versions of this work in progress. Elizabeth Dillon helped me to focus and highlight key points in the argument. George Lipsitz supported this project from its earliest days. His detailed comments on the penultimate draft proved once again that he is the hardest-working man in American studies. Jan Radway's feeling for scholarship and the varieties of intellectual experience continue to exemplify the highest standards for work in our field. Joane Nagel has read almost as many drafts of this project as I have. Her enjoyment of clear writing, passionate argument, and the intricate intertwinings of emotional life with structural determination motivated me to write the strongest book I possibly could.

My family has now seen me through two of these long projects. Their patience can never be fully rewarded. My mother-in-law, Kathy Brown, has smiled, quietly and supportively, at every mention of this project for the past seven years. I could never have formulated a project on greeting cards were not for the expert use to which my own mother, Lee Shank, can put them. Shari and Claire make the books worth writing, the house worth cleaning, the laundry worth folding, and the day worth greeting. This book is for Claire and both of her grandmothers—for the surprising continuities that disruptions render visible.

A Token of My Affection

Structured Feelings amid Circulations of the Heart

At the beginning of Frank Capra's *Mr. Deeds Goes to Town*, Longfellow Deeds lives in a small town where he makes a comfortable, though not luxurious, living by writing greeting card verse. After inheriting a fortune, he moves to New York, where he encounters the greed, corruption, and cynicism of modern urban life, a world structured by harsh competition, artificial sophistication, and deceit. Even after this move, Deeds believes that he can still live according to his own feelings about right and wrong; he can continue to rely on his ability to judge the character of others and his good common sense. Throughout the movie, Deeds's honesty and sincerity is contrasted with the manipulative struggle for advancement that seems to characterize modern society. As the plot proceeds, Deeds finds that his basic faith in the values common to greeting card verse—the importance of being true to your friends, of respecting your family members, of speaking simple truths as directly and sincerely as possible, and, of course, of finding just the right person to love forever—is deeply challenged. The woman he had fallen in love with had been deceiving him, even going under a false name to get a story for her newspaper. The men charged with administering his business dealings conspire to have Deeds declared insane for wanting to give away his fortune. Even his consistent willingness to tell the truth becomes evidence of his disconnection from reality.

During his sanity hearing, Deeds ignores the advice of counsel and refuses to challenge the charges raised against him. As the evidence mounts—including the cracked testimony of his old neighbors who had always thought that Deeds was "pixilated"—Deeds's head slumps lower and lower to his chest. Only at the moment when the court declares that

Deeds must be institutionalized does the reporter, Louise "Babe" Bennett, break out of her self-imposed silence and declare to the court that she has been involved in the deceit, that Deeds truly is a good man—even if he is "too sincere, too honest" to live among the greedy and cynical of New York—and that she really and truly loves him. In the end, Deeds's faith has been redeemed. Babe did turn out to be a good person; their feelings for each other had been authentic; Deeds's sincerity and honesty are recognized and valued for the simple yet important virtues they are. In Capra's film, the world of greeting cards and small-town America is directly and firmly opposed to the sophisticated and corrupt world of urban business. The triumph of Longfellow Deeds is the triumph of plainspoken virtue over the deceitful manipulations of commercial society.

Like *Mr. Deeds Goes to Town*, *A Token of My Affection* is a fantasia on the intertwined themes of greeting card discourse and American business culture. It follows the development of the modern greeting card industry from the 1840s, when valentines were a seasonal complement to the more consistent traditional printing and stationery businesses, to the 1960s, when the expansion of card-sending occasions and special titles for cards led to the dominance of five large firms that relied on fordist techniques of machine-based assembly-line production to sell billions of 50-cent cards per year. Although incidents from the history of greeting card production lie at the center of my narrative, my larger argument is not limited to the movement from handcraft to factory. By American business culture, I do not mean to refer to an isolated set of relations, formations, and actions characteristic solely of business endeavors, but to a range of beliefs and assumptions that, though derived from those practices, actually have a much wider range of application, and indeed come to place limits and pressures on life choices and situations typically thought of as outside the realm of business. I am most interested in using the story of the development of the greeting card industry to interrogate the relationships among the organization of material production for the market, the rise of large-scale business organizations, the social tensions produced when large firms began to require large numbers of managers and professionals (more than a single family could provide), the accompanying transformations in the shape and duration of kinship structures, the disruptions created in and through social affiliation, the shifting functions as well as the changing means of displaying emotional eloquence, and the dominant forms of subjectivity constructed in those social material contexts.

That list might look like a causal chain, linking a determining base to a determined superstructure. But I do not mean to imply such a linear process. Although I use greeting cards as an entryway into an analysis of the whole "social material process," I follow Raymond Williams's assertion that determination is a multidirectional and interlocking setting of limits and exerting of pressures.[1] Social consciousness is not simply determined by material processes, but neither, of course, is it a wholly autonomous force. The analysis of greeting cards appeals to me because it offers the opportunity to investigate what are often assumed to be widely separated poles of social life—hardheaded business competition and the soft expressions of love and social connection—in an arena where they are undeniably and profoundly connected to each other. I treat greeting cards, therefore, not only as meaningful symbols of emotional eloquence and social connection, but as primary evidence for understanding the processes whereby hegemonic and difficult-to-question assumptions about the relationships between feelings of love and affection and the procedures proper to business are sunk into the heart of American culture.

Greeting cards provide remarkable insights into the dominant structures of feeling produced as modern capitalism developed and evolved into the forms we live among now. As highly profitable commodities whose conditions of production and distribution matured from small-scale, handcrafted production for the market to industrial mass production, from family-owned firms to large-scale business organizations, greeting cards carry the marks of intensive economic competition and for-profit calculation. As symbolic products used by a variety of people to display emotional eloquence and maintain social connection, greeting cards explicitly and overtly detail the shifting forms of love and affiliation that were experienced by the individuals whose lives were shaped and structured by these major economic changes. The analysis of modern greeting cards reveals the fundamental power of economic organization to enable and constrain experiences of longing, status, desire, social connectedness, and love; to shape the construction of subjectivities; and to structure and partially determine the most private, internal, and intimate of feelings. It can also show the ways in which feelings of love and affiliation affect and channel economic flows and systems of material production.

When Williams laid out his most concise discussion of his key concept of structure of feeling, he defended the use of the term "feeling" because he was "concerned with meanings and values as they are actively lived and felt," not with organized and coherent representations of ideological positions. In fact, the notion of a structure of feeling is intended to focus critical discussion on

> characteristic elements of impulse, restraint, and tone; specifically affective elements of consciousness and relationships: not feeling against thought, but thought as felt and feeling as thought: practical consciousness of a present kind, in a living and interrelating continuity. We are then defining these elements as a "structure": as a set, with specific internal relations, at once interlocking and in tension. Yet we are also defining a social experience which is still in process, often indeed not yet recognized as social but taken to be private, idiosyncratic, and even isolating, but which in analysis (though rarely otherwise) has its emergent, connecting, and dominant characteristics, indeed its specific hierarchies.[2]

Greeting cards are dialectical images that precisely convey characteristic impulses and tones, affective connections to the structured relationships within the social material processes out of which they come. Yet, as Williams insists, such affective connections are not simply "epiphenomena of changed institutions, formations, and beliefs, or merely secondary evidence of changed social and economic relations."[3] They also display a relatively autonomous force and direction. In the case of greeting cards, this relatively autonomous force can be thought of as the longing for a shared language of feeling through which love and social affiliation can be spoken and, through speaking, reproduced and disseminated, acting agentively in the world. This longing for a language of feeling speaks back to the social and economic institutions and structures that produce it. Greeting card manufacturers know the force of this longing. They think of it as the unpredictable—indeed, capricious—nature of consumer demand. The greeting card market is the institution where the longing for a language of feeling meets the structuring effects of large-scale business organizations driven by for-profit calculation.

A hint of avant-gardism sneaks into Williams's discussion of structure of feeling. He insists that the effort to find these structures "in solution"—that is, before they can be seen as coherent and consistent chunks of ideological matter—focuses attention on the barely emergent, on the aspects of art and literature that reveal the advanced forefront of cultural expression. It might be hard to imagine mainstream greeting cards as emergent in this way. Indeed, in 1971, Webster Schott, then editorial director of Hallmark, was quoted contrasting the culture found in middlebrow journals with the culture of greeting cards: "The culture as represented by *Esquire* and *The New Yorker* doesn't begin to describe most experience. Being here [working for Hallmark] has confirmed for me that [cultural] history is a lie. The media culture might be the point on the arrow; we are the shaft." Schott went on to insist that the shaft is much longer and a much better guide to the direction of the arrow than the point. "What percentage of the population will read a book tonight?" he asked. "Two? Three? Today twenty-five million people will send a greeting card."[4]

Faced with such evidence of the dominant mainstream status of greeting card discourse, one might be tempted to dismiss these cards as, indeed, dead chunks of ideological matter, testifying only to the calcification of feeling in an overly commercialized, rationalized, and bureaucratized world. This is the position Stephen Papson takes in his article "From Symbolic Exchange to Bureaucratic Discourse: The Hallmark Greeting Card," in which he conceptualizes greeting cards as the sneakiest form of corporate domination. "Buried in the insignificance and innocence of the greeting card is the corporate invasion of everyday existence," he insists. Similarly, Leigh Eric Schmidt narrates the impact that greeting card manufacturers had on the commercialization of American holidays as they conspired with florists and retailers to profit from family celebrations. Indeed, I have had

lengthy discussions with many male colleagues who share some version of this perspective, insisting that they never send greeting cards
and wondering what one could really learn from looking closely at
these disposable imprints of mass-produced sentiment. Of course, one
fact that has remained consistent throughout the twentieth century is
that nearly 80 percent of all greeting cards are bought and sent by
women—which is not to say that female academics have wholeheartedly celebrated greeting card use. Luna Lambert's history of the gift
card is respectful and appreciative of the chromolithographed Christmas cards exchanged during the late nineteenth century, but it does
not essay an analysis of the cards themselves. Melissa Schrift, however, is horrified by the "icons of femininity" that late-twentieth-century
greeting card manufacturers produced for women to send to one another, finding a preponderance of "patriarchal language and imagery"
in studio cards. In her very important analysis of kinwork, Micaela Di
Leonardo shifts the discussion away from the content of cards to uncover the important social functions that they fulfill, though she is
hardly celebratory of the conditions within which this work is performed. Even Eva Ilouz's intriguing investigation of the "political
economy of love" relies methodologically on the capacity of greeting
cards to express relatively firmly established class distinctions. In each
of these academic studies, greeting cards are treated as relatively coherent and consistent evidence of the damage done to domestic practices of emotional communication and social connection by the intru-
sion of masculine, capitalist, and technological motives.[5]

The problem with these arguments is not that they are critical of
greeting card production, discourse, and practice. Instead, the problem
derives from their shared, if unspoken, theoretical division of the social
into separate realms, one of which is organized for economic production, the other of which ought to be protected from the imperatives and
motives characteristic of those processes. While none of these scholars
overtly proclaims the validity of a separate-spheres understanding of
American cultural history, the structures of their arguments reveal the
continuing covert strength of the assumptions that underlie that approach. Even the work of as sophisticated and nuanced a sociologist as
Arlie Hochschild laments the "commercialization of intimate life," as

though at some point in the past the economic determination of private life was insignificant. These assumptions are truly powerful and difficult to escape, but that escape is one of the theoretical and methodological goals of this project. Rather than seeing greeting cards as already concretized evidence of the economic invasion of what had previously been havens in a heartless world, I want to take seriously their status as evidence of the structures of feeling produced as part of the whole social material process in dominance from 1840 to 1960. This will require rethinking the relationships among factory and home, profit and love, contract and community. It will require reopening questions about the connections between intimate personal feelings and the public institutions that dominate our systems of material production. Above all, it will demand that we abandon the comfortable thought that we already know what greeting cards are and how they have functioned. Modern greeting cards simultaneously contain the longing for a shared language of feeling, the utopian desire for a world of material and emotional abundance, and the expression of the very attitudes toward life that limit and disable those utopian desires. They are, therefore, precisely dialectical images, those objects that Walter Benjamin studied as he tried to uncover not the "economic origins of culture," but "the expression of the economy in its culture." Greeting cards are the dialectical images that precisely figure the intertwining of material production and human longing in the modern era of the United States.[6]

In this book, I make four key assertions. The first is that, between 1840 and 1960, greeting cards became significant objects used in the cultural display of emotional eloquence and social connection in the United States. Second, these aspects of private life were not experienced by the users of greeting cards as a separate and distinct arena of private life. I argue that emotional life was conditioned by industrialization and the rise of modern forms of bureaucratic organization, just as the operations of modern business were shaped by feelings of longing and desire. In addition, the use of cards to document social connection demonstrates the intertwined patterns of business ambitions and social life. Third, emotional communication in a culture structured by business is fraught with danger; the acknowledgment of emotional connections can seem equivalent to an announcement of vulnerability. The values of competition and efficiency that dominate modern business partially determine the possible forms of emotional communication, resulting in a predominance of displaced and condensed clichés and stereotypes. Finally, the stereotyped images and sentimental language found on the cards do not hide the social tensions that produced the need for them. Rather, the cards reveal and, at times, revel in the experience of these tensions—with an almost carnivalesque yet forced gaiety.

Chronologically, the book addresses three distinct periods. This approach reflects the impact that economic and social transitions have had on popular feeling and makes a claim about the history of private emotion and popular longing. In the first period, 1840 to 1890, I place the use of antebellum valentines and late-nineteenth-century Christmas cards in the context of the market revolution and industrialization. Chapter 1 discusses the early use of commercial forms of emotional eloquence as a means of displaying an agentive interior, which was believed to be a requirement for success in the growing market economy. The display of one's interiority was a public claim that a person enjoyed the capacity for independent judgment that was both the theoretical underpinning and one of the most significant effects of the market revolution. Antebellum valentines were often written in the sender's own hand in order to claim authorship of the sentiments, though the words may have originated in a published collection of verses called a valentine writer. Commercial sources of emotional eloquence ranged from these volumes to fancy paper valentines that materially conveyed the intricacies of emotional interiors. These valentines became tools in the public representation of class difference, and the remarkable popularity of comic or vinegar valentines demonstrates the anxieties that laced the lower edges of the developing middle classes.

Chapter 2 follows the development of chromolithography and the rising importance of color in a market economy as it follows the career of Louis Prang, chromolithographer, art educator, and Christmas card publisher. Prang's project of spreading democracy through popularizing aesthetic education clashed with the use of his lavishly colored cards by urban elites. Christmas card exchange modeled the circulation of commodities among those families benefiting from the increase in productivity that accompanied the rise of industrialization, as they used such exchanges to demarcate publicly the boundaries between themselves and those who were not receiving the fruits of increased productivity. The Christmas card presented Prang with a sentimental commodity whose discursive imagery held the capacity to critique its own use, as Prang's firm increasingly imaged contradiction and conflict on cards with an overt message of joy, love, and abundance. The chapter closes with a reading of *The Rise of Silas Lapham*. Lapham's story parallels Prang's in many intriguing ways, not the least of which is the failure of both men's firms to make the transition to modern large-scale forms of business organization.

In the second period, 1906 to 1957, I trace the development of the modern greeting card industry and the evolution of modern greeting card discourse and practice as overdetermined outgrowths of the rise of the modern corporation. Chapter 3 details the early consolidation of the modern greeting card industry out of individual firms that had been publishing valentines, Christmas cards, and post cards. It argues that the intense competition that characterized business operations during the post card craze created sufficient anxieties among the early greeting card producers that they formed a national association to stabilize prices and coordinate a national market while still maintaining intense competition. Business associations, both industry-based, like the National Association of Greeting Card Manufacturers, and community-based, like the Rotarians, were means of negotiating the conflicting values of competition and comradeship, both of which were necessary for and grew out of modern business practice. A business theory of friendship developed that worked to contain the potential emotional disruption that vectors of affect could produce in a market society shaped by large-scale business organizations. This theory of momentary yet still significant—indeed, powerful—connection lies at the center of the generic elaboration of greeting card discourse. Greeting card manufacturers worked out a visual and verbal language of displaced and condensed clichés, images of masquerade, and idealized and nostalgic representations of plenty in order to reinforce the discursive separation of work and feeling. Within this discursively divided frame, the modern business of producing a shared language of feeling responded to the real need for abstract, highly regularized, and familiar formulas of commercially available emotional expression.

Chapter 4 draws heavily from the Norcross Greeting Card Collection at the National Museum of American History, which contains the complete publications of two of the "top five" major greeting card firms: Norcross and Rust Craft. It details the strategies of identification, displacement, and masquerade that characterize the discourse of modern greeting cards. During the first half of the twentieth century, greeting card manufacturers developed the concept of "sendability"—the component of any card that, in the beliefs of the industry, most directly determined its marketplace success. They understood sendability to be the capacity of any card to represent the relationship between the sender and the receiver. The industry's efforts to develop sendability resulted from its recognition of the structural conditions at the heart of its business. In order to be profitable, a card had to represent recognizable aspects of a specific human relationship sufficiently well to be purchased by thousands of different people. The use of stereotypes and clichés enabled both an identification with the feelings announced through the card and a displacement of those same feelings into the words and bodies of another. If the main function of the greeting card was to establish the objectivity of an emotional relationship in a culture that emphasized the mobility and fungibility of feeling, the initial task of each card was to construct the possibility for social recognition without imposing too strong a set of obligations on that recognition. The conditions of modern life required mobile and flexible expressions of tentative affiliation. This strategic use of the visual and verbal language of others both confirmed the legitimacy of the feelings being enunciated and protected the users from being too closely identified with them. Greeting cards of the second quarter of the twentieth century relied consistently, but not exclusively, on images of socially disempowered persons to voice the sentimental feelings of those using the cards. The use of ethnic and racialized stereotypes reinforced the ability of the largely white users of these cards to both claim and disavow the purchased sentiments. Although Mother's Day and Father's Day cards could not rely on these strategies, they developed their own discursive means of constructing simultaneous identification and displacement.

Chapter 5 relies on the greeting card collections saved by several families to demonstrate the construction of social networks during the middle third of the twentieth century. Extensive collections of Christmas cards saved by families along the East Coast and in the Midwest supplement smaller valentine and miscellaneous card collections that document the use of greeting cards to display emotional eloquence and objectify social networks. The Collection of Greeting Cards at the Popular Culture Library at Bowling Green State University contains large numbers of used valentine, birthday, sympathy, Easter, and Christmas cards that testify eloquently to the felt need for a shared language of emotional communication and social connection. It was while working in this collection that I first discovered the objective power of greeting card discourse. These used cards, already sent in order to objectify an ephemeral social connection between two people, make clear the hegemonic saturation of emotional communication by their soft language. Even when individuals compose their own additions to the sentiments preprinted on the cards, they obey the conventions of the genre. When they are concerned that the meaning of the preprinted verse is not clear or is insufficiently emphasized, they underline key words in the sentiment. When Jack and Edith, a married couple with two children, sent each other cards that varied only slightly over fifteen years of birthdays, and when they added no other words beyond "love" and their signatures, it became clear that they meant what the cards said.

Finally, chapter 6 presents evidence that the transformations in systems of material production that we think of as the shift to postfordism are evident and operative in the greeting card discourse of the final quarter of the twentieth century. I argue, however, that the adoption of postfordist strategies of production and distribution within the greeting card industry did not entail the abandonment of large-scale business organization or of the machines of mass production. What it did require is the development of complex systems of information management and a shift in the basic terms of evaluating the possible negative and positive outcomes of any business endeavor. Whereas fordist management techniques produced a subjectivity that was shy of risk, postfordist managers had to develop the capacity to work in high-risk conditions that carried a large probability of failure. The subjectivity characteristic of these work conditions finds itself initially articulated in the studio cards that first appeared in the late 1950s and more elaborately displayed in the "from-me-to-you" cards of the late 1980s and early 1990s. Both styles of cards acknowledge the fundamental gap between the ideological promise of postindustrial capitalism—the promise of unlimited growth that will eventually raise the material conditions of all—and the dominant felt reality of loss, failure, and disappointment. Whereas studio cards turned the experience of this gap into a source of ironic humor, "from-me-to-you" cards directly address the impossibility of emotional abundance in late capitalism. They speak the impossible emotional truths of our time.

I am making some very large claims in this book. The most fundamental of these claims is that our world of feeling and our need for a shared emotional language to articulate that world is powerfully though not wholly determined by the organization of our economic life. An important corollary of that claim is that our feelings are historically variable with a certain structural regularity, changes in which trace changes at the level of the economy. The investigation of these claims led me to greeting cards, the most widely distributed mass-produced commodities of feeling. No other cultural product presents more direct evidence of the emotional contradictions at the core of the American culture of business. As a result of the intense competition that characterizes the greeting card industry, the cards cannot misrepresent the feelings they are intended to convey. Indeed, greeting cards must speak the emotional truths of mainstream American culture. Some will feel that I do not have the evidence that fully supports those claims. Admittedly, my evidence is fragmentary and disconnected, but it is overwhelmingly consistent. Public historical societies across the country are filled with tattered tokens of feeling. File folders hold old greeting cards that had been carefully saved by those who received them, for whom they conjured relationships, affiliation and affection, memories and kinship networks, lovers and neighbors, the warm image of friends and the perhaps more tepid obligations of family. These cards were kept for a lifetime by their recipients, and after their death, the cards are encountered for the first time by the children who are cleaning out their parents' belongings. Bewildered by why they were

kept, unable to identify the memories and the feelings the cards represented, the now-adult children put them out in a yard sale: old cards 25
cents for the lot. A collector of ephemera or a book trader may purchase them in order to break them up into packages of Christmas
cards, Easter cards, and valentines to sell for 5 cents per package, ten
cards per package, which perhaps are bought by another collector who
longs nostalgically for the long-gone world represented in those cards.
When the collector dies or must move out of the old family home, he
or she donates them to the local historical society, where they are kept
in packages of ten cards per Mylar envelope, each of which holds only
Easter cards or birthday cards or valentines sent from someone no one
now knows to someone else who wanted to keep them for a lifetime.
The historical society dutifully receives them, catalogs them, stores
them in acid-free folders and storage boxes, and places them on the
shelves next to the real-estate deeds and the papers of mayors and
other public figures. What can possibly be the historical value of these
mass-produced cheap pieces of paper, ink, and glittering decoration?
What can these cards possibly mean?

In the corner of my office at home is a large cardboard box. Inside
that box are eight plastic shopping bags, each filled with greeting cards
that were sent to my wife's grandmother during the last years of her
life. Most of these cards arrived during her final eight years, when she
was living in a nursing home in Higginsville, Missouri. Laura Steinman
was not an outgoing person. During the years I knew her, she rarely
said more than "Oh, hello" to me. During most of those last eight
years, she didn't say even that, as she was often beyond the reach of ordinary speech. She was not beyond the reach of cards, however. The
second Sunday of every December, from 1992 through 1999, we drove
to John Knox Village, passing the local Wal-Mart on the way, to wish
her a happy birthday. During most of these brief celebrations, Laura
sat quietly in a chair as her daughter and granddaughters fussed with
pieces of cake, scoops of ice cream, and cups of coffee. She would coo
appreciatively when she opened the small shiny presents of candy and
clothing, but the moments when Laura really smiled came as she took
the birthday cards out of their envelopes, looked at the sentiments inside, and then passed them around for all of us to share. She did not

read them out loud, and I do not know if she took the time to parse carefully the lines inside or the images on the front. But there was never any doubt that those of us in the room were all supposed to read and appreciate the sentiments printed on the cards that we had bought for her. There was never any doubt that those cards mattered. She never permitted them to be thrown away. They are now stacked next to the hundreds of other birthday cards, Christmas cards, and sympathy cards that Laura had kept in one of the five drawers she was allowed in her shared room in the home. These cards had come from her children and their families, as well as from the few friends she had kept in touch with during her ninety-plus years of small-town life. Although I am not at all certain what I ought to do with these cards now that this project has come to an end, there is no doubt that their importance for Laura is a testament to the residual power of the structures of feeling that motivated and responded to the circulations of the heart in modern greeting cards. For Laura Steinman's generation, greeting cards spoke the emotional truths of a culture structured in dominance by business, the impossible truths of a supple but still interlocking set of affective connections that set profound limits and exerted considerable pressures on the capacity of persons to imagine the possibility of complexly joyful and abundant lives.

The authors of a trend report produced for the Norcross Greeting Card Company in June 1959 pointed out that the high rate of geographic mobility experienced in the United States had led to the creation of a "rootless American" who was "in the process of breaking ties and not making new ones." They pointed out that "in the big corporations, men now expect to move every five years," and that the resulting "family separation is a very significant aspect of contemporary life." One of the "emotional and sociological factors" associated with this mobility, the report found, was that "the ties of love and/or hatred with those they've left behind, remain—are always there—gnawing away in memory and deep feeling." The authors of the trend report wanted Norcross to produce cards that addressed those ties, that recognized the emotional disruptions that gnawed away in memory and deep feeling.[7] My most profound hope for this book is that, after you have read it, you will see the ways in which the modern greeting card did address these disruptions and did respond to the powerful determinants of everyday life that were also among the determinants of its own industry. The modern greeting card, made of tinsel and tripe, was shaped by the most delicate and filigreed intricacies of the hegemonic process. As it responded to the emotional needs of a business culture, it responded in line with the fundamental imperatives of a business culture. The production of emotional eloquence and the public recognition of social connection need not become objects of for-profit calculation and private accumulation. But it is not surprising that they have. This book has been motivated by two equally strong desires: the hope of extending the shared capacities for emotional eloquence and social connection as broadly as possible, and the desire to feel no scorn for those who, when moved to speak of these things under our current conditions, seem unable to do more than buy a card.

1
Vicious Sentiments

Nineteenth-Century Valentines and the Sentimental Production of Class Boundaries

*I*n his lecture notes for October 16, 1848, David Berdan, a young instructor in linguistics at Brunswick College in New Jersey, carefully formulated his understanding of the crucial distinction between thoughts and language. "Language signifies the expression of our ideas by certain articulate sounds which are used as the signs of those ideas," he wrote. "The connection between words and ideas may in general be considered as arbitrary and conventional and the differences between languages as a different set of articulate sounds which they have chosen for communicating their ideas." Berdan had studied the classics, translating Homer, Plato, and Demosthenes. He had composed small pamphlets that answered crucial questions, such as "Was the Career of Bonaparte Good for Europe?" He lectured on the origin and nature of figurative language, arguing that although "figures of speech generally imply some departure from simplicity of expression . . . [i]t is even difficult to compose a sentence of any [length] without employing what may be called a figure of speech." David Berdan was obviously well educated; he was also self-reflective and thoughtful.[1]

Working through the problem of expression and meaning for his lecture, Berdan shifted his focus from the expression of ideas to the expression of feeling. Explaining the development of language, he stated that language had begun prehistorically as simple cries of passion. These were enough to convey the primitive feelings of precivilized peoples. By the mid-nineteenth century, however, language had "become a vehicle by which the most delicate and refined thoughts [such was his initial jotting, but after reflection, he had crossed out the word "thoughts" and replaced it with a different word, "emotions"] a vehicle by which the most delicate and refined emotions of the mind can be transfered [*sic*] into another." When attempting to explain his understanding of the effort to articulate the most delicate and refined internal states that, despite their utmost recalcitrance, must be communicated to another, Berdan found it necessary to speak of the connection between words and feeling.

A few months later, young David was putting his theory into practice. He had received a lovely, commercially produced valentine from a woman named Susan. A fancy lace-paper envelope that conveyed through its tactile complexity a certain delicacy and intricacy of feeling contained a sheet of embossed lace paper, also delicate, also intricate. Pasted onto the front of this 3- by 4-inch token were two gold-colored embossed flowers. Between these symmetrical blooms was centered an embossed scroll on which only two words appeared: "Love Truth." Free of "figures of speech," yet eloquently conveying simplicity and feeling, Susan's valentine to David inspired his own careful and hand-written response:

> While passions sigh and Cupid's dart
> Around us fly from heart to heart
> Tell me dear one will love like mine
> Be welcomed in a Valentine.
> Ah yes, for in your generous heart
> Frank, loyal, fond, and free from art
> Nor carings for light flattery dwells
> No poor and false ambition swells
> Calmly thou wearest thy own bright bays.
> Friendship the golden tie
> That binds true hearts together
> May such exist tween you & I
> To be disturbed never.
> And from this hand kind one
> Accept these lines tho few
> And from them understand
> I still remember you.
> Your Valentine

As Berdan's valentine makes reference to his own hand, authorizing this sentiment as the product of his own work, it almost admonishes Susan for her purchased token, even as it flatters her generous heart, "Frank, loyal, fond, and free from art." In Berdan's verse, Susan's artlessness becomes a mark of her sincerity, while Berdan's own true heart modestly hopes that his "lines tho few," but which came directly from his own hand, can represent the most sincere friendship.[2]

A year later, Berdan perhaps understood more fully the significance and value of the highly textured paper that Susan had sent to him. For that year's valentine, he purchased sheets of Joseph Mansell's paper, the finest embossed lace paper then available. He practiced with one sheet, on which he could not resist punning:

> This day let me on you impress
> How fond my love and true.
> And ever will to you incline
> Say shall I be your Valentine
> Oh may you live that love to bless
> My heart own none but you?

This year, for this woman, for this valentine, Berdan seemed to allow the delicate intertwining shapes of embossed lace paper to contribute a layer of significance to his expression of refined and delicate emotions. Mansell lace paper was created when a highly skilled craftsman carefully filed away the raised points of the impressions made during the embossing process. It was a treacherous procedure, best performed by only a few papermakers in England, that often ruined as many sheets as it improved. The final product was quite an expensive commodity by the time it arrived in the stationery stores of the United States. It is not surprising, then, that in order to more fully express not only his love, not only his erudition, but also his commitment, Berdan called his lover's attention to the variety of impressions—those of pen and ink as well as those of tool and die—made on this paper valentine. Not only were his words outward signs of his delicate emotions, but their impression on expensive and relatively rare lace paper was intended to add value, significance, and meaning to his token of affection. This sample exchange, from the height of the first era of popular use of commercial valentines, seems to represent a perfect combination of sincere feeling eloquently expressed with the refined taste required to chose the finest material form for its manifestation. Perhaps this was true love. Perhaps these valentines were an accurate and effective outward token of the most refined and delicate emotions. Yet we ought to be careful how we evaluate these paper valentines. It would be too easy for us to see Berdan's language of 1850 as the more authentic component of his love token, just as it would be too easy to see his use of lace paper as a sign of his or his lover's susceptibility to commercial forces. Berdan's apparently individually composed, and certainly handwritten, phrases—however sincere—were not free from art. For he had worked quite diligently to develop a vocabulary of love, a group of linguistic signs with which to convey successfully his ardor.

Before he met young Susan or, at any rate, before he turned the light of his own true love on her, Berdan had written the following valentine and addressed it to a Miss Catharine Sarah:

> While passions sigh and cupid's dart
> Around us fly from heart to heart
> Tell me dear one will love like mine
> Be welcome in a valentine?
> Ah yes for in your generous heart
> Frank loyal fond and free from art
> No carings for light flattery dwells
> No poor and false ambition swells
> I long ha wished for one like thee
> To cheer and keep my company
> For in thy presence I do find
> Love peace and pleasure all combined
> Still calmly wear these thy bright bays
> And then shalt have all others praise
> So from a heart that loves as thine
> Take this a truthful Valentine

And for Valentine's Day in 1847, Berdan wrote to a young woman identified only as Catharine P—— (perhaps Catharine Sarah, perhaps not) a very long love poem, of which I will quote only a few lines:

> I have seen a pretty lady
> Dear reader so have you;
> She wears a pretty bonnet
> The color is dark blue. . . .
> I love but one &; she is fair
> I love her for her merits rare;
> I love her for her buty [*sic*] bright,
> I love her for her form so light. . . .
> I love but one and her alone,
> I love &; her I hope to own;
> I love &; if it worth while to say
> I love tis you my Catharine P——

As we know, by 1851, Berdan's love had shifted its focus, and for Valentine's Day that year, he wrote to Susan:

> I have seen a pretty lady
> Dear reader so have you
> She wears a pretty bonnet
> And of a pretty hue . . .

What are we to make of these artful recombinations of loving phrases, of the repetition of these outward linguistic signs of delicate and refined emotions? Certainly we should not simply assume that Berdan's willingness to reuse undoubtedly effective exterior tokens of his interior states reveals a lack of sincerity. But it does force us to reconsider our own assumptions about the primacy of the written word, the long-held belief that when it comes to expressions of love, to tokens of affection, that the handwritten sentiment is always closer to the heart than the printed valentine purchased at the stationer's. Perhaps David was perfectly sincere in his feelings for Catharine in 1847 and equally sincere in his love for Susan in 1851. But we cannot read his handwriting as the guarantee of that sincerity, nor should we interpret his words as a more direct and less mediated reflection of his feelings than the paper valentine was of Susan's. If we want to know how valentines worked, what their circulation among lovers both false and true, both chaste and soiled, meant to their senders and receivers, the people who transformed Valentine's Day "from . . . an often forgotten, easily neglected Old World saint's day to . . . an indigenous, not-to-be-missed American holiday,"[3] we have to be willing to consider the widest variety of outward signs of feeling—not simply the words on the valentines, but also the paper of which they were made; not only the images that appear on the embossed cutouts glued to the surface of the valentines, but also the variegated textures produced through the process of embossing—and we must refrain from assuming that the commercial apparatus that structured the production, distribution, and purchase of paper valentines somehow intervened in the otherwise direct expression of pure feeling. The users of these valentines were men and women caught up in a commercial society, a world already transformed by the "market revolution," individuals whose interior states of being were undoubtedly shaped by calculations of interest, value, profit, and loss, whose most private feelings were at least partially determined by their public material circumstances, but whose emotions were no less powerful, no less sincere, no less authentic for having been produced in that context.

Valentines, the Market Revolution, and the Culture of Sentiment

The culture of sentiment has received a great deal of scholarly attention in the past twenty years. Building on the classic debate between poles identified with Ann Douglas on one side and Jane Tompkins on the other, cultural historians and literary scholars have worked to reshape our understanding of the relationship between market societies and the culture of sentiment. June Howard's valuable recapitulation of this debate makes a series of very important points. First, she reminds us that the nineteenth-century culture of sentiment is a direct descendent of Enlightenment efforts to define and elaborate moral sentiments. For the Scottish common-sense philosophers in particular, ethics were grounded in the possibility of imagining the feelings of others. Second, she argues (persuasively, I feel) that sentiment and domestic ideology are not the same thing and that their continual conflation in literary and historical studies needs to be unpacked. Howard also endorses the recent flowering of studies that have demonstrated the widespread existence of the sentimental male and contributed so much to the abandonment of that archaic formulation of separate spheres. Finally, she suggests that the material grounding for the culture of sentiment might be found in the processes producing the middle-class families that were the focus of so much of sentimental culture. In this section, I hope to build on Howard's distillation while emphasizing the profound intersection of the material and the sentimental in nineteenth-century valentines.[4]

The appearance and resounding popularity of commercial valentines, along with the commentary that surrounded them—in the form of fiction, articles, letters, promotional materials, and critical dismissals—can be seen as evidence of one instance of "the cultural schizophrenia of capitalist transformation," the coincidence of the market revolution and the culture of sentiment. The historian Charles Sellers finds it ironic that "a people competing fiercely to level a wilderness luxuriated in a literature of nature and love." But the culture of sentiment was an unsurprising result of the commercial transformation of everyday life. Not uniformly, not in isolation from other emergent forces or residual traditions, but powerfully and wholeheartedly nonetheless, the organization of material productive processes around the demands and concerns of market conditions spread new structures of feeling. Coinciding with the first popular peak of the commercial valentine, "the early 1840s brought market revolution to culmination in a generation of rapid growth."[5] Production for the market stimulated economic development, creating a middle class with an increasingly self-conscious orientation around the calculations of profit and loss.

One of the most persistent legacies of this commercial transformation was also the primary ideological achievement of the culture of sentiment—the construction of an authentic interior self that was believed to remain independent of commercial exploitation, of market considerations, of the social forces that would shape and determine behavior, ideology, subjectivity, and desire. By the end of the eighteenth century, the ability to render public an interior self had become the most important evidence that a person was capable of certain forms of class-bound agency and autonomy. It was by means of displaying one's interiority that a person demonstrated the capacity for independent judgment that was both the theoretical underpinning and one of the most significant effects of the market revolution. As this transformation deepened and as the common power of commerce increased, producing the tectonic forces that shaped the development of new class formations, the public demonstration of sympathy—that is, fellow-feeling—became the means whereby the interior self could be displayed. Therefore, the language of emotions became the central discourse through which selfhood, interiority, and, finally, agentive subjectivity could be evidenced.

The sociologist Colin Campbell has argued that "only in modern times have emotions come to be located 'within' individuals as opposed to 'in' the world." Upon achieving the separation of self-consciousness, the modern self became fascinated by the relationships between the inside and the outside and began to characterize these relationships by the use of such emotional qualifiers as "amusing, charming, diverting, pathetic, and sentimental." The language of feeling became the key to connecting the inside and the outside, the self and the world. Commercial valentines of the mid-nineteenth century illuminate many of the conventions that shaped emotional eloquence in a developing market society at the moment when emotional eloquence was key to the demonstration of agentive subjectivity for an expanding proportion of the population. The diversity of responses to the commercial distribution of emotional eloquence in the form of mass-produced valentines can help us understand both the role of the authentic interior self and the intricacy of the social networks that helped consolidate these middle classes. Nineteenth-century valentines can help us see the complex structures of feeling that connected private emotional life and public business at this crucial moment in the development of commercial society.[6]

The work of literary scholars has shown how the reading of novels functioned as one of the primary cultural processes through which the culture of sentiment was nurtured and extended. Nancy Armstrong's formative *Desire and Domestic Fiction* describes the conventions that structured representations of the private interior self as that aspect of an individual capable of standing apart from market forces. Armstrong argues that English domestic fiction functioned "both as the document and as the agency of cultural history," working to establish the psychological reality of the interior self it described and locating that self in the domestic interior of the private home. Extending her analysis to conduct books, Armstrong suggests that this genre of domestic literature worked to literalize the fictional representations of the self by articulating codes of behavior that could function as outward signs of this interiority. These books put forth "the illusion . . . that there is a self independent of the material conditions that have produced it and that such a self can transform itself without transforming the social and economic configuration in opposition to which it is constructed." This process of self-transformation was the utopian dream of conduct books and domestic fiction alike. The political viability of this dream was the issue that divided Douglas and Tompkins.[7]

Gillian Brown's *Domestic Individualism* began the important work of linking the ideal self constructed in domestic fiction to the experience of ownership, the material possession of sentimental objects produced in and proliferated by the growth of a market-based society. Brown saw that the forms of selfhood identified with women and the domestic sphere were not simply resistant to market structures, as Jane Tompkins taught us to see, nor were they merely expressions of "the political sense obfuscated or gone rancid," as Ann Douglas insisted. Instead, the "hostility toward the market" expressed in sentimental culture, particularly in domestic novels, "represents a psychology of individuality in a market economy." Domestic individualism was a form of possessive individualism insofar as the self was exteriorized through the personalization of sentimental possessions.[8]

Lori Merish's valuable extension of Brown's argument traces a genealogy of the sentimental attachment to objects back to the Scottish common-sense philosophers. As the Scots were interested in establishing links among virtue, property, and commerce, they constructed a gendered rhetorical chain that relied on the association of women with luxury to convey both the pleasures and the dangers of the refinement, politeness, and sensibility that came with an increased access to goods. Merish builds on this discussion of the origins of liberal sensibility to link a "passional investment in property" to the elaboration of refined sentiments. She argues that caring for luxurious goods provided an opportunity to develop the emotional skills of "sentimental possession." This passionate engagement allows the modern sensitive subject to enjoy her emotional attachments precisely as extensions of her self, whether these attachments were to objects or persons. In Merish's analysis, Adam Smith's theorizing of sympathy as the capacity for imagining the feelings of others and, therefore, the very glue capable of holding together the social, connects rather neatly with his later theorizing of effectual demand as the determiner of price. The invisible hand of the marketplace required a concept of the self and of self-interest; it worked only when the free desires of independent beings met one another in commercial transactions. The operations of both the economy and the social depend on the ability of interior selves to connect with the desires and feelings of others. The shared enjoyment of sentimental possession was one means of developing these capacities. One could take pleasure in refined objects as a way to demonstrate one's interior qualities even as the object could enable a triangulation with the desires and tastes of another person. As Merish puts it, "The sentimental subject is produced and sustained by attachment to and caring for a limited, domestic world of goods." Despite this interest in the functional power of objects, Merish still awards prime causality to the structuring power of narratives, focusing on the work that popular philosophy, sentimental novels, and autobiographies do to naturalize the simultaneous development of an interior self, a private sphere of consumption, and the increasing power of market forces.[9]

In her study of mourning and middle-class identity, Mary Louise Kete theorizes sentimentality as perhaps the necessary verbal mode through which emotional collaboration can take place in a market society. She defines sentimental collaboration as "the exchange of sympathy which establishes the ground for participation in a common cultural or intellectual project." Kete is primarily interested in describing the characteristics of sentimentality as a "supra-verbal" mode of expression, but she contributes an important methodological point by insisting that the "the poetics of sentimentality is best revealed by attention to quotidian verse that celebrates not the sublime, the individual and the possibility of dissent, but the domestic, the familial, and the possibility of consent." Kete begins her book with an analysis of "Harriet Gould's Book," a scrapbook in which Harriet, her friends, and her family pasted sentimental verse, scraps of poetry that reflected on their everyday lives. The exchange of sympathy through the circulation of gifts (like the poetry given to Harriet) created a social network, a community that found its reason for being in the confrontation with loss. Kete argues that the sentimental is a mode of expression that brings individuals together in the face of this ever-present experience. Loss could come through death, through persons moving away to follow fortunes elsewhere, and through the breaking of the bonds of friendship. The sentimental, for Kete, is the mode used everyday to reinforce those bonds of affection that are the only guardians against such loss and the only effective salve for the wounds that loss causes: "The distinguishing function of the poetics of sentimentality is . . . to reattach symbolic connections that have been severed by the contingencies of human existence." She goes further to argue that the exchange of sentimental gifts—typically marked as sentimental by the language that was the key element of the gift—not only provided evidence of social networks but also made present objective evidence of the interior self:

> Again and again, what this poetry by everyday, ordinary, non-elite Americans shows is that the inalienable possession of self fundamental to liberalism is produced through a free circulation of gifts of the self. This circulation of selves engages those who participate in a joint effort—a collaboration of sentiment—to convert something established under temporary conditions and through a voluntary action of will (the individual self in this case) into something permanent and eternal.

Within the culture of sentimentalism, the circulation of sentimental objects helped create and sustain a social network of sensitive modern selves.[10]

The work of these literary scholars is complemented by the analyses of cultural and social historians. Karen Halttunen's pathbreaking study of antebellum urban middle-class culture, *Confidence Men and Painted Women*, details the development of "sentimental middle classes [that] erected barriers to define their own social status through the exclusion of others," even as they "sidestepped the difficult issue of class distinctions." Halttunen argues that the class system then developing in the United States established itself in private, where "individual claims to gentility were assessed according to sentimental criteria. To be genteel, simply stated, was to be sincere, and sincerity was not an economic category, it was a matter of morality." Sentimentalism neatly allowed for the elision of the vulgar economic considerations that were ultimately the chief determinant of class in the young republic. As Stuart Blumin argues in his masterful synthesis, *The Emergence of the Middle Class*, the economic changes that were to have such profound effects in American private life during the nineteenth century appeared initially and largely as changes in the scope of social networks, in the range of distinctions made between salaried entrepreneurs and wage-earning artisans, and the myriad ways in which the built environment of the workplace and the home reinforced and extended these distinctions.

Yet Blumin goes on to demonstrate that "middle-class formation" went beyond the reorganization of work to include experiences in the domestic sphere, which "were influential, perhaps even crucial, in generating new social identities." He argues that the middle classes developing in antebellum America shared a set of feelings that grew out of and corresponded to the activities that characterized everyday life. While middle-class identity may have made "fewer explicit claims on the consciousness of middling folk, it was more fundamental as an expression of . . . those things through which individuals located themselves in society." From 1840 to 1870, the culture of sentiment developed as an elaborate means of marking the social discriminations that were central to the consolidation and further development of this early and uncertain set of middle classes. In Halttunen's words, "Sentimentalism offered an unconscious strategy for middle-class Americans to distinguish themselves as a class while still denying the class structure of their society, and to define themselves against the lower classes even as they insisted they were merely distinguishing themselves from vulgar hypocrites." Throughout the early to mid-nineteenth century, the culture of sentiment maintained a harsh discipline. If a person failed to perform properly the ever-increasing complexity of its codes, the discourses of sentimentalism professed to have revealed that person's true vulgar nature, which might for a time have hidden beneath the outward signs of gentility, but which could not maintain its disguise under the intense scrutiny of the middle-class parlor. The harshness of the judgment—failure to perform the codes indicated a flawed character—reveals the high stakes that were involved in these judgments and the real fluidity and permeability of the class lines that they were intended to maintain and enforce.[11]

From the earliest moments of the market revolution, the production of an interior self was a class-bound accomplishment and a class-structured necessity. As David Berdan made clear in his lecture on linguistics, the language of emotional communication was the delicate material out of which this self—the locus of refined internal states—was woven. Wholly in keeping with the dictates of sentimentalism, the self of the early nineteenth century was created in and by the effort to demonstrate its existence through the use of sentimental codes that, by demanding the searching revealing of the self, participated in its construction. Authentic interiority was dependent on the possession and expression of moral sentiments. Karen Lystra argues that the full existence of this interiority (which she terms the "romantic self") could be revealed only in private—in the private world of sincere feeling, within an already sympathetic group of friends. As outward representations of internal feeling, the words, gestures, and gifts exchanged by sensitive modern selves had to appear wholly inwardly motivated, purified of self-interest and social ambition, free from the taint of the market, independent of the profit-calculations that so evidently shaped and determined the social world in which these selves were operating. The authentic interior self was created as a resistance to market determinations, as the basis of moral efficacy within market societies, yet it was wholly a creation of these conditions.[12]

The convulsive eruption of new forms of employment, new technological developments in production and transportation, new social environments, and new social networks resulted in a widely dispersed popular demand for a profusion of commercial forms of mass culture that addressed the anxieties and contradictions of sentimentalism. In the past twenty-five years, as scholars have attempted to understand the varieties of everyday life in the nineteenth century, popular fiction that detailed private feeling and domestic life, along with the etiquette books that described the sentimental code of conduct, have become key sources of evidence for understanding the culture of sentimentalism that was characteristic of the new middle classes of the nineteenth century. Curiously, commercially produced valentines have not received the attention due them for their potential evidentiary and textual value. As widely popular, commercially distributed, handcrafted productions that attempted to speak of the heart, these tokens provide key insights into the complexities of determinations that gave rise to the structures of feeling characteristic of the middle classes. As we will see, commercially produced valentines—both the sentimental and the comic—were quite useful in the maintenance and reproduction of class distinctions, even as they provided external sources for emotional eloquence.[13]

From Love Letters to Valentines

As Karen Lystra's analysis of nineteenth-century love letters has shown, the link between emotional eloquence and the middle-class status associated with commercial and professional occupations was tightly drawn and widely recognized. She argues that "the nineteenth-century Victorian experience of love was rooted in the concept of an ideal self. Not fully expressed in public roles, this ideal self was meant to be completely revealed to one person only. . . . The feelings and behaviors of love were deeply shaped by the idea that completely unfettered self-revelation should be reserved for intimates and indeed defined intimacy." The privacy that nurtured romantic love was a sort of shell protecting the initial tentative publication of the self that was required for success in a commercial society. "Writing a love letter either affirmed one's power with words or demonstrated one's ineptness with the language," Lystra argues. "This had class meaning for verbal skill indicated control over the self, and self-control was the basic indicator of middle-class standing." Writing a passionate love letter was not simply the demonstration of control over the self; it was even more the demonstration of emotional eloquence in addition to control. The expression of emotional states required the most highly developed verbal skills. Verbal skills were evidence of the ability to perform mental labor. And, as Stuart Blumin has persuasively argued, the ability to perform mental labor was an indicator of future earnings and true middle-class status. By the 1840s, expressions of love and passion had become one of the central means of establishing and maintaining the class boundaries that were being produced in the industrializing and commercialized society of the urban northeastern United States. The circulation of such expressions was a key process in the formation of families and other forms of social affiliation that were central nodes in the economic network. The display of one's verbal skills in the most delicate and refined areas of expression, therefore, was fundamental in the courtship process.[14]

If a young man such as David Berdan could demonstrate in his love letters and in his valentines the eloquent elaboration of complex and intricate feeling, he was demonstrating his potential class position. The effective claim to middle-class status would have a profound impact on his prospects for marriage. Marriage was the primary link in the chain of social networks that were consolidating the new class. Emotional eloquence, however, was not pursued consciously as an overt demonstration of class. Class consciousness as such was not a dominant factor in explicit commentary of the period; why should we expect it to have appeared in love letters? Yet young Berdan was quite aware of the need to reveal his most sublime interior states as part of his courting. If he repeatedly relied on standard phrases to render public his sensitive interior, he was at least partially motivated by the powerful if unconscious determinants of class anxiety. Although Berdan was clearly practicing the mental labor already characteristic of the middle classes, his brother, John, was a butcher. In the 1840s, a butcher was an ambiguous occupation with respect to middle-class formation. A successful butcher could have been operating as a merchant, building the wealth and economic security that accrued sentimental respect and sympathy. An unsuccessful butcher, however, could just as easily have been earning the wages of the manual trades. I do not know how successful John Berdan was, nor do I have any evidence of his own sense of class or personal status. But it seems fair to suggest that the class standing of the Berdan family was in flux, and that David's efforts to court Catharine and Susan were not free from the anxieties of an uncertain rank. I am not surprised, therefore, that, in his wooing, he relied on familiar phrases that had already demonstrated their ability to convey the most refined and delicate emotions that characterized his authentic interior self.[15]

David Berdan's handwritten valentines were dream images, shaped by convention, directed by the lineaments of genre, and aided in their expression by the previously repeated gestures of romance and romantic desire just as much as any commercially produced token of affection. This does not mean that Berdan's love was inauthentic, a reified, abstract, and, therefore, false outpouring of a commercially tainted interior. To the contrary, Berdan's longing for affiliation and feelings of love and affection were quite probably among the most authentically utopian effects of the economic and social determinants he lived within. The culture of sentiment was not simply the obfuscation of political will; it also represented a hope that the crystalline interiors forged from the fires of adversarial economics and social competition could do more than reflect the prismatic colors of those forces. The culture of sentiment hoped that the sincere effusions of these interiors would not simply reproduce those forces, but redirect them, reshape the channels through which they flowed, and, in so doing, change the means whereby the quality of social life was evaluated. Sympathy, the very capacity for fellow feeling, was the mirror image of self-interest, but it was also the basis for truly moral sentiments.

Valentine Writers

Of course, David Berdan's handwritten sentiments might not have sprung from his own heart, but could have been borrowed from one of the hundreds of valentine writers that had been published over the previous century. Emotional eloquence had been commercially available in the United States for decades. In 1820, George Moses Horton, a slave who lived and worked on a plantation near Chapel Hill, North

Carolina, "was selling love poems for a quarter, fifty cents, and occasionally seventy-five cents, to male students" at the nearby university. In the Northeast, the market for emotional eloquence was typically served by bound volumes of short love poems known as valentine writers. By 1847, *Strong's Annual Valentine Advertiser*, a promotional brochure published by one of the major valentine emporia operating in New York, hawked valentine writers at a variety of prices in every prepackaged lot of seasonal material. T. W. Strong referred to himself as an engraver. In addition to producing and selling a line of stationery and business forms, he imported valentines, fancy paper, and valentine writers from England. He also published his own valentines, using the rather simple technologies of lithography and hand-tinting to produce both comic and sentimental images and verses for sale throughout the Northeast. Strong's agents traversed New Jersey, no doubt stopping at stationers and bookstores near Brunswick College. If a local shopkeeper bought one of Strong's $10 or $50 lots of valentine material, he would have received between fourteen and forty valentine writers. Strong carried two different categories of these books. *Strong's Universal Valentine Writer* claimed to offer sentimental and satirical verses for all situations. In 1847, these relatively large volumes retailed at $3, while the smaller valentine writer sold for 37 cents. There was considerable variety among the booklets that Strong published and distributed, but among those that any store in New Jersey could acquire would quite probably have been the *Gem Valentine Writer*, a 2- by 3- inch chapbook with a printed and filigreed cover, and *Love Points Inscribed to the Valentine Writer*, almost the same size with a female figure lithographed on the cover. These small packages of emotional eloquence were about forty pages in length, with each page holding from one to three verses, each of which ranged in length from four to twelve lines. Many of the earliest valentine writers sold in the United States had been imported from England. Once paper became more widely available in North America, some firms, like Strong, found it cheaper to set their own type and copy selected verses from many of the competing imports or, on occasion, to commission a local wit to compose a few additions for their particular products.[16]

Strong published *Love Points Inscribed to the Valentine Writer* in 1849 and again in 1850. Like most of these collections of previously published verses, this booklet was prefaced with a clever demonstration of the verbal acuity and, therefore, the authority of its composer and compiler, who termed himself "a Green-un." This author of Strong's *Love Points* wished to establish his or her verbal skill by playing off the multiple meanings condensed in the title of the collection:

> In this little volume is presented to the public a collection of entirely original pieces for the Valentine Writer. We trust there are few to whom someone of our "points" may not be *in point*; and if we may be so happy as to assist any bashful swain, and over sentimental maiden, in coming to *the point*—our effort, at least so far as they are concerned, will not be *pointless*.

In accordance with the conventions of such prefaces, Green-un emphasized the originality of his enclosed verses, an originality that probably could be strictly defended. Very few of the differently titled valentine writers surviving in archives are exact replicas of one another. As is generally true for commercial mass culture, the valentine writer allowed for great variation within the strict limitations of its generic outlines. The authors of these volumes unquestionably collected elements from previous versions. In some cases, they borrowed entire verses; in other cases, they copied only lines or common similes; almost always, they adhered to the apparently widely understood requirements of the genre. Because these were products offering a service for hire, they had to promise and occasionally deliver an eloquence that was both recognizable yet not too common. Because they were competing with other volumes, they could not simply reproduce what the others had to say. Originality—which is to say, a quality of unrepeatability, of evident variation within comforting reiteration—was an essential contributor to their value. Thus the originality of each valentine writer was loudly proclaimed on its cover, on its title page, and in its preface (if it had one). Through their demonstration of the wit and cleverness of their authors, such prefaces were intended to provide a promise of the value of the verses to follow. Some of these prefaces were masterpieces of the genre, rendering explicit the contradictions of commercial emotional eloquence, even as they argued for the specific usefulness of their product.[17]

One relatively late valentine writer, published in England in 1857 and imported soon after to the United States, offered, in addition to its *Collection of New and Original Valentines*, an *Introductory Treatise on the Composition of a valentine by a Master of Hearts*. The treatise begins by highlighting an appalling absence in the market for emotional eloquence. For over thirty years, this wit declared, lovers have been forced to rely on the hackneyed "roses red and violets blue," and recently, valentine writers had been nearly driven out of the market by paper valentines. "Not only have the existing collections of Valentines not been improved," wrote the Master of Hearts,

> but they are now not to be met with at all; and those who wish to pay the compliments of the season to their friends are obliged (unless inclined to hazard an original composition) to fall back on the above-mentioned perennials, or else make use of those senseless lace-paper gew-gaws, which are a degree worse still; or, again, if it be in a satirical rather than a sentimental strain they wish to indulge, they are driven to those trashy—nay, often worse than that—those coarse and sometimes disgusting productions which, soon after Christmas, begin annually to people the hucksters' shop windows, in the shape of penny picture-Valentines. The gap in literature remains, then; and, like the devoted Quintus Curtius of old, I prepare to shy myself therein, exclaiming most emphatically as I disappear beneath the surface. REFORM YOUR VALENTINES!

After providing a brief yet humorous history of the holiday, the Master of Hearts turned to describing the "practical use of this book":

> Of course, in writing a Valentine, the very best way of all is to *write an original one*. Whether you would soften the hard heart, or give a hard hit at the soft skull, it must be obvious that nothing

can be so telling or so pungent as an immediate emanation from your own heart, or a direct inspiration of your own brain. And I shall be quite content for you to throw aside my book (supposing only you have duly bought and paid for it), if what I have said induce you to rely upon your own resources rather than those of the fancy-paper maker, or the coarse caricaturist. If, however, you are *not* disposed to go to the trouble of writing for yourselves, and do not think it *infra dig.* to use another's brain (as we all do use each other's in one way or another), let me offer you the small modicum I possess; or, at all events, let me stand between you and the present trash which goes by the name of Valentines.[18]

This author and purveyor of sentimental and satirical verses drew a qualitative distinction between preprinted paper valentines and those copied out in one's own hand: "Write at least with your own pen, and let the matter be selected, as far as possible, by your own judgment: so will one step be gained. And, even though you still employ the 'mercenary bard,' it is hoped and believed that the reformation of your Valentines will have begun." Sincerity of feeling and expression maintained its value even within the commercial market for emotional eloquence. The mark of one's own hand, along with the personalized tools of pen and ink, could splatter a coating of authenticity onto the borrowed phrases.

Was the Master of Hearts simply arguing from necessity, reaching for principles that would easily come to hand for an author of valentine writers in competition with producers of paper valentines? Perhaps. But his guidelines might also help us locate a lived measure of authenticity within the transatlantic commercial society; they might help us situate the meaning of emotional eloquence within a commercial material base. This author does acknowledge a certain social grounding to authorship—we all use one another's brains in one way or another—but he refuses to allow all distinctions to melt away: if we select the materials ourselves, and put our mark on them in some unmistakable signature, we have begun to make them ours, to have reformed our valentines. To have altered these objects, these phrases, through copying in one's own hand, is to have transformed their significance. Using one's personal pen and own hand to scratch out borrowed phrases forces that language to pass through the body of the sender—it enters through the eyes and exits by the hand, encountering the sender's internal emotional states along the way. The purpose of emotional eloquence, even if the eloquence be purchased from the mercenary bard, is still the external expression of internal states of feeling. In commercial culture, the ability to render one's own interior apprehensible to others remains the necessary step in the promotion and circulation of sympathy and fellow feeling, the prerequisite to love and affiliation, the basic element in sentimental courtship. Again, perhaps self-servingly, the Master of Hearts refers to the hazardous quality of attempting to write an original verse. It should be clear that such efforts were dangerous; in its piquant potential—its telling and pungent quality—an original verse could reveal too much. Expressions of love were treated quite seriously. There was much at stake. It might have been better to write an original valentine—if that original were well formed—but it was far better to borrow and rearrange previously successful phrases, either generated in one's own heart or looked up in a book, than to hazard an unsuccessful and potentially humiliating failure of emotional expression.[19]

Valentine writers acknowledged and documented the pain as well as the delights of love. One early English writer included a verse proclaiming:

> My panting heart is now inditing
> My trembling hand is also writing
> A line or two, to let you see
> Your folly and your cruelty.

Entitled *Hymen's Revenge*, this writer was published about 1805 in London. It included the following verse, which not only may have been used when the exact circumstances called for it, but easily could have been varied to match the qualities of any person to whom it might have been addressed; for "charms" will always rhyme with "arms," "hair" will always rhyme with "fair," and, with a bit of a stretch, "waiste" can forever line up with "surpas't":

Hard to describe those matchless charms,
Which long I've wish'd within my arms,
Yet I'll attempt—thy nut brown hair,
Thy skin, like snow white lillies fair;
Thy taper fingers and thy waiste,
By Venus self can't be surpas't . . . thou are half divine,
Dearest, do let me call thee mine.[20]

Beyond the common rhymes and the predictable references to hair, skin, and figure, the author of this verse offers a skillful combination of these typical elements within the requirements of poetic scansion, demonstrating the ability to link these common figures in lilting lines of verse. This is not poetry for the ages, but it is poetry for a moment, for a specific moment of courtship, communication, and promise. While very similar verses can be found in almost any writer from this period, this valentine, carefully modified to fit the physical description of the recipient and dutifully copied onto lace paper, could be confidently delivered by hand or post, with the sender secure that the loved one would receive just this set of phrases from no one else. This verse, therefore, could mark the sentiment that for that one moment defined their love. A simple moment of emotional eloquence for a common, yet always unique, experience.

Commercial Valentines

Such phrases were often copied onto one of the earliest forms of commercial valentine. This consisted of a sheet of lace paper, with a simple lithographed and sometimes hand-tinted design in the center, around which was penned—in the sender's own hand—a brief verse. One such valentine, probably dating from the 1840s, quietly demonstrates the anguished fear of failing to achieve emotional eloquence:

Accept this offering
Sanctioned by the day.
And let it whisper all,
I'd wish to say.[21]

How eloquent, really, is that word, "whisper," that breathy acknowledgment that the moment of emotional expression is fraught with hazards, and that the demands created out of the mutually conflicting drives of sympathy and self-interest are often beyond the individual expressive capacities of the valentine's sender. Without verbally specifying the intricacies of those internal states, the sender of this valentine has relied on the shared understanding of the holiday, its lessening of the penalties for misplaced ardor and therefore its encouragement of the more hazardous expressions, and the objective aspects of the offering itself, to articulate all the sender might have wished to say.

Between 1844 and 1849, Frances J. Crocker, the great-great-granddaughter of Isaiah Thomas, received dozens of handwritten valentines, inscribed on fancy colored paper. As a daughter of one of the more prominent families in Worcester, Massachusetts, she had many suitors. Her gentlemen friends were aware of their competitors and recognized valentines as an arena within which they could compete for her affections. For Valentine's Day in 1847, Frances's heart was compared to a music box, for which only the sender of this valentine had the magic key:

> Your heart is a music box, dearest!
> With exquisite tunes at command,
> Of melody sweetest and clearest,
> If tried by a delicate hand;
> But its workmanship, love, is so fine,
> At a single rude touch it would break;
> Then oh! By the magic key mine
> Its fancy-like whispers to wake!

The music-box conceit could have been original to the sender of this verse; it could just as easily have been found preprinted on a bound page in a bookshop. The origin of the metaphor does not matter so much as the meanings it suggests and the eventual effectiveness of its articulation of interiors. Combining the tactile metaphors of musical performance and craftsmanship as a means of discriminating between his own magic key and the rude touch of others, this would-be lover longs to conjure out of Frances the music of her heart. He emphasizes the delicacy of his hand even as he compliments her heart's fine work-manship, resulting in an elegant articulation of interiors that suggests not simply manual but also emotional dexterity. (We will come back soon to other means of articulating this felt link between productive skill and emotional labor.)

That same year, another anxious lover wrote to Frances:

> Oft I bless you for the vision
> Of something bright and rare
> That flit across my daily path,
> My daily path of care;
> And I know that many love you,
> Many sue on bended knee;
> But whate'er you are to others,
> you're all the world to me.

This valentine blends the sight of Frances with the expansive embrace of the world, describing the common feeling that the vision of the loved one can actually represent and contain all the world, a feeling known to every lover. Both these valentines are written on fancy paper with silver and blue flowers ringing the edges. The flowers add a layer of delicacy, but they do not approach the complexity of the lace paper that would soon become a central component of the commercial valentine.[22]

Soon after commercial paper valentines were introduced, their buyers, senders, and receivers began to take advantage of the emotive qualities of the object itself to represent aspects of the private internal feelings of the sender and the almost equally private meanings of the relationship. Karen Lystra has argued that the expression of the au-thentic interior always took place in private and that privacy was rec-ognized as essential to the mutual explorations of each lover's authen-tic interior self. Thus love letters were never opened in public and were very rarely shared. Although they were important artifacts of the cul-ture of sentimentalism, commercial valentines, which rapidly grew in popularity from the late 1830s through the 1870s, were never treated as the equivalent of love letters, even though valentines shared several of their purposes. As it did in love letters, the emotional language in valentines functioned only if it was believed to be sincere, for it had to represent the authentic emotional states of its senders. In addition to being conveyors of sentimental language, however, valentines were always objects. They differed from love letters in that one of their chief attributes was their ability to display, in at least a quasi-public fashion, their complex representation of sentiment. As physical objects created to be publicly displayed, valentines also expanded the means whereby feeling could be embodied and shared.

A short story that first appeared in *Godey's Lady's Book* in 1850 illustrates this difference. "Kate's Valentine" tells the story of a young woman who, "like most young ladies of her age . . . thinks independently, and generally speaks what she thinks." At the beginning of the story, Kate declares her antipathy toward valentines. "If any one were to send me a Valentine . . . I would take it as a direct insult to my common sense," she declares. Her uncle, the narrator of the story, wagers that she will one day receive a valentine from a certain young man who has been courting her and that she will actually enjoy it. Kate vehemently denies this possibility and accepts the wager. When the morning of February 14 arrives, Kate receives a large valentine delivered by the "Dispatch Post." She immediately whisks it away and opens it in the privacy of her room upstairs. Several more valentines arrive throughout the course of the day, but Kate does not comment on any of them. The next day, her uncle begins to inquire about the valentines she received, but Kate demurely refuses to reply. When the young man comes to visit that evening, however, Kate is wearing a new bracelet on her arm. The bracelet had come with the early-morning anonymous valentine, and Kate has decided that it was a gift from her favorite but quite softspoken young man. She wears it only when he visits, and it becomes a sign of their growing involvement. Eventually the uncle reveals that it was he who gave her the bracelet, and that he allowed her to believe that it had come from her young man. By the time the truth is revealed, however, the courtship has been successfully concluded; Kate is about to marry her beau. The bracelet, the valentine, had done its work, regardless of who had actually sent it. Glittering on Kate's arm, the bracelet was obviously an object that could be displayed. It was different from a love letter in that it did not need to remain completely hidden from others, and it made no attempt to demonstrate verbal skill. But the bracelet worked like a valentine to the extent that it did function to signify and externally represent an emotional relationship that was growing in significance and importance. Valentines quickly became important quasi-public expressive objects in the culture of sentimentalism. Their circulation established the objective, if tentative, reality of sensitive modern selves articulated in a social network.[23]

Comic Valentines and the Policing of the Middle Classes

Universal valentine writers had to include sentimental *and* comic or satirical verses imaginatively originating from diverse persons and aiming, like Cupid's darts, at others. The larger valentine writers often categorized their verses by specifying the subject positions of the sender and/or the receiver. The oldest English writers tended to focus on the social status of the sender and the receiver—emphasizing the specifics of fortune, of age, of the beauty, grace, or learning (or the lack thereof) of the participants in this social exchange. They often entitled their verses "From a Gentleman to a Lady," and followed such essays with suggested responses "From the Lady in Answer." Gradually, however, valentine writers began to emphasize specific differences of occupation in addition to qualities of beauty, age, and grace. As early as 1805, *Hughes's Second New and Original Valentine Writer* proclaimed that it was "Adapted for Various Trades and Professions." By 1849, Strong's *Love Points* identified almost all the senders and sometimes the receivers of its valentines by their occupations and created verses that pledged an identity between work and the personal expressions of love. The physician would prescribe the powders and pills of love; the blacksmith's true hand would fain grapple with an iron heart; a baker could deliver the staff of life. *Love Points* went on to describe the love of many tradesmen in such terms, but it also included comic satirical verses that described the inadequate courtings of occupations such as green grocers, carpenters, and sailors. Perhaps not surprisingly, wine and silk merchants were figured as the source of sentimental verses, but no satirical verses were addressed to them.[24]

Comic valentines had been a part of the valentine craze from the earliest years of its commercialization. The hazardous quality of emotional expression has long provided a source of comedy to observers, and comic valentines began as a means of poking fun at misplaced ardor. Thus the earliest comics focused on the differences of fortune, beauty, age, and grace that commonly mark inappropriate love. In his discussion of the commercialization of Valentine's Day, Leigh Eric Schmidt argues that merchants promoted the use of paper caricatures as satirical representations of "adversarial relationships," struggling to expand the commercial reach of the holiday to encompass "annoying neighbors, exacting bosses, harsh schoolmasters, unattractive suitors, and domineering wives." This is no doubt true. Comics were a sort of mass-culture charivari, as Schmidt asserts. But in his emphasis on the collaboration between merchants and gender conflict, Schmidt does not fully explain the growing popularity of the comics. Comic valentines exposed the seams in the social fabric, ripping away at the loose stitches that patched together a society divided not only by gender but also by race and by class.[25]

As Schmidt points out, Strong barely mentioned comic valentines in his 1847 promotional mailer. By 1853, however, comics were a major component of his business. Other printing houses, most famously McLoughlin Brothers, specialized in the production of comic valentines. While the traditional concern of Valentine's Day with matters of love and courtship encouraged the producers of comics to focus on gender conflict, structuring their social critique as a private concern focused on love and marriage, more often than not, comic valentines carried multiple meanings. They demand to be read as contemporary popular statements about social conflict. Most preprinted commercial comic valentines, in fact, address inappropriate love only as a result of other forms of unseemly behavior derived from and associated with the conditions of work or social status. In Strong's *Comic Valentine Writer*, satirical verses are addressed to a barber, a cook with a rolling pin, a groom, a fishmonger, a brush maker, a butcher, a carpenter, a cobbler, an apothecary, a greengrocer, a pawn broker, a tailor, and a "black or person of color."[26] These occupations and the sign of racial difference mark the shifting lower reaches of the developing white commercial middle classes. Comic valentines were as centrally involved in the re-production and transformation of class during the market revolution as were the sentimental variety. Comics were eagerly, playfully, and vi-ciously sent to and from the participants in this process of economic restructuring. The occupations and characteristics mocked in comic valentines mark the shifting boundaries of the middle classes in forma-tion throughout the nineteenth century and into the earliest years of the twentieth. As their attention moved through the decades from sailor, carpenter, and tailor to policeman, clerk, and secretary, comic valentines documented the changing shape of the middle classes as they were experienced by those undergoing the transformation. The disruptions of uncertain class status drove the popularity of comic valentines, producing a taste for the particular pleasures that one could derive from mocking the ambitions, desires, and tastes of others com-peting for a meaningful place in an anxious world.

Comic valentines were cheap to purchase and easy to send. The anonymity of the sender was guaranteed by a postal system that added injury to insult by charging the receiver of the mail for the postage. Often referred to as penny-paper valentines, these comics consisted of one sheet of cheap paper, onto which was lithographed a quick carica-ture and a very brief verse. McLoughlin Brothers created valentines that explicitly mocked the pretensions of workingmen and -women. One valentine addressed to a "teamster" read:

> As a teamster you're putting on such a high air,
> You are a whole team and donkey to spare
> Like a show-man's vain monkey you sit on the seat
> And run smash and bang 'gainst all things on the street.

"The Pride of the Mills" depicted a young woman standing in front of the textile factories built by the Boston Associates, holding a copy of the *Lowell Offering*.[27] Many comics attacked those believed to be too old to be wooing. "Miss gray hairs and wrinkles" is warned away from the marriage chase (figure 1.1), as is the "frisky old maid," who reveals her sentimental nature by carrying a "new novel." Men, too, were the objects of such scorn. The gaping teeth and bald head of a "nasty old

Figure 1.1
"Miss Gray Hairs and
Wrinkles." (Norcross
Greeting Card Collection,
Archives Center, National
Museum of American
History, Behring Center,
Smithsonian Institution)

Miss gray hairs and wrinkles, don't look quite so cold,
Don't let it surprise you to find yourself old;
The old family record, with truth on its page,
Tells a horrible fact about your present age.
Your Pa or your Ma may have said you look'd young
Some twenty years since,—but now you're among
The *old maids* of this world, without chance for a beau,
For Cupids' grown *gray* since he cut you, you know.

Huestis, 104 Nassau st., cor. Ann, N. Y.

bachelor" cannot be hidden by his fancy clothes, and the many valentines that attack such men demonstrate the negative side of the evolv-
ing practice, described by Mary Ryan, of young middle-class men post-
poning marriage for the purpose of firmly establishing their
professions and class status (figure 1.2). Of course, if a man chose not
to wait, but began his courting before solidifying his standing, he could
equally become the recipient of a satirical comic. Clerks were an especially common object of critique. As a relatively new profession with
profoundly ambiguous job requirements and future possibilities, the
clerk could claim considerably more status than his fortune or professional autonomy might actually deliver. The comic addressed "To a
Clerk" criticizes the drudgery that frequently defined this occupation,
and questioned the legitimacy of any fortune so obtained (figure 1.3):

Figure 1.2
"Nasty Old Bachelor."
(Norcross Greeting Card
Collection, Archives Center,
National Museum of American
History, Behring Center,
Smithsonian Institution)

Figure 1.3
"To a Clerk." (Norcross
Greeting Card Collection,
Archives Center, National
Museum of American History,
Behring Center, Smithsonian
Institution)

The plan of your future I plainly can see,
A slave to your books and bottle you'll be;
Unless, indeed your employer discovers,
The demon, embezzlement, over you hovers.

Young men who chose clothing to display status claims were a frequent target for the darts of comics. "The swell clerk" has spent his earnings on a "natty suit of clothes." This valentine mocks his choice by asserting that the suit will be stuck in "a pawn-shop before the month is out," and the clerk will be revealed as "a dude who has an empty head, and owns an empty purse" (figure 1.4). Some comics dispensed with the standard four-line verse and simply caricatured their subjects through the image and a slogan, such as the "true Billingsgate Fishmonger" (figure 1.5). Blacksmiths, bricklayers, and tinsmiths were common targets (figures 1.6–1.8). Working-class women employed

Figure 1.4
"The Swell Clerk."
(Norcross Greeting Card
Collection, Archives Center,
National Museum of American
History, Behring Center,
Smithsonian Institution)

THE SWELL CLERK.

Go away you homely little dude, or I'll hit you with a feather,
I really think t'would make you wilt, though I'd prefer it leather.
As for your natty suit of clothes, that you love to sport about,
You'll stick it in a pawn-shop before the month is out.
The girls think you are silly, or what is even worse,
A dude who has an empty head, and owns an empty purse.

Figure 1.5
"The True Billingsgate
Fishmonger." (Norcross
Greeting Card Collection,
Archives Center, National
Museum of American History,
Behring Center, Smithsonian
Institution)

Figure 1.6
"My Lovely Blacksmith."
(Norcross Greeting Card
Collection, Archives
Center, National Museum
of American History,
Behring Center,
Smithsonian Institution)

outside or inside the home were equally likely to receive barbs addressed to their occupation. Along with the frequent depiction of maids, the nursemaid and the milliner were common objects of vicious sentiments (figures 1.9 and 1.10).[28]

In the complex interweaving discourses of class and ethnicity, the mark of drink was a sign of difference from the native-born middle classes, and an obvious target for comic valentines. One milliner's "bottle nose doth show / Where the profits on the bonnets go." At some point, one of the producers specializing in comics discovered that, relatively quickly and easily, a bit of red ink could be daubed onto the noses of their caricatures, adding a distinct tinge of middle-class morality to their mockery. Such bits of color probably added considerably to the appeal of these cards, as this trick of manufacturing soon spread comic accusations of working-class pleasures across ambiguous occupations. The milliner could own her own shop, as

Figure 1.9
"Nursery Maid."
(Norcross Greeting Card Collection, Archives Center, National Museum of American History, Behring Center, Smithsonian Institution)

'TIS alas too true as I've often heard said,
You're a careless unfeeling sham nursery maid,
Pray who would wed charms such as thine,
Or have such a slut for a valentine.

could the tinsmith; the clerk could be a junior partner in a rising firm. But if they displayed a taste for liquor, they were demonstrating the liquidity of their class ambitions.[29]

While comic valentines often illustrated racial differences, I have never seen a comic from this era produced to be sold or sent to an African American. J. Wrigley, a manufacturer of comic valentines in New York, created a hostile antiabolitionist comic that read in part:

> You nasty, Black Republican
> To hug the sooty African
> How sweet to you her stench must seem.

Even the comic addressed to "a black" in Strong's *Comic Valentine Writer* is as concerned with class as it is with race, participating as it does in the powerful American tradition of blackface minstrelsy. The lines read:

My dingy dear, when you appear,
My heart goes pit-a-pat;
So black your face, your lips to grace, and nose so very flat.
Your woolly hair, I do declare,
Appears to be divine.
Then stray no more, sweet Blackamoor
But be my Valentine.

Of all the comics in this writer, this one alone had no response following it. It was clearly meant to be sent not to a person of color, but to a person who would have been insulted by being addressed as a person of color (figure 1.11). Whereas most comics directly insult the receiver, stating firmly that a love match would be impossible with a person like that caricatured, this comic asks the blackamoor to stray no more. Obviously the classification was believed to be sufficiently insulting in itself—so insulting that whoever had received it would not think of replying. As Eric Lott and numerous others have carefully detailed, the discourse of racial difference played a complex role in the formation of working classes in the antebellum period. Recognizing the policing function of comic valentines, this blackface token of sentiment placed its receiver even lower than the white working class.[30]

The popular ingenuity of comic valentines demonstrates the intensity of the lived conflict we understand as classes-in-formation. The social relationships that were policed and disciplined by comic valentines were akin to the social relationships that were produced through the use of sentimental valentines. While the comic valentine illustrated the humorous yet harsh capacities of inappropriate love to mock differences of class and gender as well as ethnicity and race, the sentimental relied on the sweet tones of sincere feeling and the implied achievement of an agentive interior self to discriminate the same differences. Both genres relied on paper and ink and standardized gestures, both verbal and visual. Both took strategic advantage of the potential for anonymity that printed communication and the postal system offered. Both were indicative of and revealing of the new and complex social conditions within which the exchange of these tokens took place. They were equally concerned with the formation and the policing of desire,

Figure 1.11 "Dingy Dear." (Norcross Greeting Card Collection, Archives Center, National Museum of American History, Behring Center, Smithsonian Institution)

both carnal and material, within new, confusing, and apparently endless opportunities for longing.

The Material Culture of Valentines

One of the most important ways in which valentines represented desire, emotional relationships, and authentic interior states was through their condition as material objects. Most obviously, valentines were visual, often saying as much through an image as they did through their sentiment. One Strong valentine from the 1840s shows a couple sitting before a statue on a park bench, proclaiming "affection, fair and truly." This valentine fit Strong's category of "Sentimental No. 2," valentines "of . . . nicely tinted or colored lithographic vignettes, with inscriptions to imitate manuscript." The object qualities of valentines were not limited to their visual imagery, however. Any time spent among collections of antebellum valentines forces one to consider their layered tactile complexity. Most commercial valentines produced in the 1840s were made of a single sheet of paper, occasionally but not always embossed or laced. If the verse—either original or copied from a writer—were handwritten, often the only complement to the verse was the delicacy or intricacy of the paper's design. The special qualities of the paper were precisely what marked this early form of the commercial valentine—it was the paper (and, when necessary, the valentine writer) that was purchased at the stationers. By the middle part of this decade, many commercial valentine makers were printing a simple lithographed image onto the paper. Typically, the more complex and delicate the embossing of the paper, the more simple the lithographed image; conversely, the plainer the paper, the larger and more detailed the image (figures 1.12 and 1.13). Strong offered valentines that combined extensive lacework with elaborate images, but these valentines sold for upward of 50 cents each—beyond the reach of all but the most financially comfortable lovers. But even mass-produced valentines displayed individualizing variation. With hand-tinting, each valentine would differ from its otherwise identical siblings in the location and amount of color added. The effects of the hand could be seen in the slight variations in the patterns of embossed and laced paper as well.[31]

Figure 1.12　Mansell lace-paper valentine: "Thy Name Is Now the Magic Spell." (Norcross Greeting Card Collection, Archives Center, National Museum of American History, Behring Center, Smithsonian Institution)

Figure 1.13 "I Cannot Long These Pangs Endure." (Norcross Greeting Card Collection, Archives Center, National Museum of American History, Behring Center, Smithsonian Institution)

Only high-quality rag paper could withstand the embossing pressures that produced the textured surfaces of valentines. Embossed stationery had been produced in Germany, Austria, and England since the last decades of the eighteenth century. The first English patent for embossing was granted to John Gregory Hancock in 1796. By the second decade of the nineteenth century, H. Dobbs and Thomas de la Rue were making embossed stationery and playing cards. Jonathan King, one of the earliest collectors of valentines, worked for Dobbs toward the end of the nineteenth century. According to King, it was in 1842 that an Englishman named Addenbrooke came up with the idea of placing the embossed paper back onto the die that had produced the texture, stretching the paper tight against the die, and then filing off the uppermost surfaces, "leaving the finely-cut, lace-like threads of paper safely embedded in the die." Charles Dickens described paper embossing as "a tedious and expensive process," requiring "a great number and variety of punches . . . to execute a design." Transforming the embossed paper into lace "requires great nicety of touch not to tear the paper." Each step in the process, from the initial cutting of the die, to the tempering that hardened it, to the embossing, stretching, and filing of the paper, required the combination of concentration, dexterity, and care that suggests the intimate attentions of love: "This was the so-called lace paper which became the foundation of so many beautiful and expensive Valentines from 1845–1865." By the 1850s there were thirteen lace-paper makers operating in England, the most famous and successful being Joseph Mansell, who was exporting white, gold-colored, and silver-colored lace papers to North America.[32]

In 1850 most commercial valentines were either single sheets of plain paper, lithographed with a simple image and a brief verse, or single sheets of embossed lace paper folded over to allow the inscription of sentiment. Comics never used lace paper, certainly out of concern for the cost—why spend good money on a cheap insult?—but also for reasons more closely connected to the quality of the sentiments expressed. I argue that one of the important functions of valentines was to materialize the quality of the emotional relationships they represented. During the 1850s, lace paper became more easily available throughout the northeastern United States; it quickly became an almost necessary component of the sentimental valentine for its ability to suggest delicacy, refinement, and complexity. No such implications were required for a comic's policing of desire. The flatness of the paper and the two-dimensional quality of the images were the perfect complement for the comic's harsh caricatures.

The years between 1847 and 1858 saw the greatest diversification of commercial valentine styles. In New York, the trade was dominated by engraving firms like T. W. Strong, Robert Elton, Fisher & Brothers, McLoughlin Brothers, and J. Wrigley. Although they continued to produce sentimental valentines, by the mid-1850s these firms tended to emphasize their lines of comic valentines. Comics were cheaper to produce, as they continued to rely on the relatively simple production techniques of lithography and hand-tinting that had been the basis of commercial valentine production in the 1840s. Insofar as the complex crosscuttings of class formation intersected more frequently with everyday life than did the sentimental effusions of love, the potential audience for comics was considerably wider than that for sentimental valentines. In short, comics quickly became more profitable. In fact, by the 1880s, *Harper's Weekly* would bemoan the fact that Valentine's Day had become more closely associated with satire than with sentiment.[33] But this taste for images of class struggle over gestures of love did not eliminate the genre of sentimental valentines. For by the end of the 1840s, with the advent of lace paper, the intense competition among commercial valentine producers to create ever more elaborate tokens of affection, and the technical innovations of a young woman from Worcester, Massachusetts, the expressive potential of sentimental valentines increased dramatically.

Esther Howland and the Texture of Sentiment

No other producer of commercial valentines understood so well their potential for the tactile communication of complex feeling as did Esther Howland. Between 1855 and 1879, Howland's valentines became one of the most immediately recognized commercially produced symbols of both interior complexity and the class status that both required and produced those interiors. To this day, her valentines are prized by collectors for their visual and haptic intensity. In fact, Howland has been the object of numerous articles addressed to popular audiences and collectors of ephemera, where she appears as the perfectly self-supporting yet sympathetic domestic figure capable of uniting both sides of sentimental culture—market-driven production and exchange combined with sentiment and sympathy. Her symbolic importance among collectors of valentines and popular historians has led to a series of incredible claims. She has been falsely credited with producing the first commercial valentines on this continent. Most accounts of her business claim that she was earning $100,000 a year during the 1850s, an utterly fantastic sum. Howland does seem to have initiated the portion of the Howland family business that was devoted to valentine production, distribution, and sales. She does seem to have been in charge of the design and production process. She does seem to have been the person responsible for many—though certainly not all—of the stylistic innovations that transformed valentine design in the 1850s. But there is no evidence for the extravagant claims that "it was considered a privilege to work for Miss Howland, for she paid liberally and the work was light and pleasant," or that she "monopolized the business in the United States," or that she should be credited with inventing mass production and the "progressive assembly" of products. The Howland family business included stationery and book publishing, and valentines were a small part of that business. While she certainly controlled the design and quite probably directed the production of the family's valentines, Howland herself ran the company publicly for only a brief period during the 1870s. Leigh Eric Schmidt has suggested that the hagiography surrounding her can be explained by the need on the part of merchants to feminize the holiday, and to eliminate as much as possible the crass motives of profit and expansion that helped drive much of the merchants' behavior. According to Schmidt, "Stories about Howland help 'feminize' valentines and 'engender' the impression that 'feminine' sentimentality lies at their foundation, and thus lessen the 'taint' of commercial (and male) self-interest." While this is quite probably true so far as it goes, this interpretation ignores the structural link between sentiment and self-interest, as it fails to acknowledge the powerful utopian longings for the unification of sentiment and self-interest produced in market societies or the potential ability of valentine exchange to address those longings. Howland has taken on such a critical role in the history of valentine production in the United States because of her ability to represent the possibility of a specialized commodity-production-for-the-market purified by sentimentalism. As a domestic woman designing her own commodities, she has been presented as the dialectical unity of the contradictory cultural forces that emerged from the market revolution. The commercial success of her business, her ability to understand the material culture and the utopian promise of valentines, and the probably not-quite-true stories about her charming and dainty workplace have all become important markers of the deep need for a more profound meaning for human sociality and economic production than simple accumulation.[34]

Esther Howland was born in Worcester in 1828 to Southworth Allen Howland and Esther Allen, who demonstrated their class aspirations by sending her to Mount Holyoke Academy in South Hadley. The education at Mount Holyoke Academy was largely religious, focusing on the behavior and approach to life deemed appropriate for the women of the white, native-born middle classes who had been given the responsibility for ensuring the character of the nation's children. By the time she returned from the academy in 1848, her three brothers were working in her father's bookbindery and stationery store. Southworth Howland's main business was the compilation and production of schoolbooks that were used throughout New England, but he also produced and sold engraved cards and paper forms appropriate for a variety of uses, from wedding invitations to business purposes.

The mythical story, which I will follow for a moment, partly because of the significance of the myth and partly because there are no other sources, begins when Howland spies some English valentines that her father had imported for sale in his shop in downtown Worcester. It is curious that the oldest versions of the story do not recount her receiving one of these valentines, but make it clear that her first encounter with the expressive form that would become the basis of her lifework took place in her father's store: "In 1849 her father added to his stock a few imported valentines, the first which ever had been seen in Worcester. This bright young girl thought it would be no great task to make even prettier ones than the European love missives and told her folks so." At first she constructed her valentines out of scraps of embossed paper cut from envelopes. She pasted these decorations onto plain sheets of paper, positioned a few scraps of embossed and lightly colored lithographed images in the center, scalloped the edges of the paper, and asked her brother with the best handwriting to inscribe some brief verses. The myth emphasizes her ingenuity and creativity. Every version of the story insists that she fashioned her initial line of valentines from the scraps and detritus surrounding her in her father's workplace.[35]

Every version of the story also details the immediate success that greeted these humble homemade commercial valentines. After Southworth Howland approved of his daughter's prototypes, he ordered basic supplies of lace paper from England and small colored images from a lithographer in New York for the following year's season. He used his own printing plant for the verses that, throughout Esther's career, remained short and rather insignificant in the final construction of her valentines. Her brother Charles carried samples during his next sales trip and, the story goes, came back from that one trip with orders for $5,000 worth of valentines. Remember that the family's business combined book publishing and stationery. Charles was quite probably visiting the family's regular out-of-town customers and simply showing them his sister's valentines along with his regular merchandise. Even if we consider the $5,000 figure to be exaggerated, a likely projection backward to 1849 of turn-of-the-century dollars not adjusted for inflation, the success was astonishing. *Strong's Annual Valentine Advertiser for S. Valentine's Day, Feb. 14, 1847*, a publication not known for understatement, valued Strong's entire valentine stock, including papers and envelopes, at $15,000. If Howland's initial orders amounted to one-fifth that of the legend, it was an auspicious beginning for a young woman assembling scraps of color and lace according to the whims of her heart. Whatever the contemporary dollar value of the orders placed with Charles, Howland's designs were well received in the marketplace.

The first year's designs are gone, but surviving examples demonstrate Howland's awareness of the crucial significance of texture as the material foundation of a valentine's emotional representations. Before

Howland's success, the vast majority of valentines sold in the United States were flat, with two-dimensional woodcuts or lithographed images. In 1847, Strong reported employing "ten engravers on wood, three excellent lithographers, letter press and lithographic printers, thirty colorists, and other ornamental artists." Extrapolating from this proud description of Strong's technology and from the samples still found in archives, the focus of these valentines was the image, the picture created by printers and colorists. Even the most expensive valentines that Strong produced, those that retailed for $1 or more, simply complicated the two-dimensional image by, for example, enclosing it inside a fold-open flap, and, at the most expensive price points, attaching tiny gilt-edged mirrors, feathers, bits of hair, velvet, and silk. Strong and the other New York valentine manufacturers recognized the demand for texture on valentines, but their response to this demand was accumulative, not innovative. They added bits of texture onto the surface of their paper valentines, whereas Howland transformed texturing and layering into the structural principles of her production.[36]

Howland's valentines, and those of her followers and imitators, began with a sheet of plain paper. Onto this was glued a very thin sheet of colored glazed paper. Onto that was glued several small strips of paper that had been folded three times. These were the "lift-ups," which raised the lace paper and its ornaments above the colored paper, emphasizing the fact that this valentine was a three-dimensional object. The lace paper was as often gold or silver as it was white. Onto the lace paper was pasted numerous very small embossed and colored ornaments, typically flowers, garlands, birds, and cupids (plates 1 and 2). Inside a Howland valentine, you might find a standard-length verse, but the sentiments were never as significant as the dense textured layering that was responsible for the tactile complexity of her valentines. To our eyes, they appear gaudy and overwrought, virtually impossible, as they assault you with their riot of colors and forms. But that was not the way they were experienced in the middle of the nineteenth century. Howland's valentines were beloved tokens of intricate feeling. They were not the means of displaying verbal skills, but relied on the haptic pleasures of complex material objects to represent their profound condensation of sympathy and self-interest.[37]

As the legend continues, the orders so overwhelmed Howland that first year that she hired "four or five girls" to help her assemble the valentines, and they set up their operations in the attic of the family's home. Apparently, the assembly line was a model of compassionate management. Esther designed the patterns, and the young women joyfully put them together. "She was a strict but just forewoman," and "each girl had a space of her own, and a pattern to copy as exactly as possible." The workspace was well lighted and spacious. "Much laughter went along with the love, in the creations." Snipping, folding, assembling, pasting, and painting hundreds of similar items in a brisk line of rapidly swinging elbows and fingers, the female assemblers seem in these descriptions to attain the limited autonomy and joyous fellowship of the republican artisan's shop, though Howland's operation was as clearly structured as any of the new middle-class commercial operations. Production was physically separated from sales, but with production located in the Howland home, something of the earlier workplace relations was retained. Howland, "always . . . fond of the society of young girls," accepted many of them as apprentices who lived with her until they were married. These stories told about Esther Howland's early days as a mass producer of valentines are a fantasy of redeemed manual labor, of the survival of artisanal relations into the era of mass production.[38]

Worcester was a town of manufactories. A business guide published by Henry Howland in 1856 states that "the principal business of Worcester is mechanical, including the manufacture of an almost infinite variety of articles for different and distant markets, as well as for home consumption."[39] The town had developed as a regional center of mass production for the market of machinery, tools, iron and brass wire, cotton and woolen goods, boots and shoes, musical instruments, firearms—in short, the widest variety of consumer and business goods that it was possible to mass-produce. Industrialization was firming class lines. From Worcester's leading families came the directors of firms, the merchants who traded and shipped these goods. Places in the production line were held by unmarried girls and women, young boys, and recent immigrants. One might expect, therefore, that the descriptions of Esther's republican assembly line were utterly fanciful, with very little truth in them.

Yet in 1858, *Harper's Weekly* printed an article about valentine production and use that detailed the "nimble fingers of expert young ladies," stating that about 75 percent of all workers in the valentine industry were women and that their wages varied from $3 to $8 per week, year round. In 1864, Charles Dickens's journal *All the Year Round* reported a visit to "Cupid's Manufactory," a modern greeting card plant in London. There is no clear indication of which English company was the one visited, but it probably was that of either Thomas de la Rue or Marcus Ward, the two leading English makers of valentines at the time. Cupid's Manufactory housed the presses and dies that embossed, printed, and colored the paper, as well as the assembly line that so fascinated the fans of Esther Howland. But Dickens's description of the industrialized production of valentines also contains many of the key points in the fantasy of sentimentalized mass production: "In following the progress of our valentine from the embossing-room to the finishing department, we have passed in review about sixty hands, nearly forty of these being girls, the rest men and boys. In all the departments the work struck me as being of a healthy and cheerful kind. The rooms are well lighted and airy, and the girls exhibit none of the languor and weariness which are painfully apparent in the workrooms of the milliner and dressmaker."[40] Why would this be true? Or, if not true, why would the production of sentimental valentines become a site where could be located fantastic dreams of pleasant work performed by happy and decently paid workers in the early era of mass production, assembly line work, and hardening class lines?

Mass-produced sentimental valentines of the middle decades of the nineteenth century offered new means of externalizing a person's agentive interior. They expanded the possible forms that such an externalization could take beyond the display of verbal skills, beyond the promise of an educated place in the new commercial middle classes, to include the recognition of the complexity of material forms and the changing needs of manual work. They exemplified the capacity to combine artfully and expressively machine-made parts with hand assembly and finishing. The sentimental valentines of Howland and those who expanded on her work helped shape the imagined fantasies of sentiment, sympathy, and love for an economic system in transition from artisanal workplaces to industrialized factories. They helped ensure that the culture of sentimentalism would survive this stage in the modernization of the economy, and helped expand the range of this culture to include the broadest reaches of a middle class defined by its capacity to externalize its most refined and delicate feelings, its authentic interiors of self-interest and sympathy, in the form of lace paper, embossed hearts, and heightened color. In their materiality, their restricted use of language, and their undeniably mass-produced repetition, sentimental valentines objectified the most powerful subjective effects of the market revolution. Linking love with material production, interiority with the sensual textures of complex objects, and the changing conditions of work with the possibilities for affection, affiliation, and marriage, the production and exchange of commercial valentines helped establish the matrix of emotion and interiority as the crucial ideological construct through which questions of subjectivity, agency, longing, and belonging were deliberated until the forces of industrialization and the development of large business organizations began again to reshape middle-class structures of feeling.

2

The Nineteenth-Century Christmas Card

The Chromo-Reproduction of Sentimental Value

"Surely a new Pandora has been sent forth by the gods!—a most lovely, bewitching Pandora, who has opened her mysterious box, and poured upon the world its yearly blessing,—a rainbow-hued shower of Christmas cards!" So began Janet Huntington McKelvey's 1886 essay, "The Christmas Card," the winner of a competition sponsored by Louis Prang & Company for the best expression of "what ladies think" about the relatively recent American adoption of the practice of sending Christmas cards.[1] For a little more than ten years, Prang's artists, chromolithographers, printers, and salesmen had been collaborating in the design, production, and distribution of elegant, colorful cards created for exchange among friends, relatives, and business acquaintances at Christmas and on New Year's Day. The expression of special holiday greetings at this time was an old practice, dating back centuries. But the modern Christmas card tradition of purchasing and sending a printed card was an invention of the nineteenth century.

Commissioned by Henry Cole, an English reformer and educator, and designed by John Calcott Horsley, the first modern Christmas card was printed, published, and sold for the Christmas season of 1843.[2] Cole was an educator, and among his many projects was the improvement of children's literature. He believed that the illustration of children's books should be of the highest quality, and the stories should draw from traditional folk tales. This project was attacked in art journals and newspapers. Cole's ideas were termed "vague speculations, Utopian in their character." Opponents tried to block his appointment to the position of superintendent of schools in England because of his attempts to "wed art and manufacture."[3]

The Horsley–Cole Christmas card had been created as a fund-raiser for the children's literature project. Approximately a thousand copies of this simple lithographed card were sold to the public for 1 shilling each. The sentiment on the card is plain, "A Merry Christmas and a Happy New Year to You," but the design renders explicit the social function of this card. The center scene depicts a celebratory meal, with an extended family joyfully drinking together. This domestic scene is flanked by images of charity. To the left, a young man feeds an older woman and a young child. To the right, a young woman provides shelter and comfort to what seems to be an even younger mother. The happy, well-fed family in the center represents the key holiday theme of material abundance amid extensive social bonds. The charity scenes on the margins represent a noble conde-scension willing to share the fruits of seasonal abundance with those outside the nurturing social networks of extended families. Yet the decorative arbor that distinguishes the three scenes marks a clear boundary between those inside and those outside the social network. The faces of the drinking family are turned toward the users (both the sender and the receiver) of the card, including them in the represen-tation of wholeness, safety, and abundance. The faces in the charity scenes, however, are turned down and away. The overall effect of the card is to draw a distinction between the family of abundance and those cast aside by the industrial economy. This wedding of art and manufacture represents a fractured social whole as it positions the Christmas card as an imaginary field displaying the contradiction of inequality amid abundance.[4]

Variations on the Horsley–Cole card were published in England and the United States in the following years. William Egley created a card very similar to the Horsley–Cole card in 1848 that featured mul-tiple scenes of seasonal festivity. In the early 1850s, R. H. Pease de-signed a card to promote the family's variety store in Albany, New York, as a commercial source of seasonal abundance. Both of these cards clearly copied elements of the Horsley–Cole card, yet each em-phasized pleasure and consumption while dispensing with social obli-gations or any reference to charity. After the English adoption of the German technique of chromolithography, printing firms such as

Charles Goodall & Sons, Marcus Ward, and Thomas de la Rue added Christmas cards to their lines of valentines, stationery, personal cards, and posters. Growing in popularity through the late 1860s, these cards most often replaced any reference to human-produced abundance with nature imagery, tending to thematize the innocence of seasonal rebirth and renewal through flowers, small animals, and cherubic-faced children, emphasizing a sentimental representation of a presocial joy over against the rationally organized industrial means that enabled their production and supported their circulation.[5]

Although Louis Prang did not create the first American Christmas card, and he certainly was not alone in attempting to exploit the American market for these cards that developed over the second half of the nineteenth century, his overt public struggles with the contradictions of art, industry, discipline, and abundance give us an entry into the collapsed paradox of mass-cultural production and the problem of social affiliation within an industrializing world. Throughout his career as a chromolithographer, Prang mass-produced images representing the structures of feeling that organized rational business discipline along with ideologies of family joy and social obligation, and combined them into a consistent, if internally fractured and contradictory, whole. He worked to promote aesthetic education through the production of relatively cheap chromolithographic prints that aimed to distribute widely images with the visual complexity of oil paintings. The resulting "chromo-civilization" debates laid out the basic terms of the mass-culture debates that would be played out in the twentieth century. When he turned his factory to the production of Christmas cards, Prang focused his sentimental business acumen on a commodity whose discursive imagery held the capacity to critique its own means of production. A Pandora's box it was, and so it continued to be, as Prang's firm increasingly imaged contradiction and conflict on cards whose overt message remained joy, love, and abundance. This chapter focuses on Prang as it traces his economic and emotional investments in the industrial printing processes of chromolithography, his belief in the educational value of mass art, and his exploration of the dialectical imagery of the Christmas card as it became an important social tool in the rapidly industrializing northeastern United States. Prang's cards and career together illustrate the transformations in social networks produced by industrial capitalism.

Louis Prang was born in Breslau (then a part of Prussia) on March 12, 1824. His father was a successful cloth printer. In an autobiographical sketch, probably written when he was seventy, Prang described his father as a "Huguenot" and his mother as a "Calvinist," perhaps suggesting something of the origin of his taste for combining business and social uplift. A sickly young man, Prang did not acquire much formal schooling. At the age of thirteen, he began to work in his father's firm and developed an extensive knowledge of printing on a variety of materials using a wide range of processes. In his twenties, he joined a "Democratic Club" in Silesia, and after the failure of the 1848 revolutions, he left home, taking a variety of jobs with his father's friends before deciding to move to the United States in 1850. His autobiography makes it clear that he had multiple motives for this move—the political pressures were a factor, but Prang claims to have been just as strongly moved by his feelings for a young Swiss woman he had met on his way to Paris at just the moment when she was moving to Ohio. Autobiographies can present evidentiary challenges, but this apparent confluence of sentiment and politics was not atypical for Prang. He soon settled in Boston, where he married that young woman, Rosa Gerber, on November 1, 1851. After years of struggling to turn his handicraft skills into a productive business partnership, Prang had his first commercial printing success when he was commissioned to design an "ornamental business card" for a former partner (figure 2.1).

Spurred by this successful attempt at combing art and manufacture, Prang adopted the printing technique of chromolithography in 1857 and became a master designer and printer of business labels. A major commission from Preston and Merrill, a flavor-extract company, gave him the opportunity to develop the design style that he would exploit throughout the remainder of his career as a chromolithographer. As Prang described it: "The principle was simplicity, breadth and directness. A simple fruit as large as the span of the label would allow; little ornamentation to leave the sign of the fruit conspicuous and plain lettering; coloring strong and natural to catch the eye and explain the object at a glance."[6]

This design exemplifies the structural principles of chromolithographic commercial illustration. The first principle, however, was not simplicity. It was, rather, an effort to emphasize the natural over the cultural. The dominant image of the fruit represents the organic source of the flavor extract—the nature out of which the commodity had been drawn. The coloring, with its immediately perceptible vitality, artificially highlighted the customer's consciousness of the naturalness of the fruit. Chromolithography, with its capacity to intensify saturated colors, can compensate for the flatness of printed business labels, contributing a third dimension of artificially suggested naturalness to the commercial appeal. The language was kept simple; the lettering, plain. The limited ornamentation focuses attention directly on the fruit, suppressing as much as possible any reference to human production. Chromolithography had made it possible for deep color to be mass-produced. It was an industrial craft system that expanded the range of visual production beyond the handicraft level. In the hands of those who mastered the craft, chromolithography produced color-saturated images that rival the representational power of oil paintings. With its capacity for mass-producing these pictures, chromolithography linked industrialization with realistic images, participating in an aesthetic process of naturalizing the newer forms of economic production. Prang's principles for the design of business labels describe this crucial ideological function. The color of the fruit on a business label was made possible only by an industrial craft process, and it was the color of the fruit itself that was wonderfully capable of masking that industrial process with its beauty. All other ornamentation and lettering were subordinated to this naturalizing function.[7]

At the time Janet Huntington McKelvey wrote her prize-winning essay, Louis Prang & Company was located in Roxbury, Massachusetts. The firm had achieved significant regional prominence during the Civil War, when Prang sold lithographed copies of maps of famous battle scenes. When the war ended, Prang turned his presses to the printing of "chromos," mass-produced copies of popular paintings. He also produced business cards, flyers, album cards, and a host of variations on the intersecting themes of industry, color, business, and art. It was not until the mid-1870s that Prang hit on Christmas cards as the perfect prismatic synthesis of his conflicting impulses toward artistic education, social uplift, and surplus value. By 1885 Prang's firm was dominating the domestic Christmas card market, reaching customers across the United States even as his cards were celebrated internationally for their beauty. At this point, after years of marketplace success, Prang seemed to want an explanation of his Christmas card strategies, an articulate justification of the aesthetic, technological, and business decisions that he had made. Typically, for this master of mass-cultural reproduction, Prang thought to use the words of others, and so sponsored the essay competition won by McKelvey.

In numerous circulars published throughout 1885, Prang promoted the competition and enumerated the issues that each entry must consider. The prize-winning essay would do the best job of detailing (1) the social influence of the Christmas card, (2) the artistic influence of the Christmas card, (3) the proper elements of design for a Christmas card, (4) the extent to which Prang's very best cards—as determined by a series of artistic competitions—met the standards outlined in the essay, and, finally, (5) the extent to which Prang's entire line met these standards. McKelvey's essay addressed these issues with the artificial naturalness appropriate to the task.

As McKelvey wrote in her essay, the most important function of the Christmas card was "to carry the Christmas message of good-will and love from friend to friend." All the other necessary aspects of the best Christmas card derived from this social function. McKelvey argued that Christmas was about the gift of Christ's love and that the exchange of gifts at Christmastime was but an earthly representation of that original gift of love. Furthermore, for McKelvey, the exchange of material things was only a means of giving "the far sweeter gifts of kindly regards and wishes." Two general characteristics contributed to the effectiveness of the card for this social purpose. First, it was a highly condensed representational object whose use-value was capable of determining its content: "The Christmas card [is] a token of love pre-eminently; a long drawn out 'Merry Christmas,' placed in beautiful form as a reminder of the beauty or tenderness of the giver. Everything about it must be subservient to this message, must aid in giving it force." There was no more direct means of conveying the essence of Christmas giving, the expression of social connection, but to send cards whose content—design and sentiment—reflected this social function.[8]

Second, the card had the potential to be the perfect Christmas gift because it was not expensive. As McKelvey put it, "The Christmas card should certainly be within the reach of those who are not rich in this world's goods." The social collective created through the exchange of Christmas gifts should expand beyond the dominant and powerful. She asked: "Who has greater need of expression of sympathy and fellowship, than the one who lacks costly gifts? The card will differ, therefore, from other gifts in not being so valuable intrinsically, as for the love which it carries. It must be a simple tribute of broad, freely given affection; and hence it should be *inexpensive*,—as inexpensive as is compatible with two other characteristics of a good Christmas card, —*popularity* and *artistic merit*." As if the message were not clear, she continued, "The genuine Christmas card . . . must be within the grasp of the *people*." It is worth taking a moment to unpack the argument here. First of all, the beauty of the card, its aesthetic merit, serves to represent the beauty and tenderness of the sender. It is an objectification of the sender, not merely a token sent to flatter its recipient. Second, the disadvantaged must be able to send cards, not just receive them. In fact, those who lack costly gifts have a greater need to express sympathy and fellowship. Unlike the Horsley–Cole card, which clearly marked the distinction between those able to give and those who could only receive, McKelvey's essay aims to include "the people" as full agents in the discursive game of Christmas card exchange. Its primary value must be sentimental value, yet its artistic merit must remain high. Perhaps most important, its value would not be intrinsic to the object itself; rather, its use-value could only be realized in exchange.[9]

The central problem that McKelvey laid out in the remainder of her essay was how to reconcile the competing demands of popularity and artistic merit. How could the image, mass-produced as a commodity for sale, retain aesthetic value? Although "the card successfully fulfilling its mission must please the people," McKelvey assured her readers that this mission would not necessarily lead to the use of garish colors and awkward or trite scenes. As she wrote for Prang, "It is only because the public taste has been so long fed on such abuses of nature, that it has become perverted. . . . The most ignorant child in all this land will grasp after a delicate flower, or lovely bird, and its eyes will sparkle with delight."[10] Representational images of nature loom here as a universal standard of aesthetic value and proper content even, or perhaps especially, for industrially produced objects. McKelvey asserted that the natural joy inspired by a colorful vision of the world as it is can raise the taste of the public (who are figured here as ignorant children). Not surprisingly, these issues of art, taste, pleasure, education, the popular, and the value of images of nature in an industrializing world were issues that had driven Prang throughout most of his career.

Chromo-Civilization: The Social Meaning of Color

Prang's maps of Civil War battle scenes built the capital needed to construct his first modern factory. At the end of the war, he returned to his first love, chromolithography, again focusing on commercial illustration: album cards, trade cards, and business labels. Printing for business had long been central to Prang's success. From his first independent commission to create an ornamental business card to his successful design of flavor-extract labels, Prang's printing innovations had been prompted primarily by commercial concerns. It is not surprising that this would be true for a printer. What is surprising is that a printer would strive to blend the harsh tones of his business imperative with the subtle gradations found in the art world in an effort to illustrate the contradictions of industrial abundance. Color, with all its cultural ramifications and social resonance, became the grounds of this merger. Chromolithography was a means of reproducing color with a visual intensity that matched the acceleration of rapid industrialization, the quickening outreach into new markets, and the sensual luxury of heightened sensation. Indeed, the early criticisms of chromolithography attacked its crudity; critics claimed that it necessarily produced harsh contrast and oversaturation, aesthetic qualities perhaps appropriate to business announcements but clearly too brusque for art. Prang spent ten years countering this criticism in letters to editors, commentary in his own journal, and, most important, his next line of highly popular products—Prang's American Chromos.

Museum curator Peter Marzio has argued that chromolithography was a "democratic art" and that Prang's genius was "his ability to understand popular taste." Prang clearly believed in the capacity of mass culture—specifically, the chromolithographic reproduction of popular oil paintings—to appeal to and educate a popular audience. He wanted his pictures to reach out beyond the elites who were already trained in the use of visual material to display distinction and taste. Prang was not alone in producing chromos for the American marketplace. Competitors included Currier & Ives, Strobridge & Company, and Otto Krebs, among others who were exploiting the popular demand for pictures. This demand was part of the drive to master visually—to objectify and to render knowable—the explosion of new goods and new social relations that were the outgrowths of an industrializing economy. But Prang saw more than a market; he was not interested in simply producing visual entertainment. I do not want to claim that Prang held a more profound understanding of the ideological work of images than did his competitors. But he explicitly linked his work of making popular pictures available for a mass audience to Martin Luther's desire to place vernacular Bibles in the hands of common people. Uninterested in merely providing efficiently what the market demanded, Prang aimed not simply to divine a democratically determined common denominator of taste. Instead, he wanted to intervene in the mass production of images, to provide these images as a means of continually raising popular taste in a perpetual, never-ending process of individual salvation and self-determination (that is, Protestantism in an age of competitive consumerism). Prang argued that under the influence of a commonly available Bible, "Mental culture became possible for whole nations." He saw his own work as continuing this process. Chromolithography, he believed, was "art republicanized and naturalized in America. . . . As the popular taste improves the subjects will be worthier of an art which seeks to give back to mankind what has hitherto been confined to a few."[11] In the middle decades of the nineteenth century, mechanical reproductions of visual art were not rare. Lithography, woodcutting, and plate engraving were techniques that made available formally organized visual stimulus. But chromolithography added vibrant color. Why was the intense color of chromolithography so important?

 Ellen Gruber Garvey has built on a suggestion made by Neil Harris that the end of the nineteenth century saw the flourishing of a popular desire for color in illustration. Harris provocatively proposes that color is the "most pictorial" of all visual qualities and accurately, I believe, suggests that color illustration became a battleground for matters of class and taste. In a careful analysis of nineteenth-century scrapbooks, Garvey shows how young women, and sometimes men, relied on color as an organizing principle in their attempts to come to grips with a new consumer society. Color enabled the organized arrangement of trade cards, valentines, labels, and post cards, each of which dealt with widely varying topics, onto a single page of a scrapbook. Garvey concludes that the introduction of color into illustrated promotional materials helped young consumers learn a visual language that aided the negotiation of shops overflowing with new products. By the end of the nineteenth century, color had become a key element of visual perception that allowed for the discrimination of consumer goods accompanied by their temporally specific implications of taste and class.[12]

I want to explore these suggestions further in an effort to outline some of the specific meanings that a heightened awareness of color could carry when it entered the printed realms of commercial illustration and cultural expression. The taste for color should not be regarded as merely a new skill needed for the expansion of competitive consumption. Similarly, the chromo-civilization debates cannot be reduced to a simple struggle over pure art in the unending battle for class distinction (as if such struggles were ever simple). For many educated northeastern art critics, chromo-civilization signified something very different from the democratization of art. It carried all the polluting traits of any art/technology hybrid: it blurred the lines between art and commerce; in its very ability to copy the hand, it displayed the mark of the machine; in its promise of democratic access, it suggested mediocrity; with its overt affiliation for and promotion of sentiment, it threatened to feminize all visual art. In his responses to critics and in his promotional literature, Prang contested every one of these charges but the last. He seemingly had no problem with promoting sentiment or feminizing art. In Prang's understanding, the use of color was linked to the values of sentimental reform. This is not surprising, because chromolithography became popular at the moment when color became a crucial issue in the struggle to reorganize the dominant means of production. Vibrant color became an important means of signifying the symbolic presence of the natural in an industrializing world. Not coincidentally, the issue of color and the color line was reinforced as a seemingly natural division between those who deserved the fruits of industrialization and those who could only, at best, produce the raw materials out of which the new economy was being built.

By the end of 1865, Prang was concentrating his energies on the production of chromos—chromolithographed copies of oil paintings. During a recent trip to Europe, he had hired the English lithographer William Harring, "an all around artist in lithography." One of Harring's earliest successes was a copy of a genre painting by A. F. Tait called *Ducklings*. This chromo had no trouble selling for $5 per print—about ten times more than the previously accepted price for chromolithographic prints. Writing more than twenty years later, Prang asserted in his autobiography that "this picture seemed to me to be peculiarly fitted to test the popular appreciation." Of course, it was his first popular success, and, in hindsight, it would not be surprising for it to seem peculiarly fitted. Nevertheless, it is interesting to see the explanation that Prang gave for this success. He described the painting as "five downy chicks cunningly grouped on a green plot of grass . . . exquisitely painted." The chromo itself was successful, Prang claimed, because "the people felt interested in the subject and in a print which resembled so closely an oil painting. $5.00 was not thought too high to gratify a desire for a good picture to decorate a bare wall and to make a living room more cozy."[13] As outlined here, well after the fact, the goal of the chromo was to reproduce an inexpensive, but not cheap, picture good enough to make a living room more cozy. A room becomes cozy when it is warm and sheltered. Five ducklings, facing one another in innocent sociality, their downiness testifying simultaneously to their youth and to the pictorial skill of the artist, succeed in appealing to that taste for pictures organized around the basic use-value of making a domestic interior feel warm and sheltered. Curiously, intensely colored images of young animals seemed to convey an innocence and a security that assuaged the anxieties surrounding and assaulting the white middle-class domestic interior immediately after the Civil War.

Soon after the initial success of *Ducklings*, art critic Clarence Cook attacked chromos in the *New York Tribune*. His argument was simple: when chromolithography is put to copying oil painting, it is engaged in imitation: "A clever imitation . . . can teach nobody anything, nor benefit anybody; and as every art has its own particular application and field of work, we hinder progress by every effort to wrest it to the cheap imitation of the results of some other art." Prang conceded, "Chromolithography is in itself an art to reproduce, to imitate, not to create. It can never obtain an 'individual and independent' character." In his letter to the editor of the *Tribune*, Prang never contested his own standing as a printer; what he challenged was the dominion of language as the sole expressive medium available to common people, and the idea that education in art could only be a unilateral, top–down process:

> The education of the million demanded the power-press for lit-erature, and now it claims chromolithography for the art of painting. The mental process of culture in art is the same as of all other culture. A poorly written book, not bad in its spirit and ob-ject, is always better than no book at all: it gives an impulse, which is followed up by a demand for better books: and, by com-paring and criticizing, the taste for good books is created. So in art a poor picture is better than none, and in the course of time will create a demand for better and for the best.[14]

Focusing on the question of reproduction, Prang left the basic aes-thetic question unanswered ("not bad in its spirit and object") or, rather, suspended. Instead of exploring that space between spirit and execution, Prang drew attention to the social process whereby the quality of books and pictures are determined. Once a demand has been created, once a market for symbolic goods has been established, com-parison and criticism lead toward an ever-improved standard of taste. Comparison and criticism are not imposed from the top but are tech-niques inherent in the democratic appropriation of symbolic goods. Prang's commitment to aesthetic improvement and his belief in its democratic inevitability contrasted sharply with the pessimism of his critics.

The chromo-civilization debate heated up when Prang began send-ing chromos to leading northeastern intellectuals, asking for endorse-ments or testimonials about the value of these prints for decorating the home and improving the tastes of the masses. Prang mailed chromos to Lydia Maria Child, Harriet Beecher Stowe, William Dean Howells, Ralph Waldo Emerson, and Frederick Douglass, among others. He also mailed copies to leading journals, including, most famously, the *Nation*. Over the next several years, a series of editorials appeared in this journal that firmly situated the terms of the debate about the place of chromolithography, the function of reproduction, and the possibilities of mass-culture-based aesthetic education.

The *Nation* acknowledged that Prang's work, selling "hundreds, and in some cases thousands, of their chromos," had achieved a national presence, being "as common in Chicago as in Boston." Furthermore, the quality of Prang's chromos was of the highest caliber among its mass-produced genre. The *Nation* also granted that chromolithography might have a legitimate role to play in art education. But two barriers prevented Prang's chromos from serving a positive function in the promotion of art in the eyes of the *Nation*'s critics. First was a technique that Prang had introduced in order to add depth and verisimilitude to his chromos. The final processing of each print involved stamping it with a stone laced with lines that was intended to impress on the flat paper surface of the chromo the image of having been produced on textured canvas; this final stamping was followed by a coating of varnish. According to the *Nation*'s critics, such a violation of materials, a deliberate attempt to imitate oil on canvas, was an outrage, "quite unnecessary and inexcusable." This trick threw "discredit on the whole matter and [made] the pictures merely merchandise."[15] In essence, this charge repeated Cook's criticism. Prang's chromos tried too hard to copy oil paintings, and in the process made clear their intention to borrow illegitimately some of the cultural capital that had accumulated to the older technique. Prang seemed to accede to this intention when he claimed that his work had value because of its ability to resemble "so closely an oil painting." Yet Prang asserted over and over again that he was not trying to deceive his customers into believing that they were buying oil paintings. His trademark was always visible either in the bottom-right-hand corner of the print or on the label on the back. Furthermore, he had his lithographers sign their prints, adding the mark of a second creator to the image. Prang was trying to imitate the qualities of oil painting, but he was not trying to steal their aura. As Prang had put it in his response to Cook:

> Good paintings are lessons of beauty, and blessings to our do-
> mestic and social feelings: oil paintings represent nature more
> truthfully and more satisfactorily to the unsophisticated mind,
> and this makes them preferable to all others. Adopting these
> views, the reproduction of good paintings is to be desired as a
> popular benefit, and the process which can best do the work, in
> spirit and in color must be the only one adopted, and, as it hap-
> pens that chromo-lithography has no rival in the field, of course
> we have to take it up and welcome it, with all the ardor of a pro-
> gressive democratic nation. Art, artists, the millions of people,
> will reap a benefit from this invention which very few at present
> can adequately estimate.[16]

The addition of lines and varnish to chromos came from a desire to match one of the great expressive qualities of oil painting—its ability to convey depth and texture—purely for its ability to convey complex visual information through the representation of nature. If, when look-ing at a painting, one could perceive the lines that testified to the layer of canvas supporting the oil paint, then for Prang, that was a crucial part of the perception. Similarly, if the accumulation of oil on canvas led to a certain shininess, then the addition of varnish to a chromo only reproduced that visual experience. The value of an oil painting derived from its capacity to represent nature truthfully. The value of a chro-molithographic reproduction was its capacity to expand the possible users of these truthful representations.

The second criticism raised by the *Nation* was more to the point; "The art question, however, is this: Are these pictures good as pictures; good to have and to look at; good in their influence on people who do not have much original art within their reach; good at teaching people to feel and understand nature?" The *Nation* took on the aesthetic ques-tion directly, defining the sole legitimate task for mass reproductions of visual art. Mass art could have a positive influence only on those without access to paintings, and this positive influence was only to teach these people to develop an intuitive emotional and cognitive re-lationship with nature. This was an unquestioned aesthetic function for an industrializing era. Nature was conceived of as a separate realm of experience requiring a carefully nurtured relationship. The purpose of art was to make possible visual experiences of nature that were no longer easily available. In the end, however, the *Nation* insisted that Prang's chromos could not fulfill this function because of their lack of "any true or delicate 'gradion' of color":

> Good color, that is, delicately graded color, is not to be produced by the printing press. . . . A colored reproduction must be perfect or it is nothing. What the brush of a skilful [*sic*] painter does at every touch in graduating, softening, and blending tints, leading one color into another, breaking one color over another, until there cannot be found two grains of color the size of a pinhead that shall be really the same; this is beyond the reach of any me-chanical contrivance.[17]

Color was the key to mediating the fraught relationship between nature and culture, the distinction between the nonhuman and the human. The machine's efforts to reproduce painting's chromatic ef-fects, by definition, could never succeed; the machine could never achieve the delicacy of the hand. It could only interfere with the job of teaching people to feel and understand nature. Yet by putting forth an empirical standard of visual perfection—delicately graduated color— the *Nation* only encouraged Prang's efforts. Throughout his career as a chromolithographer, Prang produced booklets and pamphlets devot-ed to teaching children about nature, and by the end, delicately grad-uated color had become Prang's stock-in-trade.

Prang continued to send his work to the *Nation*, hoping with each package to convince his critics that chromolithography could attain del-icately graded color and contribute to aesthetic education. In October 1867, the journal responded again that Prang's work failed to the extent that it attempted to reproduce the experience of looking at oil paintings. Rather than attempt to achieve the unattainable, the *Nation*'s critic ar-gued, domestic publishers of chromos ought to follow the lead of certain

English and French firms that left their products "rather flat and rather pale and wholly without pretence of being facsimiles or imitations." Apparently, as long as the gap between chromos and oil paintings remained evident, the mechanical process would not threaten the order of things. Viewers would naturally long to experience the real painting, the original. There would be no temptation to settle for the copy.[18]

Although it was important, the material condition of the copy was not the foremost concern for either Prang or the *Nation*'s critics. Fundamentally, their debate was an argument about the changing relationship of human production to the natural world, where artistic production was a synecdoche for all means of production. In an abstract industrial commercial world, where buyers did not personally know their sellers, where the production of commodities was increasingly distanced from the controlling intentions of any single person, the potential for deceptive practices was high. Such transformations necessarily required new rules for authenticating any commodity not simply for its use-value but also as the legitimate carrier of the meanings associated with it. The chromo-civilization debates were about what sorts of processes were appropriate mechanisms for producing meaning, for transforming nature into culture in an industrialized, commercialized society, and they were about how these meanings were to be valued, appreciated, and consumed. This particular version of that powerful, ongoing debate turned on the meaning and purpose of color. According to the *Nation*, finely gradated color was an attribute of nature that could be reproduced only by the relatively natural technologies of hand and brush. Only the most highly and traditionally skilled artist could approximate the natural meanings of color. The proper discernment of finely gradated color could be achieved only by years of study. Of course, any mechanical process that threatened to change the conditions of that aesthetic work could potentially reduce the value of years of study and practice. This was the common fear that accompanied the mass reproduction of art. But this debate focused on color because the increasing dominance of industrialized production and the legal end to slavery transformed the meaning of color, bringing it to the foreground of commercial exchange as well as aesthetic debates about the meanings as well as the mechanisms of production.

Evidence for this interpretation can be drawn from two more pictures that Prang copied. The first is *Barefoot Boy* by Eastman Johnson (plate 3). This became one of Prang's most popular chromos, selling thousands of copies at $5 each. Johnson was a successful genre painter whose first major success was *Old Kentucky Home—Negro Life in the South* (1859), a detailed yet sentimental depiction of comfortable leisure among decaying shacks. Its allegorical significance was ambiguous enough for the painting to be praised by abolitionists and slaveholders alike. Johnson's *Barefoot Boy* had been inspired by a poem by John Greenleaf Whittier, first published in 1855, as the sectional crisis was reaching its peak. The poem speaks of a "barefoot boy with cheek of tan" whose moments of innocence are about to end forever. The lyric connects the boy's innocence to nature, with respect to both the innate qualities of the child and the bustling world around him. The natural world depicted in this poem is a world of honest toil: bees chase flowers, tortoises bear shells, woodchucks dig cells, and ground-moles sink wells. The natural world's ability to find good honest work for all its denizens is contrasted with the adult human world, where such innocence is abandoned in the unending struggle for status and distinction: "All too soon these feet must hide in the prison cells of pride." Yet there is hope for the barefoot boy. He might grow up a republican— aware that his own joy and happiness are qualities that no millionaire can buy. The poem ends with the wish that the boy will grow up free from the "quick and treacherous sands of sin," as it scatters "Blessings on thee, barefoot boy." This poem certainly is sentimental. But it is sentimental with a purpose. In 1855, no casual mention of the word "republican" was innocent; no reference to cheek of (however delicately colored) tan could pass unnoticed; no contrast with the indolent wealthy could be misplaced; no gesture back to a time before the current ceaseless moil, with its apparently inevitable quicksand-like tendencies that were dragging the nation down into civil war, would be misunderstood. The poem's sentimentality is aimed at sympathetically linking its readers into a republican unity that valued honest toil and a more simple way of life oriented around agriculture, with a correspondingly more direct relationship to nature, perhaps even cleansed of the sins of slavery.[19]

Whittier approved of Johnson's painting, calling it "a charming illustration." But the painting itself conveys nothing of the turmoil that the barefoot boy was about to face. In the painting, his cheeks of tan and strawberry-kissed lips have lost any ambiguity. His innocence is depicted not as an affinity for the honest toil shared by all of nature, but as an isolated individual freed of any social conflict. Johnson's best work always reminded its viewers of racialized and gendered hierarchies, even when it might be accused of sentimentalizing them. This painting hides those inequalities behind an image of innocent youthful whiteness. Whereas Whittier's poem saw that innocence as an imaginary resource that could link all Americans together in a republican vision of equality and honest work, Johnson's painting figured that innocence as the attributes of a past age. The nostalgia was regularly mentioned in reviews of Prang's chromo of the painting. The *Hartford Evening Post* wrote, "To everyone who has been a barefoot boy himself . . . this picture brings vividly to mind the joys and sorrows . . . of that period of our existence which we now look back upon as filled with the romance of happiness and peace, despite the occasional misfortunes that well nigh broke our youthful hearts." Quite probably the image's chromatic nostalgia linked the commercial success of the copies of this painting to those of Tait's *Ducklings* and *Chickens*. This success was predicated on the desire to reclaim a presocial innocence, not to imagine a republican unity, but to escape the effects of the Civil War and to re-imagine its memory as a period of "occasional misfortunes." Occasional misfortunes do not require reconstruction, but something much less radical. The popular success of Prang's postwar chromo of Johnson's *Barefoot Boy* suggests the power of this longing for sentimental reunification.[20]

Not all of Prang's chromos sold thousands. One that failed to reach an extensive market was his copy of Theodore Kaufmann's *Portrait of Senator Revels* (plate 4). Hiram Revels was the nation's first African-American senator, chosen by the legislature of Mississippi to fill the unexpired term of the seat formerly held by Jefferson Davis. Kaufmann's portrait emphasizes Revels's dignity and accomplishment. Revels had been a minister, an educator, and a community organizer before he was elected to the Senate. His career had not included work in agriculture, nor had he ever been a slave. Prang sent a copy of his chromo to Frederick Douglass, who wrote back:

> Upon public grounds, I thank the publishing house of Prang & Co., for giving the country this admirable picture of our first colored American Senator. Whatever may be the prejudices of those who may look upon it, they will be compelled to admit that the Mississippi Senator is a man, and one who will easily pass for a man among men. We colored men so often see ourselves described and painted as monkeys, that we think it a great piece of good fortune to find an exception to this general rule.[21]

Chromolithographers often had produced stereotyped images of African Americans, participating in the visual elaboration of blackface minstrelsy. Prang clearly intended to challenge that practice. In addition to replicating all the tropes of formal portraiture, Prang's chromo of Kaufmann's portrait evinces the most visible of final stampings. The lines that mimic the presence of canvas beneath the image stand out quite clearly. This suggests that Prang was doubly concerned with conveying the status that accompanied an oil portrait and working to combat the tradition in commercial printed imagery to mock black Americans.

Douglass's letter went on to detail the cultural changes that the Civil War should produce:

> Pictures come not with slavery and oppression and destitution, but with liberty, fair play, leisure, and refinement. These conditions are now possible to colored American citizens, and I think the walls of their houses will soon begin to bear evidences of their altered relations to the people about them. This portrait, representing truly, as it does, the face and form of our first colored U.S. Senator, is a historical picture. It marks, with almost startling emphasis, the point dividing our new from our old condition. Every colored householder in the land should have one of these portraits in his parlor, and should explain it to his children,

as the dividing line between the darkness and despair that over-
hung our past, and the light and hope that now beam upon our
future as a people.[22]

Douglass's elucidation of the meaning of this chromo differs radically from the nostalgia that haunted the reception of *Barefoot Boy*.
Whereas the white boy is imaged in rural simplicity, inviting the spec-
tator to long for his or her own lost innocence, the black man is shown
in his professional attire, imaging mature success and stimulating hope
for the future. Revels was an early member of the professional middle
class, precisely that category that was being brought into existence
through the commercial and industrial modernization of the nation's
economy. Prang elsewhere depicted this developing class in his series
of illustrations depicting the modernization of trades. These illustrations clearly demarcated the owners and managers of expanding businesses from the skilled labor previously associated with the trade. As
Stuart Blumin remarks, Prang established in these images "a hierarchy
that sets the storekeeping business man above his handworking, artisanal employees." Prang's copy of Kaufmann's *Portrait of Senator Revels* was a vivid reminder of the radical shift in the social hierarchies of
race and class that the Civil War had made possible. Perhaps the significance of color, perhaps its rapid spread as a prime commercial indicator of taste and status, had something to do with the transition
marked by *Barefoot Boy* on the one hand and *Portrait of Senator Revels* on
the other. From a rural nation fundamentally organized around artisans, agriculture, and slavery, to an urban civilization of storefronts and
back rooms, offices and paper; from an image of the nation based on
white nostalgia to the suggestion of a polychromatic country of competing races—what better technology to image this complex set of social and economic transitions than chromolithography?[23]

The controversy over chromolithography continued through the
nineteenth century. Catharine Beecher and Harriet Beecher Stowe
recommended that young middle-class householders budget for the
purchase of chromos. "The aesthetic element," they argued, "holds a
place of great significance among the influences which make home

happy and attractive, which give it a constant and wholesome power over the young, and contributes much to the education of the entire household in refinement, intellectual development, and moral sensibility."[24] The sisters particularly recommended the purchase of *Barefoot Boy* along with three other chromos. These images were recommended precisely as a way of making a living room more cozy, of increasing the feeling of warmth and security to be found in domestic interiors. The Beecher sisters and other authors of advice books recognized that the creation of warm and secure domestic interiors was no small accomplishment. A certain domestic aesthetics was required, and these advisers recommended the dependable power of sentimental imagery as the foundation for an art that would be both uplifting and democratic. Stowe wrote for the *Atlantic Almanac*: "The great value of pictures for home should be, after all, in their sentiment. They should express sincere ideas and tastes of the household, and not the tyrannical dicta of some art critic or neighbor. . . . We should try to cultivate our taste, and then express it; but the value of family pictures in a great degree should consist in the fact that they do sincerely represent our own tastes and preferences, and not those of others."[25]

The *Nation*, of course, would have none of it. Attacking the testimonials of those such as the Beecher sisters, the journal declared, "In modern times, the term 'democratic' in all that relates to quality, is a synonym for what, in slang phrase, is called cheap and nasty. . . . We are so eager to have all men have pianos and carpets and pictures that we care little, and are every day caring less, what kind of pianos or carpets or pictures they are." In 1874, E. L. Godkin, the *Nation*'s editor, coined the phrase "chromo-civilization" as he leveled one of his last attacks on what he regarded as the shameful slide toward aesthetic mediocrity and social fakery that chromolithography represented. Godkin's attack remained directed at two characteristics of the chromo: its status as a copy and its sentimental content, so often stripped of any sense of conflict. The *Buffalo Courier* emphasized the latter point: "Upset peach-baskets, however skillfully pictured, teach no great lesson either of truth or beauty, and one turned over permanently in one's dining room would fail to attract admiration; and yet they are sold so cheaply by Mr. Prang, the great duplicator of unimportant processes and things, that they disfigure many a pretty eating-room in New York."[26]

Taking place in an era dominated by the ideology of separate spheres, the gendered outlines of this argument are clear, but they do not cover the entire story. While typically attacked by male critics and championed by women essayists, Prang's chromos used sentimental imagery not solely to delay or diffuse the conflict of raging emotions. For every image of juvenile presociality, (*Ducklings, Barefoot Boy*), Prang published images of dignity and drama (*Portrait of Senator Revels, Yo-Semite Valley*). Prang's chromos were intended to add to the warmth and security of domestic interiors and, in the process, aid the elevation of public taste. But for Prang, these domestic and aesthetic functions were firmly linked to the realm of production and social competition. Prang's awareness of this link, the inescapable presence of the whole material social process, was the basis for the aesthetic triumph of his Christmas cards.

From Chromos to Christmas Cards:
The Cultural Work of the Cozy Domestic Interior

Although he continued to produce and promote his line of chromos, Prang had begun to focus on a different form of sentimental commodity by the time of Godkin's last salvo in the *Nation*. Prang had recognized that the growing desire for color was not restricted to those individuals who were promoting flavor extracts, decorating living rooms, or covering the pages of scrapbooks. During the early 1870s, Prang's catalogs began to feature chromolithographed cards—album cards to paste in scrapbooks, business cards to promote trade, and personal cards to aid social communication. Over a period of about three years, as his production shifted from focusing on chromos and business materials to printing the emergent sentimental commodity called the Christmas card, Prang developed an intuited connection between the transformation in economic production along with accompanying shifts in the forms of social affiliation, and the social use of cards and the social function of Christmas. Walter Benjamin's concept of a dialectical image identifies those objects that capture the contradictions of their historical moment, reflecting both the material conditions of their production and the utopian desires that they addressed. The Christmas cards published by Prang were particularly evocative dialectical images that illustrated the turmoil swirling beneath the Gilded Age. The Christmas card built on traditions of visiting card use that had been established by urban elite families during the middle third of the nineteenth century. The Christmas card made manifest the longings for abundance that accompanied the internalization of discipline demanded by industrial commercial capitalism, even as it continued to participate in the social process of determining who would be included and who would be excluded from the enjoyment of that abundance.[27]

The modern celebration of Christmas in the United States is built on two apparently contradictory ethics: the Protestant ethic, which Max Weber made famous, and a complementary romantic ethic proposed by the sociologist Colin Campbell. Just as Weber's Protestant ethic is an image of the "spirit of capitalism," so Campbell's romantic ethic provides the impulse behind the "spirit of modern consumerism." The longing for salvation is a key motive driving both ethics. Campbell's spirited rethinking of Weber's connection between the material and the ideal focuses on the almost sensual pleasure that Puritan divines seemed to evince in their unending interrogation of their souls and their fates. Campbell understands pleasure to be the result of specific activities that were designed to produce a set of feelings; this link between intentional action and feelings differentiates pleasure from the mere satisfaction of needs, which is not to say that the satisfaction of needs cannot be pleasurable. Campbell specifically disavows any concept of universal pleasure that drives all humans; his theory is historically specific yet meant to be broadly suggestive. He argues that "only in modern times have emotions come to be located 'within' individuals as opposed to 'in' the world." This relatively recent internal locus of feelings allows for the manipulation of environments in order to produce certain specific feelings. The complexity of pleasure in modern life can be represented by the Puritan divine Thomas Shepard's famous line, "Grace lies in mourning the want of it." In this quote, the most desired eternal state, the goal of all Puritan activities, is recognized as a highly condensed set of feelings. Thus Campbell argues for a simultaneous taste for sensibility and aesceticism that arose out of the complementary development of Protestantism and modern capitalism. The longing for salvation, therefore, does not preclude luxuriating in the sensuous uncertainty of it. Nor does the development of industrial discipline preclude a longing for the fruits of abundance.[28]

Charles Dickens's notorious fable *A Christmas Carol* is clearly an elaboration of these two impulses. Dickens, along with Washington Irving, is often credited with sparking the promotion of the modern Christmas in Anglo-America, which established both its commercial foundation and its propensity to lament that commercial foundation during the nineteenth century. The curious and conflicted development of this midwinter festival has prompted a recent spate of significant research into the commercial history of Christmas. Rather than reproduce that work, I intend to build on it, focusing in particular on the prismatic capacities of the Christmas card to illustrate the material infusions of these twin ideological extracts.[29]

During the mid-nineteenth century, and particularly in the urban Northeast, the week between Christmas and New Year became a key holiday period that simultaneously celebrated and gave a break from modern commercial industrial life. The historical transitions in the traditions of gift giving particularly marked the social and economic bases of the holiday. In those sections of the country less industrially organized, Christmas remained more traditionally carnivalesque. The rhythms of agricultural life fit more neatly with a week-long break from work—filled with status inversion, feasting, and communal indulgence—during the shortest days of the year. Industrial production for a market, particularly production that could continue year-round in heated and artificially lighted interiors, demanded a shift in the meaning and therefore in the precise means of celebration. The common nineteenth-century critiques of the holiday, that it was overcommercialized or, simply, too materialistic, were displaced and condensed reminders of the social function of the gift and of the holiday itself. In traditional societies, the exchange of gifts marked the lineaments of the social group, reinforcing the community bound together by kinship and economic networks. Nobles recognized their obligations to peasants, leaders to

their followers, neighboring villages to one another. As production became increasingly organized around market-based exchange, with its at-
tendant incentives to the division of labor and industrialization, gift exchange was socialized, meaning its function ceased to be primarily
economic. As gift exchange was sifted out of the realm of the economic, it became a marker of the formal structural distinction between the
economic and the social. A key function of the gift, therefore, became
its ability to mark precisely those elements of the social that resisted re-
duction to the economic. Art, and symbolic expression in general, then
became articulated to the social function of the gift insofar as the gift of
symbols minimized its use-value and therefore represented with a particular clarity the formal purity of the social. Beautiful tokens of love,
delicate sentimental trinkets, and sensuously pleasurable objects, intended to display the sympathy and fellowship of the giver and to objectify the social connection between the giver and the receiver, became
effective tools for the construction of social networks. As the items exchanged evolved from handmade tokens to store-bought and then
mass-produced objects, the gift did not lose its capacity to reinforce social connections. In an increasingly urbanized, commercialized, and industrially based society, the midwinter holiday itself provided for the
delineation and the celebration of the social collective engendered by
these modern conditions of existence. Gift exchange survived in modern Western societies as more than an archaism. To the extent that social collectives, from kinship networks to nations, were believed to carry
some kernel of independence from the market, gifts carried the burden
of that alternative organizing principle.[30]

The modern Christmas card developed under these conditions,
merging the functions of the holiday gift with those of the visiting card.
Card exchange was already an elaborate system that contributed to the
building of business as well as social connections. The increasingly fine
and subtle class distinctions among the developing middle classes were
abstractions built out of hierarchies of kinship networks and business
connections that card exchange traced and made visible. Kenneth Ames
has surveyed etiquette books published between 1845 and 1881 in order
to determine the social rules of visiting card exchange. His analysis con-
firms the critique leveled by Thorstein Veblen in 1899, that the eti-

quette of card exchange was a form of conspicuous consumption that demonstrated a family's capacity for honorific wasteful expenditure. The etiquette books prescribed the delivery of cards between noon and five o'clock in the afternoon, precisely during business hours. Typically, then, wives, mothers, and daughters took on the tasks of visiting and card exchange, along with the intense negotiation and unstable reproduction of status that the game enabled. The entire system of card exchange required a detailed knowledge of overlapping kinship and business hierarchies. For one family to accept the card of another and then to deliver its own card in return indicated a relatively equivalent social status. Single gentlemen were allowed into the game, typically using their business cards in place of personal cards, which indicated their relative social independence along with a claim to a corresponding relative economic autonomy. According to Veblen, this game of cards required a display of leisure in that only those families (or single businessmen) who were free from work obligations in the mid-afternoon could play. Veblen went on to argue that the adoption of this game by the middle class (which he termed the pecuniary class) reflected a top–down process of emulation and status ambition. What Veblen failed to recognize was that the game of card exchange was in effect a system of tracking the shifting values of families in what amounted to a market of kinship and business connections, and that, like all markets, it was open to any with the requisite social capital to venture even as it was subject to the shifting demands of all its participants.[31]

In his study of etiquette books, Ames found a system of elite business and visiting card use that insisted on a plain vellum card with pure black engraving as the visual and tactile mark of the status distinction necessary even to enter the game of card exchange. Equipped with the wrong materials, one's card simply would not be recognized. As Maude Cook, an etiquette book author from the end of the nineteenth century, put it, "The stress laid by society upon the correct usage of these magic bits of pasteboard will not seem unnecessary when it is remembered that the visiting card, socially defined, means, and is frequently made to take the place of, one's self." She then asserted that "any ornamentation whatever upon a card savors of ill-breeding or rusticity."[32] Just as Veblen's theory was hampered by his dogged insistence on a top–down model of social influence, Ames's analysis is skewed by his sources. Neither etiquette book authors nor social scientists of the late nineteenth century considered the middle classes to be capable of changing the game. But if one acknowledges the market system that underlay the exchange of cards and if one examines again the issue of color, the market-based power of the middle classes becomes evident. Etiquette books of the period assumed the same top–down model of social emulation that Veblen worked from. They prescribed a set of behaviors that they claimed were those of "the best society." It can be safely assumed that those who purchased these guides were interested in such prescriptions, especially when faced with the overwhelming consistency of certain basic propositions published across scores of sources. But the actual practices of the middle classes were not based on simple emulation. While the basic operating principles of this game of social recognition remained the same—accept only the cards of those individuals or families that you want your cards accepted by, or trade your cards only for cards of equal or better value—the highly competitive retail market for the purchase of these cards recognized a powerful demand for color and decoration that directly contradicted the prescriptions of the etiquette books, suggesting also a transformation in the values produced in the social game of card exchange. This demand for color marked the opening of a new front in the commercial production of this basic equipment for the competitive activity of social network building. It was a further elaboration of the battles over status and taste on which the chromo-civilization debates had been based. But in the development of cards, there is no doubt which tastes, or which class fragments, won.

The business cards, visiting cards, and hidden name cards that were sold by card companies across the northern half of the nation were covered with color (figures 2.2 and 2.3). Many cards sold by the Ohio Card Company and the Atlantic Card Company simply applied a scrap of embossed chromolithography to an otherwise plain off-white card, decorating the corners or the edges of the cards with flowers or birds. A special category of cards called hidden name cards enjoyed a brief vogue. On these cards, a chromolithographed embossed scrap, usually in the shape of a hand holding flowers, formed a flap covering the name

Figure 2.2 Illustrated visiting cards. (Courtesy, The Winterthur Library: Joseph Downs Collection of Manuscripts and Printed Ephemera)

Figure 2.3 Illustrated hidden name cards. (Courtesy, The Winterthur Library: Joseph Downs Collection of Manuscripts and Printed Ephemera)

on the card. The "rusticity" of its presenter perhaps conferred a sort of shyness that required its receiver to lift the flap to see who had left it. In 1873 Prang took hundreds of samples of his own chromolithographed cards to an international exhibit in Vienna. These cards did not rely on the simple technique of attaching colorful scraps but had been illustrated using the same principles that Prang had developed for his successful business labels, integrating color more fully into the design. Chromolithography enabled the representation of bold colors; the eye-catching qualities of these colors were naturalized through the choice of fruits, flowers, or animals as decorative items printed onto the card itself, not attached to the card as potentially superfluous decoration; the lettering was left simple, with just the person's name or the company name placed directly in the center of the card.[33]

Much of the appeal of Prang's decorated business cards derived from their luxurious display of color. The vibrant intensity of this color had been deliberately designed to "exceed the limits of absolute necessity." Regardless of the emphasis placed by art critics on delicately gradated color, Prang and his customers clearly enjoyed the boldly sensuous chromaticism his stones could produce. By 1876, Prang had found an academic authority that helped him contest the *Nation*'s formulation of the purpose of color in art. Wilhelm Von Bezold was a professor at the Rolay Polytechnic School in Munich who worked on the psychophysics of color. When Edward Pickering, professor of physics at the Massachusetts Institute of Technology, brought this work to Prang's attention, he proved eager to publish it. Bezold's *Theory of Color in Its Relation to Art and Art-Industry* was useful for Prang because it clearly distinguished two factors that differentiated decorative art from representational arts such as painting. According to Bezold, painters rely on subtle contrasts that can create a psychological experience of color where that color is not physically present. Because their goal is not to present color but to use color to represent something else, painters take advantage of the capacity of color to depict the presence of things that are absent. Decorative artists, on the contrary, desire to present color itself, and too much emphasis on subtle contrasts produces a "lowering of fullness": "It is the task of decorative art to enrich and enliven the objects of daily use by the addition of new forms and of colors which exceed the limits of absolute necessity."[34] Prang's chromolithographed business cards coated these symbols of the self with the luxuries of saturated color. The full presence of color in business and visiting cards became the sign of an orientation of the self toward the market—both the economic market and the market of social relations, an orientation that was fundamentally necessary for an individual to assume one of the new positions only just being produced out of the dramatic economic transformations of the late nineteenth century. More than a symbol of the self, these cards were a symbol of a self in relation to economic and social networks. The struggle over color was a struggle over which class fragment would dominate and what would be the signs of that domination. Increasingly, victory went to those social units (whether single gentlemen or families) who were conscious of and able to maneuver within their relationships to a variety of markets. Bold color became the sign of that dominance.

In his autobiography, Prang claims that the wife of his English agent, Mrs. Arthur Ackermann, saw his colorful business cards in Vienna and gave Prang the idea of inserting a "Merry Christmas" or a "Happy New Year" into the center of the design. Ackermann was no doubt thinking of the English Christmas cards that Charles Goodall & Sons and Marcus Ward had been making since the mid-1860s. These cards relied on the familiar visual language of flowers, birds, and animals to naturalize the colorful display of social connection. Prang's catalogs of the late 1860s and early 1870s show that he was already selling something that he was calling Christmas cards. These cards followed the same principles of design as, but were significantly bigger than, his business cards. Prang had been producing these for sale to churches that distributed them to their members. Ackermann's suggestion gave Prang an insight into the social use of cards that drew from and extended the practice of exchanging business and visiting cards. With holiday sentiments inserted into the space of the business card, Prang's Christmas cards were able to merge the sensuous social actions of holiday gift exchange with the process of evaluating kinship and business networks, reinforcing the efficacy of market orientation within the specifically social space of the gift. Functionally and symbolically, these cards testified to the inextricable intertwining of home and business, and the accruing social power of the orientation toward the market within both these nodes of the social process. Prang wrote about the importance of this linkage when he described his newly completed modern factory:

> Family and home have their rights; business has its duties; both must be attended to; and our ideal in this direction was always . . . to have home and business connected in such a way that each may be strengthened by the support of the other. The interests of the home ought to be cultivated in the breasts of our business-man as well as the interests of trade; and an interest in the business of the husband and father ought to be cultivated in the hearts of the wife and children, who, while making his home cosey [*sic*] and attractive, will also share in the hopes and joys of his out-door life.[35]

The cards then became the signs of a consciously constructed social collective whose productive capacity as well as systems of consumption and reproduction—both the factory and the cozy domestic interior—were organized into marketlike systems of evaluation. This market structure revealed itself in the strategies of card exchange that delineated the social value of the agents competing for status within that collective. Families exchanged cards with the other families in their social networks. Over time, one might be cut off while another might be welcomed in. A network might expand, change shape, or die off, depending on the mutual assessment of those participating in it. Prang's Christmas cards participated in the work of social reproduction to the extent that they became effective tools in the productive social work of card exchange. The goal of this productive work was the construction of social networks made up of warm and secure domestic interiors, and the display of bold color was a mark of the radical reorientation of social life around the market. But his best cards were not simple sentimental apologies for the appropriation of surplus value by a dominant class. These cards reveal the seriousness of the purposes to which they were put. During the last quarter of the nineteenth century, Prang's primary customers for these cards consisted of the still-blurry middle classes made up of the families of skilled craftsmen, professionals, and managers. Those who succeeded recognized the agentive mediation of market structures in the struggle for social dominance. But as units struggling in a market system, these families were uncertain of their position; they were made anxious by the turbulence of social transformations. Prang addressed this market not with reassuring bromides about the natural dominance of his customers, but through consistent reminders of the precariousness of their material standing and the responsibility that each participant in the social network shared for defining the social collective.[36]

This complex of social and economic representations—a set of dialectical images that displayed the material foundations of business networks and kinship status built on an extended practice of calculated exchange—was the Pandora's box opened by Prang's Christmas cards. But it took several years before Prang's synthesis of visiting cards and Christmas gifts could take on the visual representation of the material conditions of their production. It was not until 1880 that Prang completed the transformation of his factory from a primary focus on chromolithographed copies of oil paintings to a focus on Christmas cards. Across this transformation, much of Prang's motivation remained the same. He continued to publish art education pamphlets and illustrated books for children even as he continued to print business labels. Prang's three diverse projects of promoting aesthetic education, contributing to social uplift, and expanding the sale of sentimental commodities each contributed to the process of constituting the market-oriented social units demanded by an industrialized commercialized productive system. Whether individuals or families, these agents in the operations of market systems were constituted in part through an engagement with art. As Prang described the aim of his company: "For many years, it has been our dream, by day and by night, to popularize art and art ideas in the homes of our America,—not alone because of any financial benefit likely to accrue from it, but from the higher aim of contributing our share to promote the social pleasures of our country men." In one of his journals, Prang quoted Lydia Maria Child's articulation of the role of art in the process of distinguishing individuals out of the masses:

How plainly is it indicated, in the progress of the world, that the masses are everywhere to be raised into distinct individuals. A few centuries ago, only the wealthy inhabitants of palaces could possess beautiful pictures. . . . Now thousand and thousands of farmers and mechanics ornament the walls of their houses with handsome pictures. . . . Even negroes, whom we have so long kept shut up in the dark cave of ignorance, are coming to a perception of the beautiful.[37]

As mentioned before, Harriet Beecher Stowe insisted that the decoration of homes must reflect the tastes of those who live in them, not some anonymous abstract standard. According to like-minded reformers, aesthetic education contributed to social uplift insofar as it promoted the development of individuals capable of functioning as agents in a variety of market systems—represented most clearly in the market for symbolic goods. The highest value upheld in the countless paeans to the democratic diffusion of art was the ability of art to raise the taste of each individual. But this process could also profitably be understood as a crucial practice of subject formation. An alertness to formally organized symbolic expression contributes to the competitive success of market-oriented individuals who must be sensitive to the ever-changing nature of values produced through marketplace exchange. Prang saw Christmas cards as a central line of sentimental commodities that could contribute to aesthetic education and social uplift by emphasizing the social power of the market-oriented individual in the construction of kinship and business networks.

In 1880 Prang hit on the idea of sponsoring competitions for the best artistic designs created expressly for his Christmas cards. Each of these competitions provided a way for Prang to locate new designs while it contributed to the aura of artistic prestige (and the implications of increasing individuation) that he liked to associate with his products.[38] An exhibit of the entries for his first competition took place at the American Art Gallery in New York during the first half of June, and the competition was judged by three employees of Tiffany's. They awarded the first prize to Rosina Emmet, a student of William Merritt Chase.[39] Although criticized by many of his fellows for devoting so much of his energy to education, Chase advocated the teaching of art in order to avoid having to "please the vulgar taste" of potential buyers.[40] His reputation for "vigor and health" helped combat the association of art with decadent gentility, and his overt affectation of bohemian styles inoculated him against charges of pandering to a public.[41] Emmet's association with Chase contributed to her legitimacy in Prang's eyes, and her design became part of the year's Christmas card line.

In the *Boston Advertiser*'s announcement of the results of the contest, the description of the winning cards suggested a link between the value of vivid colors and particular social qualities that might characterize the agents in a social market: "However dangerous may be the use of vivid color in an unpractised hand, pure color cannot profitably be discarded, even in favor of the more thoughtful and emotional modern harmonies. We need now to strive after strength quite as much as after refinement; and the present design shows the strength and healthy freshness which come from a successful endeavor after decided effects."[42]

The market for artistic Christmas cards associated the value of pure vivid colors with the strength and healthy freshness that were the result of intentional action. The aesthetics of Prang's Christmas cards highlighted the cultural production of agents in the market-oriented society of the late nineteenth century, a society seemingly bifurcated into business on the one hand and domestic life on the other, but a society unified by its increasing adoption of market systems for the assessment of value in all spheres.

In November 1880, Prang announced a second art competition, to be held on February 21, 1881. He sought to confirm the aesthetic legitimacy of the process and to add a certain prestige to the winning cards by asking the well-known artist John La Farge and the architect Stanford White to join Samuel Coleman as judges. The contest was again to be administered by the American Art Gallery in New York. That year the results sparked considerable controversy. One of the qualifications for winning the contest had been that "the designs must be original and appropriate to the Christmas season." Although four prizes were awarded, most of the seasonally oriented entries were so technically inferior that the judges awarded two of the top prizes to artists whose work made not even a tangential reference to the holiday.

On February 27, an anonymous letter appeared in the *New York Tribune* in "defense of the judges." Signed "Decorative Art," the letter began by reminding its readers that Prang's goal was not simply to find popularly pleasing designs, but to establish Christmas card design as a legitimate form of decorative art. Furthermore, Prang had chosen as judges "artists who, by their work in the two departments of fine art and of decorative art, have the right to speak with authority upon the best and most effectual methods of developing this branch of design." The initial reaction of these judges to the bulk of material submitted was overwhelmingly negative. They were appalled that they were required to treat seriously designs that showed "an ignorance of the simplest technical principles of art . . . evidenced by the most deplorable results." Yet the letter writer felt as though he had to defend the judges from the charge of considering only technical matters. They were not blind to the importance of ideas, but "the first great lesson which the competitors needed to learn was that technique was an absolute requisite to the satisfactory expression of good ideas." The judges were not adverse to the power of feeling—they conceded that many of the inferior cards were inspired by lofty ideas. But evidence of an inspiring ideal by itself was not sufficient. Powerful and effective artistic expression, even the decorative art found in Christmas cards, required an individuation of those ideas produced through the discipline of technique. As the author concluded, "[The judges] have set their faces against bad workmanship as the great failure of the work submitted, and they have placed the seal of their approval upon strong and original ideas as the great necessity in all decorative art. Their verdict is unmistakable in its opposition to all tawdry sentimentalism."[43]

The effort to legitimate decorative art in Christmas cards had sliced through the shared cloth of sentimental imagery. This was an art competition, sponsored by a business that was striving after a competitive edge. But the ostensible public aim of the contest was to produce images that would reinforce social values of love and domestic warmth, specifically those noneconomic values associated with the holiday season that ran counter to the impulses of competition and efficiency that dominated business organizations. What seemed to distinguish tawdry sentimentalism from strong and original conceptions in the eyes of the judges was not the abandonment of holiday themes of love and abundance, but the discipline of pictorial technique. Aesthetic discipline in decorative art required not simply the meeting of a set of prescribed standards but the artistic individuation that mastery of technique enabled, an individuation required by a society driven to constant reorganization by the agency of market structures. According to the judges, the social values of love and domestic warmth could be expressed best through the efforts of disciplined competitive individuals. For the next several years, Prang's Christmas cards showed the effects of these judges' collective decision. From 1881 until 1890, Prang's best cards achieved the individuation of legitimate decorative art and, in the process, created the powerful dialectical images that signified sentimental seasonal abundance and warmth amid the contradictions of competitive industrial production and acquisitive accumulation. These images continued to function as Christmas cards—as gifts exchanged in the development of the social network—because they addressed the anxieties of market-oriented subjects in process.

Prang held a third competition, in November 1881. He was clearly still feeling the sting of the previous contest when he devised a double system of judgment. The company would award prizes for both the most popular card, as voted for by all those who attended the general exhibition of the cards, and the most artistically distinguished, as judged by invited artists and critics.[44] Apparently the thinking was that this bifurcated system would address both the popular market of Christmas card buyers and the interests of those capable of consecrating the company's products as legitimate art. But that November a striking concurrence among the views expressed by the popular voting and the opinions of the invited judges resulted in the top popular and the top artistic awards being given to a single card. It is quite possible that some tinkering took place in the judgment process. In the circular that Prang had sent to potential entrants into the competition, he had underlined the possibility that one card could win both competitions (and both monetary prizes).[45] It does seem at first glance quite unlikely that the profound split between the judges and the public that had been evidenced in the previous contest could be so easily resolved only a few months later. But this almost does not matter. Regardless of whether or not a manipulation of those allowed to vote or a selective tabulation of the votes took place, what matters for my purposes is the particular design by Dora Wheeler that benefited from the process. The card is an extraordinary representation of the gap between the sentimental ideals that had been common to Christmas expression and the material realities of inequality produced through industrial production along with market-based systems of distributing goods and status (plate 5).

In a circular published only a few days after the contest was judged, Prang described Wheeler's design as

> in the highest degree artistic. The leading thought, symbolically rendered, is that of the light of the world rising to dissipate the darkness which encompasses poverty-stricken mankind. A desolate woman, standing on the globe and leaning against a barren, snow-laden tree, gazes intently in an agony of expectation towards a vision in the clouds of the Virgin with the Christ Child in her arms. Two thinly clad little children, frightened by what they do not understand, cling closely to their mother's side, in search of aid and protection. The contrast between these groups, one of heavenly beauty and promise in a sun of light, the other of poverty, intense expectation, fear and desolation, produces a most striking effect.[46]

Indeed, the contrast could not be more striking. Compare this card with the Horsley–Cole card that initiated the commercial Christmas card tradition. The Horsley–Cole card distinguishes between those living in abundance and those in need of charity, including its users in the innermost circle of success. Wheeler's card strips away the smug complacency of the family in abundance, centering the card's focus on the family in need. The imagery might still be termed sentimental; the card focuses on families with children, and it represents the possibility of Christian salvation. The motto on the card is "Good tidings of great Joy!" But this card makes no promises about the earthy deliverance of that joy. It does not suggest the smooth resolution of conflict. It does not beckon nostalgically to a simpler past, nor does it frame children as presocial innocents. In Prang's own description, the earthly children are frightened and desolate. They are not sitting warm and cozy by the fire waiting for Santa to deliver the fruits of industrial production and acquisitive accumulation.

Prang sold this card for $1, $1.50 with fringe. It was his most expensive card for the 1882 season. I have no idea how many copies he sold. Luna Lambert says that Prang's prize cards never sold very well. She suggests that their purpose was promotional, to call attention to Prang's other products. Prang certainly took advantage of every notice that this card received. He quoted a London paper, the *Queen*, that praised the card as "a true 'Christmas Card.'" The pricing suggests that, contrary to Janet Huntington McKelvey's later urgings, only the most well-off would buy this card. But the card was purchased, and it was given away. What did those who sent and received Wheeler's card think of it? Did they identify with the family clinging to the tree in agony and fear? Did they thank heaven that they were spared such a life? Did they consider opening their own social networks to include this desolate unit? Did they feel safely separated from them? Perhaps the image seemed wholly spiritual. Did its senders and receivers feel reassured that the poor would always be taken care of, in the next world if not in this one? Remember McKelvey's description of the social function of the Christmas card. How could this image work to reflect the beauty and tenderness, sympathy and fellowship of the sender? It could function in this way only by conjuring the real existence of such families in need. This card had to have reminded its users—those successful market-oriented individuals—of the real limits to the social networks produced through gift exchange in a market economy and the corresponding precariousness of a society built on competitive capitalism and acquisitive accumulation.

A second card from the 1882 season quite probably sold more, as several copies can be found in collections stored in archives across the country. Picturing angels dropping toys from the heavens, this card displaces the source of abundance out of the realm of the social, seemingly emptying all conflict out of the productive process (plate 6). It provides a powerful contrast to Wheeler's design. That card's sentiment, "Good tidings of great Joy," is here transformed into "Christmas

Scatter Many Joys about you!" Unlike Wheeler's card, this design leaves no question about the objects responsible for seasonal joy. The tumbling leather-bound book, the shining trumpet, the bookmarks and dolls, are saturated with rich color; the angels dispensing these joys are youthful and innocent. In fact, intense rich colors soak through the clouds holding the crescent moon, floating across a deep blue sky that lightens softly into a sunset over a small village. This card represents the nostalgic, sentimental side of Prang's productions, a sentiment without a critical function, the *Barefoot Boy* to the *Portrait of Senator Revels* of Wheeler's card. This card flatters its receiver as it congratulates its sender. Here, sympathy and fellowship perform no transformative social work. They simply reinforce the networks constructed by those successful market-oriented individuals blessed by a productive process beyond their control, one that seemingly produced no negative consequences for anyone.[47]

Another card from that same season demonstrates Prang's awareness of the value of the warm and cozy interior (plate 7). This card depicts the home as an idealized shelter, with solid thick walls. Yet those walls clearly mark the boundaries of this shelter. Outside, icicles hang heavily from bare tree limbs; inside, happy faces shine with the warmth of social inclusion. The liminal condition figured on the card, as the guests standing on the porch are welcomed with "A Hearty Christmas Greeting," is clearly temporary. They will either be invited into this house or be summarily turned away. They are either part of the social network or not. As a clear representation of the significance of such networks, this card images the consequences of inclusion or exclusion. The idealized home, with its warm and cozy domestic interior, remained a regular theme of Prang's cards. One card from 1886 emphasized the imaginary condition of this ideal. A large, beautiful, detached house sits alone on a well-tended lot, inviting the "humble hearts" evoked by a stanza from Thomas More's *Ballad Stanzas* to find peace inside (plate 8). Yet the entire scene is imaged as a fantasy, placed as it is in the smoke and flames of a blazing fireplace. What might have been the function of this fantasy? Did the circulation of cards with this image call attention to the difficulty of the materialization of the dream-wish it depicted? Probably not. More likely, it confirmed the significance of the fantasy, reinforcing the symbolic power of the ideal home. But the very need for effective reminders suggests again a possible awareness among those who bought and gave away Prang's cards of the precariousness of their comfort, of the need to continually reinforce the means of its reproduction.[48]

What were these means? Prang recognized the integration of home and factory in his vision of the social process. And just as he recognized the symbolic value of the idealized home, he produced sentimental visions of the idealized factory. His own descriptions of his firm's modern, spacious, clean, and warm interior speaks to a taste for order and clarity that accompanied his focus on technique and workmanship. Prang was an advocate for industrialized craftsmanship. Although he continually praised his chromolithographers, artists, and pressmen, he was equally proud of his "sixty-horse steam boiler," his "twenty-horse Corliss engine," and his steam presses. Prang shared the prevailing opinion among chromolithographers that mechanical pressings could be of equal quality to hand pressings. For Prang, the workings of the machine were not a hindrance to artistry or a secondary apparatus that industrially and unconsciously reproduced the results of the skilled craftsman. Instead, the proper operation of the machines was subject to the same requirements of delicate attention and careful technique as the drawing on the stone. In particular, Prang highlighted the skill necessary to apply ink to the lithographic stone, a process he called the "rolling of the stone. This rolling is an operation partly mechanical, partly scientific: it demands a steady eye, close observation, and dexterous manipulation, in order to meet the requirements of artistic excellence in the results." In 1880 a description of Prang's operation published in the trade journal *Paper World* claimed: "The chromo-lithograph printer must be at once an artist in color and a printer of rare mechanical skill." According to this journal, the combination of craftsmanship and artistry suffused Prang's entire operation. For even the business office was "so entirely devoid of the conventional counting room stiffness, and so full of artistic suggestion that one feels, the moment he enters, that he is in a place where the difficult undertaking of making System and Beauty go hand in hand has for once been accomplished." Whether this meld of aesthetic efficiency was real or simply imagined is irrelevant next to the power of the desire that it renders explicit. The joy taken in skillful work, the blending of strong ideas and learned technique, the combination of sentiment and business, of system and beauty was the fundamental requirement for salvation. In Prang's own words, "Thus only are we able to live a perfect life, and can we hope for a happy old age."[49]

The idealized organization of Prang's business operations reflected the aesthetic qualities of his best work. Thorstein Veblen named this the "instinct for workmanship," which he termed an imminently pragmatic and teleological instinct that, because it is developed in interaction with an environment, is highly sensitive to competition and changing standards. In its traditional form, the instinct for workmanship was "concerned with the ways and means of life rather than with any one given ulterior end." It represented precisely the careful attention to technique that Prang's judges required from award-winning Christmas card designs and that Prang himself ascribed to the operators of machine-driven presses. As Veblen simply put it, "Much of the functional content of the instinct for workmanship is a proclivity for taking pains." A historical shift in the organization of production, however, forced a mutation in this instinct. The separation in modern businesses between the skilled workers who produced the goods and the managers, salesmen, and owners who organized the work and oversaw the pecuniary aspects of the firm resulted in the channeling of this instinct among the middle classes into the accelerating competition organized around calculations of profit and loss. In this arena, the instinct for workmanship, previously a positive value, became purely an accounting for financial advantage, a habit of calculation measured against an abstract, depersonalized, but apparently objective standard. In Veblen's narration, the instinct for workmanship under modern business conditions suffered a fall from the highest form of honorable motivation to the "self-regarding sentiments of emulous rivalry." The instinct for workmanship is a collective instinct. It directs the aspirations and desires of individuals into a social mirror from which can be reflected the communally recognized value of their efforts. Stripped of any body of sensuous material with which to work, allowed to operate only in the realm of calculation, this desire for purposeful work became the basis for a totally abstracted longing for pure advantage, for the most abstract forms of capital, not for the functional investment of energy and desire in the production of items of use.[50] If it is possible to drop Veblen's harsh judgment of this adaptation, I would like to adopt the view that the social use of cards reflects the pecuniary channeling of Veblen's instinct for workmanship. The modern development of Christmas cards resulted from the merger of the taste for beauty—the sensuous pleasure taken in qualities abstracted from use, such as full, vibrant, decorative color—with the calculated production of social value that lay behind the previously elite game of card exchange. Chromolithographed Christmas cards as produced by Prang and his rivals captured, if only for a moment, the union of beauty and system.

Prang's Christmas cards were tokens of industrial beauty whose systemic means of production reinforced the longings for the warm and cozy interior they so often imaged. But even as the home was figured as a site of warm fantasy that recognized the difficulty of this achievement, the scene of production also appeared as a dialectical image of struggle and progress. The Christmas card industry was a highly competitive field that reinforced the anxieties of modern social and economic life. Prang captured these anxieties in one particularly ambivalent card from 1890 that shows Santa whipping his reindeer in a frantic race against a train (plate 9). Santa's sleigh and reindeer are rendered in loving detail, even to the presence of gifts in the back of the sleigh. But the vision of the train rapidly dissolves into steam. A sardonic sun grins at this scene of competition and struggle while the motto on the card states, "This race is full of mirth and fun you see: / At Christmas so the human race should be." The image on the card suggests that the struggle to keep up with advancing forms of industrialization—whether actualized in any one field of production or simply imagined as a continual condition of economic life—is fierce and frenzied. Santa is forced to whip his animals, driving them ever faster just to keep the slightest bit ahead of the train. Yet the sun claims that this race is full of "mirth and fun." What could possibly be the source of mirth in this scene? Perhaps the sun is rising, grinning at the sight of Santa not yet finished with his labors. Possibly the sun recognizes the already evident dominance of the train and mocks Santa's reliance on outdated forms of transportation.[51]

A reading of this card that focuses on the apparently intense competition between the train and Santa is reinforced by a speech that Prang delivered in 1897 to the Boston Women's Club on the topic of trusts and monopolies. The speech begins with Prang claiming not to want to talk about this topic, because it was impossible to present himself as a "Saint": "I cannot point to the monopolist as the other fellow whose sins I scorn to follow. We business men scheme and work for a monopoly, every one of us. We live in an age of monopoly. Monopoly is, under present social conditions, the goal of comparative safety from the wild rush for a comfortable seat in the chariot of life." Under these social conditions, Prang went on to suggest, it was not mere greed that provoked businessmen to chase after monopoly, but fear. "The impelling cause," he said, "is simply the knowledge that under present conditions of our social organization some one will be left on the roadside to starve and every one is naturally anxious to escape this terrible fate." For Prang, for this 1848er, monopoly was a direct effect of the private ownership of the means of production. The possibility of private ownership lead inevitably to the competitive desire to control one's own fate through dominating and controlling the means of production, even as it inevitably resulted in the starvation of others: "Monopolies will flourish . . . until the fundamental principle that man is born into this world with equal rights to its opportunities for supporting life, shall become a fact." Perhaps this card of Santa versus the train represents one of Prang's most forceful and direct critiques of the social conditions under which he labored. Maybe the key word in the motto is "should": "At Christmas so the human race *should* be."[52]

There is another possible interpretation. Perhaps the race is full of fun because the chores of the night have been completed and the scene really depicts a playful romp between those who are jointly responsible for producing the gifts for exchange. Perhaps this is not a frantic fierce competition between handicrafts and industrial production, or a struggle resulting in either the dominance of monopoly or the fate of starvation. Perhaps Santa and the train always frolic together in the celebration of their mutual endeavors, in recognition of the different yet mutually supportive functions they perform in the project of establishing the economic and social bases for the dominance of market-oriented individuals. And if the sun is rising in the morning, then both the train and Santa are headed west, away from the East Coast where the union of their work is so familiar as to require no overt claims, and toward a land that appears, at least on this card, to be empty. Maybe this is what the sun means by linking the race between industry and handicrafts to the spirit of the human race. Perhaps the race that the sun refers to is precisely that race who benefits from an economy of industrial production and a social system constructed at least in part through gifts that mark the specific function of the social while rewarding and including those with an awareness of the agency of markets. Perhaps this card marks the dominance of Western industrialism and the processes of racialization that distinguishes between those who receive its benefits and those who do not.

Two last cards from Prang's line might help us to think once again about the racialized social collective that was constructed through the exchange of his cards. In 1885 Prang published a card that represented a sexually ambiguous but racially identified doll, hanging from a bit of mistletoe (plate 10). The message reads:

> Just over from Japan,
> hear my jolly little plan.
> Hang me under the mistletoe,
> to get a little kiss, you know.

Fringed in red, the card itself soaked in red, its eroticism is unmistakable, yet the figure on the card is not a person, but a toy, a doll dressed in a kimono, hanging from a twig of holiday decoration.[53] It is an object, not at all a subject: the projected capacity of desire, perhaps, but not a person capable of desiring. Within the market-oriented logic of Christmas card exchange, then, this card figures the Asian as an object of exchange, not an agent of exchange. The Asian becomes a token used in the game that results in social recognition, and the social collective created in the game of card exchange is thus racialized, marked as non-Asian.

Of all the cards created by Prang, the most intriguing one I have found is entitled "A Modern Santa Claus" (plate 11). Perhaps the richest mass-culture image produced in the United States in the last quarter of the nineteenth century, this card shows a black peddler draped in his wares, a bicycle wheel forming a halo around his head, his white teeth shining in a smile reminiscent of but not wholly indebted to blackface imagery. To his right (the viewer's left) a fine lady's ankle slips back into her fancy carriage, or prepares to step out. As with so much of this card, the direction of this gesture is impossible to disambiguate. Is she stepping out of the carriage to purchase a trumpet or a pair of shoes? Or is she slipping back into the carriage satisfied with whatever goods she has garnered from the peddler? The immediate questions, of course, involve the central figure. Is this black peddler the "modern Santa Claus?" If so, what does his blackness signify? In his dissertation treating consumer culture among African Americans, Patrick Mullins points out that although most peddlers in the postbellum North were recent European immigrants, black peddlers were common throughout the South from the late nineteenth century into the 1920s, with the peddlers "typically [selling] to both White and African American consumers." Furthermore, when black peddlers were depicted in southern newspapers, they "often were reduced to standard racial stereotypes. The caricature of the foolish, humorous Black peddler with a rickety cart, old donkey, and modest wagon of mediocre vegetables made African American marketing and White consumption from them seem innocuous."[54] This card, with its suggestion of satisfied exchange, is clearly not produced to ridicule the concept of African-American marketing. Should this card, then, be placed next to the portrait of Hiram Revels, as an indicator of the movement of African Americans beyond slavery and beyond agriculture into a commercial class? Or is this Santa a token of the labor that produces the wealth of the United States, reminding us that the northern commercial economy also grew on the backs of black laborers? Is his smile strictly the servile grimace of blackface, or is it the sign of a successful commercial transaction? Other key questions concern what it might have meant for one market-oriented subject to buy this card and send it to another one. While the detail and the evident humanity of the black image on the card raise it above traditional blackface stereotypes, we have to remember that this card was more than probably purchased, sent, and received by whites. If the figure of the Asian on the preceding card marked one racialized boundary of the circuit of card exchanges, does this figure perform similar work?

To pursue for a moment the work of racialization that card exchange participated in, I want to consider two texts. The first is the first chapter of *The Souls of Black Folk* by W. E. B. Du Bois. In "Our Spiritual Strivings," Du Bois describes how he first became aware of being, as he put it, "a problem":

> In a wee wooden schoolhouse, something put it into the boys' and girls' heads to buy gorgeous visiting-cards—ten cents a package—and exchange. The exchange was merry, till one girl, a tall newcomer, refused my card,—refused it peremptorily, with a glance. Then it dawned upon me with a certain suddenness that I was different from the others; or like, mayhap, in heart and life and longing, but shut out from their world by a vast veil.[55]

Thus, dramatically, Du Bois situates the functionality of card exchange in the reproduction of racialized difference. If the cards result in a market evaluation of the worth of social units, the refusal of young Du Bois's card was a judgment of relative worth. But this example might be too clear, too obvious. It might also seem to undercut my previous argument about the production of market-oriented social units, replacing that strategic concept with the more familiar one of racialized social hierarchies. The key point here is that market orientation does not abstract one from racialized structures but interacts with and reinforces racialization.

In order to support this contention, I will turn to another famous literary example, *The Rise of Silas Lapham*, by William Dean Howells. This novel, published in 1885, situates the upper-middle-class white family in relation to the changing means of production, the shifting organizational patterns in business, and the struggles to accrue value—both social and economic—through the operations of fluctuating markets. It precisely locates the traditional reproductive family as the nexus

between schemes of economic production and regimes of social reproduction. Here the happy family experiences the stresses that accompany the globalization of capitalist systems of increase and the transition
from family-based firms to modern corporate structures, along with
the careful, even if implicit and unspoken, social negotiations that accompany love.

The Laphams are precisely a social unit in touch with fluctuating
markets. Silas Lapham himself is a paint manufacturer who, by splash-
ing his bold colors on local rocks, has spread the sign of his products
across the New England landscape. The paint firm began as a partnership. But Lapham drove out his early partner, instinctively reacting to
the impression of weakness that Rogers, the partner, exhibited in his
business dealings. Once the partnership was dissolved, the company
became a family proprietorship. Although he has hired some managers
and split the firm into departments, Lapham retains control of the crucial operations of the business, keeping some dealings secret from all
his employees. Lapham's personal and managerial relationship to his
firm mirrors that maintained by Prang. All the managers report directly to him, and he is accountable to only himself. Howells has
Lapham's wife point out "that his paint was something more than business to him; it was a sentiment, almost a passion. He could not share
its management and its profit with another without a measure of self-
sacrifice far beyond that which he must make with something less personal to him."[56] Lapham's paint firm is not a modern corporation. The
paint itself is based on a mineral ore that is mined from Lapham's father's farm. Lapham's pride in the ore and pride in the family's direct
connection to the source of their wealth is emphasized when he names
his premium paint after his wife—Persis.

When the novel begins, the Laphams are doing quite well—in
every sense, their stock is rising. The paint is the best available; markets are expanding. Lapham's success is remarkable enough for him to
be interviewed for "The Solid Men of Boston" series in a local newspaper. As Amy Kaplan has shown, this interview crucially raises the
question of how one might come to know others, a problem of central
significance in American realism: "Howells tries to construct a community based on character, on mutual recognition," yet this process of

recognition is necessarily indirect, profoundly mediated.[57] In the interview, the economic need for mediation is highlighted when Lapham boasts that he ships his paint "to all parts of the world." Outlining the reach of his empire, Lapham declares, "It goes to South America, lots of it. It goes to Australia, and it goes to India, and it goes to China, and it goes to the Cape of Good Hope. It'll stand any climate."[58] The market for Lapham's paint is global. Although he has commented directly on the paint's ability to handle the weather, Lapham's apparently innocent remark serves to cover other differences among those continents that remain unspoken. Clearly Howells wants us to see that it would not be remarkable for Lapham to sell to Europe or across the United States. The transatlantic and transcontinental markets were well established. The sign of Lapham's true success was his ability to reach "others." Immediately, however, Howells points out to us some of the cultural factors that are implicated in the mediations of distant markets. As another sign of his global footprint, Lapham proudly displays a drawer full of business labels that are printed in Spanish, French, German, and Italian—distinctly not in Hindi or Cantonese or Hausa.[59] The mediation of the labels reflects the imperial mediation of markets, just as the mediation of market system affects the production and exchange of cultural value.

In the domestic arena of Boston society, cards replace business labels in the mediations of the social marketplace. After the Laphams become acquainted with the Coreys, they anxiously participate in the requisite rituals of visiting and card exchange. The Coreys represent old (or, at least, older) money, their fortune having been made in the generation before the Civil War, when the patriarch had been "an old India merchant."[60] Bromfield Corey, the son of the deceased merchant, regards himself as an artist. While he reads and paints, the family lives off its investments. Although the Coreys are not proprietors of a firm, they are as dependent economically on the fluctuations of markets as the Laphams. Indeed, the family has recently suffered a "shrinkage of values" that is forcing Bromfield's son, Tom, into gainful employment. But they still enjoy a certain distinction in Boston society, a value that is socially recognized and, therefore, objective. Bromfield's artistry, never quite successful, is the mark of the family's declining but still distinctive gentility: "It was absurd for him to paint portraits for pay and ridiculous to paint them for nothing, so he did not paint them at all. He continued a dilettante, never quite abandoning his art . . . and talking about it more than working on it."[61] Bromfield Corey's non-painting is the ultimate sign of disinterest, the mark of aesthetic distinction; this disinterest signifies his rejection of complete market orientation. Lapham's aesthetic theory, on the contrary, is completely opposed to this Kantian position. He believes quite simply that in art, as in all things, you get what you pay for.

These opposing aesthetics are set off by the families' divergent economic trajectories, and the tension between culture and economics structures their encounter in the social marketplace. Although the Coreys maintain their social advantage, the decline in family fortunes causes Tom to look for work. While advising his son, Bromfield acknowledges that "in my time you would have gone into the China trade or the India trade—though I didn't; and a little later cotton would have been your manifest destiny—though it wasn't mine."[62] Howells is suggesting here that the social dominance of the cultured elite was predicated on an economic dominance that was racialized. The cotton trade had been built on slave labor; the India and China trade reflected the profound intersection of Boston shippers and merchants with the expansion of the British Empire across Asia. In each case, surplus value was extracted by the white traders. While Bromfield refused to be involved in these doings, his position of aesthetic disinterest had clearly been paid for by his father's activities. And his own unwillingness to expand the family's fortunes has resulted in his son's having to enter a business. After Tom announces his plan to work for Lapham, his father drolly comments, "You never could draw, but this scheme of going into the mineral-paint business shows that you have inherited something of my feeling for color."[63] The relationship to color not only comments on the racialization of the global marketplace, but again marks the cultural class-fracture in the domestic arena. Tom has a talent for business. He shares with Lapham the bold vigor that bright color conveys, a vigor that the paint itself conveys. It is to be used in decoration, not in artistic depiction, and, as such, it must be deep and rich in its colors. His father, an artist too refined to actually paint, develops instead his theory of the method employed by Titian, an artist whose work could easily form the standard for fine gradations of color.

The pressure on these intersecting class trajectories is heightened when it becomes evident that Tom Corey is romantically interested in one of the Lapham daughters. The somewhat hackneyed marriage plot allows Howells to show the dilemmas that arise when one's cards are not in order. Persis Lapham displays a keen awareness of their relative standing, and anxiously worries about the propriety of her family's appearance when encountering the Coreys. In particular, she frets about Silas's too-close identification with his business. Not only is "Lapham's idea of hospitality . . . still to bring a heavy-buying customer home to pot-luck,"[64] but he lacks a card that represents his self as something other than a paint manufacturer. When the Coreys pay their first visit, Anna Corey leaves behind her husband's visiting card as well as her own, putting Persis Lapham "in some trouble about the proper form of acknowledging the civility." For Silas "had no card but a business card, which advertised the principal depot and the several agencies of the mineral paint; and Mrs. Lapham doubted, till she wished to goodness that she had never seen nor heard of those people, whether to ignore her husband in the transaction altogether or to write his name on her own card."[65]

In contrast to the Laphams' dependence on their business for their standing, the Coreys have achieved a relatively independent social status. Howells makes clear the kinship structures that have shaped Boston society. Anna Corey is a Bellingham. The Coreys are, therefore, part of the "society where Middlesexes have married Essexes and produced Suffolks for two hundred and fifty years."[66] Any linkage between the Coreys and the Laphams will require special conditions—conditions constructed out of economic trajectories and realized through business. Tom Corey does enter into the world of the Laphams as an employee, one who brings special talents to the world of paint distribution. Tom's education means that he can speak many languages (though, again, he specializes in the European languages of colonization), and he promises to expand the "foreign markets" for Lapham's paint. Tom also brings a genetic trait that skipped his father's generation—a Roman nose that Bromfield sees as the visible sign of a talent for business. This physical trait stands in for internal qualities in exactly the way that skin color and hair tone mark racial identity, rendering visible and evident Tom's skills. The merger of the families is initiated for business purposes; the fortunes of the families are tied to the fortunes of the business.

But the operations of capital produce complications in the marriage plot. First, there is a softening of the general economy (quite probably based on the depression of 1873). This causes a downturn in Lapham's market. As his paint builds up in his warehouse, he begins to look for opportunities to diversify, and selectively invests in stocks. At first this seems to pay off magically. But Lapham has no real instinct for this form of workmanship. Soon the investments show the effects of the larger downturn, subtracting more from Lapham's worth. Finally, a competing paint firm enters the market. This competition has efficiencies of production that enable it to sell its paint more cheaply, undercutting Lapham's position even further. Lapham has lost his monopoly and, following the logic laid out in Prang's speech on trusts, finds himself facing bankruptcy. He thrashes around, searching out schemes for quick returns. As they fail, one after another, Lapham is forced out of business. He sells the paintworks to the competing firm from West Virginia. It hires Tom Corey to be its South American representative, gaining his business skills, linguistic talents, and Roman nose. Tom's inheritance from his grandfather, his ability to pursue markets across the empire, enables his success in the new paint corporation. When Tom marries Penelope Lapham, then, the global dominance of whiteness in the continued pursuit of markets for color is maintained, and the merger of families and firms is completed in precisely the indirect way that market orientation favors.

Lapham's firm failed to make the transition from a family proprietorship producing one line of goods to a modern corporation diversified in ownership, with hierarchies of managers vertically linked from production through distribution and with multiple lines of goods. As Howells stated a few years later, "the struggle for life has changed from a free fight to an encounter of disciplined forces, and the free fighters that are left get ground to pieces."[67] Silas Lapham was a free fighter, as was Louis Prang. Facing competition from German and English greeting card manufacturers, seeing the market shift from a focus on deep color to a fascination with the easily mailed post card, Prang sold his chromolithography plant and retired. What both Lapham and Prang lacked was the side effect of the modern complete orientation toward the market that Veblen identified as the divergence of the instinct for workmanship into purely pecuniary channels. Lapham's "practical sympathy," his desire to take care of and respect the feelings of those around him, and Prang's concern with art and aesthetic education prevented both of them from competing effectively with the more efficient firms.

The first thirty years of the twentieth century would see major changes in the greeting card industry. Although all the major firms began as family proprietorships, the most successful companies made the transition to modern forms of business organization. These transformations were not unique to the greeting card industry but represent a broad pattern that changed business practices across the United States. These economic changes interacted structurally with changes in the reproductive family to produce new structures of feeling and new markets for greeting cards. Rather than merely limiting the production of quality, then, effective business competition would drive most of the innovations in the twentieth-century greeting card industry.

3

Corporate Sentiment

The Rise of the Twentieth-Century Greeting Card Industry
and the American Culture of Business

*B*y the beginning of the twentieth century, the construction of market-oriented subjectivities no longer organized the demand for emotional eloquence. The market revolution had transformed all but the most outlying areas. The economic force that would drive emergent structures of feeling for the next half-century would be the development of large-scale business organizations. The swift rise to dominance of the corporate form began soon after the 1886 Supreme Court decision that gave the business corporation the legal status of a person. A massive set of mergers quickly followed, collapsing thousands of small firms into a much smaller number of very large ones, and, by 1920, the U.S. economy was effectively shaped by the interests of large-scale, nationally focused corporations.

Out of the rise of large-scale business organizations grew a business culture with its own set of affects and its own set of emotional needs. Large-scale business organizations were forced to hire such large numbers of managers that they had to reach beyond their immediate circle of family members and close acquaintances. Forced to deal with the contradictory needs of competitive capitalism and social affiliation, the modern corporation fostered the development of particular sensibilities and subjectivities. Modern processes of social affiliation were shaped by the mobility produced through the national dominance of these large corporations. Similarly, while working together, businessmen and -women developed feelings of affection for one another that could disrupt the purely economic calculations evaluating market performance. A somewhat peculiar business theory of friendship arose that worked with business and fraternal organizations to help mediate these contradictions. I argue that this clash between affiliation and calculation produced the dominant structure of feeling within corporate capitalism and, furthermore, that the effects of this emergent structure of feeling can be seen in the history of the modern greeting card industry. The language of emotional cliché, the displaced and condensed visual imagery characteristic of greeting cards of the first half of the twentieth century, is a direct expression of that structural collision. The development and distribution of that set of verbal and linguistic signs of fungible feeling was the great achievement of the twentieth-century greeting card industry.[1]

In 1900, ten years after Louis Prang sold his chromolithography plant and ceased to print Christmas cards, producers of valentines and Christmas cards in the United States continued to exploit the market for emotional eloquence that could be used in the construction and maintenance of social networks. Most of these printers and publishers, however, tended not to consider their operations part of the same industry. As the fascination with emotional and domestic interiority correspondingly faded, the densely layered, sentimental valentine lost much of its functional power. The pleasures of policing the lower boundaries of the middle classes remained strong, however, and the trade journals and the genteel press continued to lament the market dominance of comic valentines. The seasonal trade in Christmas cards continued to supplement the incomes of the purveyors of visiting cards and business cards, reinforcing the taste for color among the shifting fractions of the commercial classes. A company calling itself the Visiting and Fancy Card Manufactory claimed to provide $350,000 worth of seasonal and visiting cards to the trade. There were jobbers, such as the American News Company, that dabbled in valentines, and there were stationers, such as William J. Burckhardt, who would occasionally engrave Christmas cards. There were a few firms, such as McLoughlin Brothers, that continued to specialize in the publication of comic valentines while maintaining a respectable business through their publication of children's books. E. P. Dutton was publishing books in New York even as its importation of Ernst Nister's Christmas cards from Bavaria helped drive Prang out of business. The English company Raphael Tuck had established a New York office in order to exploit the relatively cheap English labor to sell valentines, Christmas cards, and Easter cards in the United

States. But the George C. Whitney Company in Worcester, Massachusetts, was the only domestic firm focusing on the production of both valentines and Christmas cards in the United States.[2]

Whitney had entered the valentine business soon after he was mustered out of the Union Army in 1865. He first worked as a clerk in a stationery shop in East Rutland, Massachusetts, but soon moved to Worcester, where he began to import lace and embossed paper and to build some of the intricate assemblages that the Howland family was making famous. Whitney's early designs were based on the Howland aesthetic, and his initial cards closely imitated Esther Howland's layered complexity. But he produced his valentines at a lower cost by relying on cheaper materials—in particular, cheaper paper. While Whitney layered image after image onto his valentines, his paper was more hard-edged, rough to the touch, not soft like the lace used by Howland. The silver and gilt took on a harsh tone; the backing paper was more stiff and cardlike. Whitney's plant was no friendly feminine assembly line, either. Although at first he built his layers by hand, using scissors and paste in the manner of Howland's ladies, Whitney quickly purchased the machine dies and printing presses that enabled the rapid mass production of printed sentiment. Industrialization brought the profits necessary to expand his production facilities. Whitney soon bought out Berlin & Jones, a stationery company that specialized in the production of envelopes. As he consolidated his operations, he began producing his own paper. He diversified beyond the production of intricate sentimental valentines when he bought out A. J. Fisher & Company, taking over its share of the comic valentine market. He soon expanded to include Christmas cards and gifts (called novelties in the trade at the time). In 1879, Whitney was able to buy out his local competitor, Esther Howland, and by 1886 he had branch offices in New York, Boston, and Chicago.[3]

Whitney's success demonstrated his awareness of the value of new corporate structures and his eagerness to exploit the efficiencies of industrial mass production and vertical integration. By the end of the 1880s, Whitney had consolidated under his own firm the production of all his paper needs. While he still had to buy ink, he could create his own lace paper—though it certainly never met the standards of Joseph

Mansell's work. He produced his own envelopes, mechanically embossed and cut out his own scraps, and even devised a printing technique that, at first glance, seemed to reproduce Howland's layers (plate
12). Yet Whitney's valentines did not evince the three-dimensional
complexity that characterized Howland's hand productions. No machine dies could layer the gold foil and insert the lift-ups that contributed a crucial depth to Howland's sentimental objects. Lacking the
equipment and the highly skilled artists that Prang had relied on to
layer dense colors, Whitney never tried to enter the market for chromolithographed Christmas cards, but instead produced printed cards
with simple images distinguished by their nontraditional shapes.
Valentines would take on the shape of hearts (figure 3.1); Christmas
cards would have the form of trees, tops, and other toys. Whitney's
firm shifted the focus away from the sensuous material of the object to
a more abstract and flatter concern with the recombination of already
successful elements of design and sentiment. Whitney seemed not to
care about the refined taste that found expression in a dainty delicacy
suggesting sincere sentimentality. Rather, his business strategy focused
on modernizing production techniques, controlling as much of his own
resources as he could, and expanding his distribution as far across the
nation as possible. He was soon the biggest producer of valentines in
the country. And he announced his success by placing his own trademark along with the retail price on the back of every card he produced.
In 1894 Whitney completed his transition from a single proprietorship
to a modern corporation with officers drawn from outside his extended family. By 1900, the George C. Whitney Company had in place the
defining business characteristics of the modern greeting card industry.[4]

The process of expansion and consolidation that Whitney's firm
experienced was part of a pattern that swept through the U.S. economy at the turn of the twentieth century. Yet Whitney's growth was
atypical of those firms producing valentines and Christmas cards between 1890 and 1910. Most of those companies remained small; most
considered their seasonal paper products to be a sideline of their otherwise more stable businesses. Those that had specialized in fancy
valentines or elegant Christmas cards found it increasingly difficult to
sell their goods profitably as the combined availability of inexpensive

Figure 3.1
Whitney valentine:
"I Can Sing and I Can
Sew." (Norcross Greeting
Card Collection, Archives
Center, National Museum
of American History,
Behring Center,
Smithsonian Institution)

imports and proliferation of smaller domestic firms entering the market at the cheaper end forced competing manufacturers to lower prices and cut costs. Whitney survived by modernizing well ahead of his competitors and, through either luck or wisdom, by having shifted his production away from what the trade called the quality market. From the 1890s through the first half of the twentieth century, the Whitney firm specialized in valentines for children. The company promoted the practice of exchanging valentines among schoolmates and created a special product line of valentines to be given to teachers. In this field, oddly shaped cards featuring cute, chubby children met the functional requirement of promoting an emotionally nurturing public classroom at just the moment when women were becoming the nation's predominant schoolteachers. Whitney's company quickly dominated this corner of the valentine market. His success in this field, along with his early modernization, kept his firm safe from the fierce competition that was in the process of transforming the two different practices of sending valentines and giving Christmas cards into the modern greeting card industry. What were the causes of this transformation? Why was Whitney's firm the only large company to survive this transition?[5]

The traditional answer given in histories of the greeting card industry is that cheap imports drove down the price and the quality of cards and that elites then dropped the practice with disgust, leaving only a lower-class demand for cheaper cards. Bad goods drove away discerning customers. Presumably, elites returned to handwritten missives and black-on-vellum visiting cards. Valentine exchange became a children's game. Ernest Dudley Chase's industry-sponsored *The Romance of Greeting Cards* explains it this way: "A disinterested, discouraged public was being offered huge quantities of cheap and tawdry foreign imports far removed from the original concept of the Christmas card. . . . Illustrated post cards for Christmas (and for Valentine's Day and Easter) appeared also, and with their cheaper postal rate of one cent, they cut into what buying market was left, and further alienated the quality-demanding public." Chase's explanation correctly highlights the fierceness of competition within the unorganized card business. But he fails to acknowledge the real forces that interrupted the development of the greeting card industry. Not only was the public being offered huge quantities of cheap cards, but they were buying huge quantities of cheap cards. This was not a disinterested, discouraged group of consumers. Valentines, Christmas cards, and other holiday cards experienced a continual expansion of the market from 1875 through the turn of the century. Relatively inexpensive imports of chromolithographed Christmas cards had made it impossible for Prang to continue selling the cards that he wanted to make. But many of the imported cards were aimed at the very same class and taste fraction that Prang had targeted. They were cheaper, but perhaps only slightly lower in quality. They lacked the social intensity of the imagery and the richness of design and color that Prang's artists and multiple pressings had created, but maintained the full visual vocabulary of emotional and material abundance that characterized chromolithographed Christmas cards. Of course, their relative cheapness helped expand the market for such cards, which was in line with Prang's intentions. As he saw it, Prang's own mission had been to raise the public taste for art, which could also be seen as lowering the capacity of his cards to function as symbols of class distinction. The very presence of color in cards used to delineate social networks was a transformation of the practice of card exchange, removing it from the province of elites, and opening it to the use of differently located persons and families. These cards were flexible social tools; they could mark the networks of numerous competing class fractions. Their use of bold color and densely layered textures presented a strong challenge to the public aesthetics of genteel elites, even as their potential for international industrialized mass production limited their effectiveness as unmediated signs of distinction. Recognizing the expanding market, new producers leaped into the business.[6]

At that point, the special economics of industrial capitalist mass culture began to take hold. Christmas cards and valentines were made of paper and ink, with an occasional extra dab of fringe, glitter, or feathers. If a producer chose not to use expensive paper or hire highly skilled lithographers, the cards themselves could be made quite cheaply. After several years of sending and receiving these cards, many users no longer located any objective magic directly in the cards. As the cards flattened, both literally and aesthetically, the predominance of any lasting affect would then result from the associations the card conjured up—the love it represented, the social network it marked. The sensuous materiality of the cards—Prang's lush colors, Howland's softly layered textures—ceased to drive the demand. It is not that the users failed to use aesthetic criteria in their choice of or appreciation of cards; rather, these aesthetics had become the genre-based aesthetics of mass culture. Valentines and Christmas cards no longer had to compete with innumerable other seasonal items for the attention of shoppers. Buyers now entered stationery stores in order to purchase these established consumer items with their own well-understood purposes. Receivers now compared this year's cards with those received the year before. At that point, valentines and Christmas cards simply competed against other valentines and Christmas cards, and their functionality took precedence over their magical beauty. In the furious economic and social transformations of the period between 1890 and 1920, it was function that drove the demand for cards, and function was served not so much by the quality of paper or elegance of colors, but by the perceived usefulness of design and sentiment.[7]

Whitney's solution of marketing for children limited the impact of the discriminating consumer as it took advantage of the most established genres of cards. It also insulated him against the next convulsive development in the world of card exchange, the post card craze. In September 1905, publishers and wholesalers of souvenir post cards in New York City reported an unusually active season. While they had expected an increase in sales during the summer vacation months, they were not prepared for the extreme growth in demand. The new display racks that helped boost sales were standing empty. Supplies were not keeping up. There seemed to be a clear need that enterprising publishers could help meet.[8]

The Post Card Interruption

Post cards had been produced and sold in Germany since the 1860s. The United States Postal Service did not approve post card mail until 1873; even then, it limited the special post card rate to only those cards officially produced by the post office. Nevertheless, 60 million cards were sold the first year they were legal, indicating a tremendous demand for these easily mailed and necessarily brief forms of communication. By 1893, the Postal Service was selling large numbers of souvenir picture post cards with scenes from the World's Columbian Exposition. These emblems of trips taken and places seen were evidence of the expanding possibilities of travel and, therefore, of the modern experience of mobility. Souvenir post cards, typically carrying a photograph of a tourist site on one side, enabled travelers to demonstrate the wonders they had seen, to provide objective evidence of their own travels, to bring the world back home. They were cheap testimonials to the pleasures of leisure travel and the joys of visual representation. The pleasures of tourism, including the purchase of pictorial souvenirs as tokens of that travel, enabled an increasingly mobile population to play with the social forces that were transforming their lives.

The use of post cards grew when the dependability of modern mail service became evident. Their popularity peaked as people recognized the ubiquity of travel and the necessity of long-distance communication. But they became a true source of pleasure only when their users began to feel the increasing possibility that kinship structures would be susceptible to the demands of a changing and increasingly national economy—that families and young people quite probably would not remain in the same towns their entire lives. On May 19, 1898, Congress allowed privately printed post cards to have the same mailing rights and rates as official government cards. Commercially produced post cards now also cost 1 cent to mail, while letters in an envelope required 3 cents. By 1900, the United States had the second-largest postal system in the world, following only Germany's. At that point, card publishers in the United States began to invest in post card production.[9]

The practice of sending souvenir post cards helped promote the mailing of holiday greetings. To the extent that Christmas card exchange remained linked to its origins in the visiting card rituals, it had retained the obligation of hand delivery. While valentines were often mailed in order to take strategic advantage of the anonymity the postal service offered, they were equally often hand-delivered. The blend of holiday cards and post cards marked a significant move away from the visiting card tradition. It recognized that social networks were no longer limited geographically. It also recognized the place of modern institutional communication systems at the heart of both social and business networks. Modern corporate capitalism developed in intimate interdependence with a national mail system. "Communication," as business historian Thomas Cochran put it, had become "the essential element in managerial control." The popularity of post cards is early evidence that communication at a distance had become an essential element in social networks as well. By 1905, American publishers had invested heavily in the capital equipment needed to produce holiday post cards. One publisher stated his confidence in the continued growth of this new market: "Big as our facilities are . . . we are continually adding to them. . . . If we were not thoroughly sure of the future of the post card business you may be sure we would not risk our capital in this way."[10]

Among the first blends of post cards and holiday cards to appear in large numbers were comic valentine post cards. Their vinegar quality rendered them the most likely valentine form to have been mailed previously. In addition, these valentines typically had been cheaply illustrated, with simple line drawings lithographed onto cheap paper. They were, therefore, the easiest genre to print onto post cards. They certainly were commercially successful. When Alfred Holzman brought out his line of cards in Chicago in 1906, he guaranteed prospective customers: "You will sell more Valentine Post Cards in six weeks than all post cards sold last year." Perhaps the emphasis on the modern and the new that accompanied post cards enabled new categories of these valentines to appear. In 1905 the Edward Stern Company advertised comic post cards that ridiculed leisure activities in addition to occupations—the Automobile Fiend, the Tennis Player, and the Golf Player joined the secretary and the policeman as potential objects of scorn. Valentine post cards were, therefore, one of the earlier mass-cultural forms that figured leisure as an arena for class distinction. Other forms of holiday cards soon followed. By 1909, the Souvenir Post Card Company of New York boasted of carrying 206 different Christmas cards, 144 Easter cards, 70 valentines, 56 New Year cards, 36 Thanksgiving cards, 12 Halloween cards, and cards for Washington's Birthday, Lincoln's Birthday, St Patrick's Day, and Decoration Day. That same year, *American Stationer* began a regular weekly column called "The Post Card World," demonstrating the importance of this line of products to the stationery business. By October of that year, this column became the place in the trade journal where the season's holiday cards were discussed. As far as the stationery trade was concerned, then, holiday cards and post cards had become the same business.[11]

Also by 1909, section 7 of the Payne-Aldrich Tariff Act had been put in place to help protect domestic publishers, including those producing post cards. Many of the German cards that had undersold Prang were driven out of the market by what their importers soon termed a "prohibitive duty." Dutton, one of the firms that had long imported German cards, was forced to radically transform its business. In the summer of 1909, it was still featuring its line of Ernst Nister's cards printed in Bavaria. In less than six months, it had ceased to promote this line at all. After the tariff was enforced, the American News Company chose to highlight its "seventy-five or more designs . . . of Domestic Cards," which, escaping the import fee, could retail for 1 cent each. With this limit on imported cards, many new firms quickly entered the domestic market. Companies in Illinois, Indiana, Nebraska, Missouri, and other midwestern states joined the publishers based in Philadelphia, New York, and Boston to produce souvenir and holiday post cards.[12]

Between 1905 and 1910, greeting cards became, in the main, an offshoot of the post card industry. The post card craze, as it was called, materialized the social changes that were transforming kinship networks. Anxieties produced out of new experiences of mobility created a set of pleasures in travel that collaborated with the technological developments in photographic reproduction and the growth of an efficient postal service to produce new markets for mass-produced tokens of social connection. These cards linked the social networks that were being stretched by the consolidation of industrial capitalism, the development of the modern corporation, and the expansion of a truly national economy. The post card craze also demonstrates the radical volatility of early mass culture in industrial capitalism. If we avoid the temptation to narrate a triumphalist saga that focuses exclusively on the success of the major companies that went on to dominate greeting card production in the first half of the twentieth century, what we see is a considerable number of individuals entering a business that could require as little capital as $100 and a shoe box. The vast bulk of these entrepreneurs left the business as quickly as they had entered it. When presented with the figures demonstrating the incredible growth of post card use, the evident protection of the tariff, and the relatively large margins that post card manufacturing and sales could produce, banks would lend money to individuals and firms that quickly faced fierce competition. This competition took place at not only the level of price, but also the level of distribution and access to retail markets.[13]

Joyce Hall, the maniacally driven founder of Hallmark Cards, was persuaded to enter the post card business when he was fourteen years old. During the peak of the post card boom in 1905, a salesman representing "one of the bigger New York firms" entered the bookstore in Norfolk, Nebraska, that was owned by Hall's brother. The drummer was looking for regional distributors and regaled the young boy with stories of the immense profits that could be his. Hall listened to the man's pitch and, once his brother returned to the store, convinced him to share the capital costs of entering the business. The Norfolk Post Card Company began with an investment of $540. The Hall brothers were jobbers; they traveled throughout the Midwest, convincing small shop owners to carry the cards they had purchased from publishers. By 1908, they were selling post cards for $7.50 per thousand, which did not allow much markup if their retailers were trying to meet the prevailing price of 1 cent per card. Two years later, Joyce Hall moved to Kansas City, separating the card business from the Norfolk bookstore and seeking a larger market for his cards. There he hit on a distribution scheme that took advantage of the same trust and, perhaps, gullibility that he had evinced when the Norfolk Post Card Company began. He packaged cards into assortments of a hundred and addressed the packages to "The Leading Post Card Dealer," with the name of the town and the state. He also included a bill for $1 plus 8 cents for postage. Norfolk had been selling the cards for $7.50 per thousand, so Hall's package price represented an increase of 33 percent, probably just covering the costs of those cards that were not paid for while considerably expanding the number of his dealers. Hall mailed his cards completely unsolicited; initially, he did not even have the name of the dealer. He also charged a wholesale rate that equaled the prevailing retail rate for post cards. Some of the packages he mailed went unaccounted for. Some were angrily returned. According to Hall, "about a third sent a check. They would get another shipment the next month, and I gradually built up quite a list. The system worked because few salesmen covered these small towns." The system also worked because Hall understood that mass culture, especially the selling of relatively cheap mass-produced commodities, benefited from the most aggressive marketing imaginable. Post cards that were bought in small towns scattered across the prairies did not necessarily carry images of places that people had visited. Any souvenir cards carried by the "leading post card dealer" in Abilene, Kansas; Higginsville, Missouri; or Guthrie, Oklahoma, more likely represented the possibility of mobility, the desire to travel, a particular longing for a particular, if only imagined, class trajectory.[14]

Not all post card entrepreneurs evinced the audacious aggression of Hall. Most simply produced flyers that described their wares and tried to find salesmen who could service and increase their accounts. Traveling drummers maintained a notorious autonomy at this time, and they would not continue to promote a line that was not quickly profitable. The competition for space on the countertops and in the drawers of small shops was often won simply by the first card company to approach each store. Many of the small companies that entered the business in the second half of the decade, therefore, found themselves losing in the ferocious struggle that followed boom times in any market. By November 1910, the columnist of "The Post Card World" was worrying that the intense competition that developed with the possibility of immense profits and the very broad appeal of the cards had resulted in deceptive business practices. The easy availability of credit for jobbers created new mid-level businesses that stimulated the wholesale demand for the cards. This demand encouraged publishers to invest their capital in productive machinery that created an actual oversupply of cards. The glut of cards produced intensive price competition among these jobbers, which resulted in many of them not being able to pay their bills. According to this columnist, the jobbers could easily avoid paying their bills by leaving town and starting over again somewhere else under a new name, but this left the publishers with unpaid accounts, causing many of them to go out of business. A few weeks later, the same column declared "The Call to Arms in the Post Card Trade," describing the "pangs of purification" that the industry was going through. To this date, the business had been characterized by "antagonistic methods," "unfair competition," "dishonest and cut-throat practices, and last, but not least . . . selling goods . . . at prices less than the actual cost of man-ufacturing." The columnist called for the industry to organize itself: "The day has passed when disjointed efforts can safely carry on the complex machinery of manufacturing and distributing merchandise in any vast line. Brains for administration and direction is required, and every trade must furnish this sort of experience and ability and become sufficiently devoted to its own interests." The post card industry had developed in a chaotic business climate of ad hoc solutions and catch-as-catch-can survival tactics. It had become an industry of response, servicing a demand driven by an emergent and barely conscious aware-ness of changing social and economic conditions.

Imagining Rational Organization

From 1898 to 1910, the practice of sending post cards transformed the production and use of greeting cards. Post cards—their production, use, and popularity—emphasized the aggressive, the quick, the mobile, and the new. In effect, a national industry publishing greetings that could be mailed at any time of the year had grown out of what had been an eastern urban practice of producing seasonal cards to be delivered. Even as post cards provided evidence of the competition of early mass culture, the ubiquity of modern mobility, and the stability of modern communication systems, they shortened the mental labor required of social connection at a distance by drastically limiting the space avail-able for a written message. The front of the card carried the preprint-ed image and holiday greeting; the back was split into two equal halves. As one side was dedicated to the address, only a small bit of card was left for any handwritten message. As a result, the greeting carried by post cards was often formulaic, sometimes reduced completely to a signature. The card itself again became the message, but this message was relatively two-dimensional. As quickly as it had risen to national awareness, the evidence of travel taken lost its novel pungency. The intersection of geographical and economic mobility worked its way through the tight language of post cards with modern efficiency. With that point made, with the anxieties of modern mobility acknowledged, the souvenir card could state only that the Florida Keys had been visited or that Niagara Falls had been seen. The holiday post card had another weakness: its message was public. Without an envelope, post cards were cheap to mail. But the public nature of any message sent—whether it was the smallest handwritten note squeezed into the space provided, or a preprinted combination of words and pictures—limited the post card's ability to convey emotional eloquence. By 1909, then, Dutton had begun to advertise "Private Christmas Greeting Cards: Just the card for the discriminating buyer seeking the personal note."[16]

The Christmas trade that year showed an evident return to envelopes. "A large part of the public that formerly used Christmas post cards bought greeting cards this season," said *American Stationer*. This retreat to envelopes was also a reaction against the flatness of post cards on the part of those seeking commercial solutions to the problem of social and emotional communication at a distance. When A. M. Davis began to produce specialized holiday cards in his shop in Boston in 1906, he was not quite sure what to call them. He sold them as post cards, but Davis soon composed short sentiments and had them engraved on his cards. Within two years, he was selling envelopes to go with the cards, and several of his holiday cards had a bit of ribbon attached to them. It was also in 1906 when Fred Rust, proprietor of a small book and gift shop in Kansas City, sold a few thousand copies of a Christmas greeting he had printed onto a sheet of tan paper that was to be folded and placed into an envelope before mailing. The Sapirstein family (later to form American Greetings) began stuffing the post cards they were jobbing into envelopes to help them sell better. Gibson Art Company began to feature something that it was not quite calling greeting cards as early as 1908. In 1910, Gibson called them "Xmas Letters," claiming that "letters with sentiment are what sells. Not mere wishy washy bubbles of thought but flashes of inspiration that fasten themselves on one's eye and compel attention." By 1909, the George Buzza Company in Minneapolis and the P. F. Volland Company in Chicago were promoting their own lines of Christmas cards.

In the whirlwind of new publishers entering the trade, of post card firms going bankrupt, and of stationers and gift stores continuing to demand seasonal markers of social connection, greeting cards struggled to define their distinction from post cards. They developed specializations not only of production but also of distribution, retail outlet, display, and use. The twentieth-century greeting card was mailed in an envelope. It combined image and words—design and sentiment—in its efforts to provide emotional eloquence and promote social connection. Whereas post cards were flat celebrations of modern mobility, greeting cards were elaborate exploitations of the disruptions caused by this movement. Ambivalent to the core, early greeting cards were coated with nostalgia for an imagined premodern community of emotional abundance even as they built a language of clichés and stereotypes that exploited the blank affections accompanying individual mobility. Their very conditions of possibility were the result of turmoil; their manifest content denied any such rupture. As the industry that produced these cards developed, it inherited the harsh competition that had characterized the early years of the post card industry. But it also quickly put into practice the post card industry's lesson about the importance of organizing. Greeting card manufacturers understood the importance of association. They enacted a powerful theory of friendship in a business culture that linked neatly with the paradoxes of their own product and the contexts of its production.[17]

The Business Theory of Friendship

Friendship in American business is complex and problematic. The affect produced through business transactions can be quite powerful. Businessmen of the early twentieth century wisely refused to underestimate it. Friendship was both a problem and a strategy in business culture. "Success," according to Thomas Cochran, "depended largely on making friends and providing efficient but largely routine service."

Friends had "potential cash value." But friendship's power also built on the class anxieties that saturated everyday life. As the sociologists W. Lloyd Warner, Marchia Meeker, and Kenneth Eells wrote in 1949, "Social class enters into almost every aspect of our lives, into marriage, family, business, government, work and play." Class aspirations are "a major determinant of individual decisions and social actions . . . the major decisions of most individuals are partly controlled by it." A businessman's circle of friends was partially determined by economic flows over which he had little control. The properly trained businessman needed to develop useful friendships while remaining wary of letting friendship interfere with complex business calculations. There was, therefore, little room for autonomy in friendship.[18]

In 1915, Elsie Clews Parsons wrote an analysis of modern friendship that underlined its troubling and unstable status. "As an institutional relationship friendship cannot expect to escape the trouble all the other institutional relationships are facing in this modern world," she wrote. In particular, "new conceptions of personality" limited friendship's claim to the permanence associated with other social categories. In a culture of personality, friendship "has been the harbinger of those free relations" that challenge the more traditional categories of society. Since it was not really a category of kinship, modern friendship carried no necessary permanence. This impermanence could be the flexible strength of modern friendship, but it was also the source of the anxiety it provoked. Friendship could arise out of the most casual of meetings— "friends made friends . . . by a smoke or a chew"—and it could disappear when those tastes were no longer shared. Friendships could grow out of business interactions or political organizations, with the knowledge that the end of a deal or a change of policy might end the relationship. Nevertheless, friendship remained a social force. It was not merely the subordinate effect of comradeship, but a transformation of the rules whereby the acquaintance could continue. This was friendship's real threat: it was a powerful sentiment, capable of transforming the network of social relations. But if it was not permanent, not a stable social category, then how was one to evaluate and respond to its pull?[19]

If quickly developed friendships were both an effect of and a technique used in modern business, they could not simply be eradicated from standardized business practices. The intensely gendered popular magazines of the period recognized the problem: business was not free from the complications of friendship, nor could friendship remain untainted by the entanglements of investment and interest. As early as December 1901, *Harper's Bazar* warned its presumably female readers about the potential friend who was, in reality, a bargain hunter: "He knows a good thing when he sees it, recognizes merit in unlikely places, has faith that misfortune cannot last forever, and that a rising market may be looked for." But the friendships that he contracts for "are often ruthlessly dissolved in the interest of more advantageous ones." A little more than ten years later, the magazine provided apparently contrary advice, suggesting that its readers not eschew but practice market evaluations of potential friendships: "If I had daughters . . . I would strive to impart a discretion which would keep girls from giving all their love and confidence to any friend before persuaded of her worth." Young readers had to somehow determine the worth of their friends yet not reduce their longing for friendship to the desire for a bargain.[20]

Throughout the first half of the twentieth century, *American Magazine* was "dedicated to the success of American men and American business." During the 1920s and 1930s, it ran several articles that directly addressed the tensions that lay at the intersection of business and friendship. While some of these articles tried to maintain a categorical distinction between friend and business acquaintance, the most interesting discussions confronted their muddled similarities. The popular poet, and author of one of the biggest selling greeting cards in history, Edgar Guest, declared in 1928 that true friendship was completely and utterly selfless. No consideration of personal gain or interest could possibly enter the relationship without polluting it. According to Guest, a friend considers only the needs of his friends. A friend is a friend for life or else no friend at all. Guest was, of course, articulating a sentimental value abstracted from the complicated relations of most readers of the magazine. With its longing for a purity of self-denial, Guest's article extended sentimentality beyond the ambiguities found in his most popular poem, "My Friend," which had been made into a best-selling greeting card for both Buzza and Hall Brothers: "I'd like to be the kind of friend that you have been to me." A less idealized vision of business and friendship had been provided a few months before when an anonymous author stated that the best friends that business can provide are those who were kind to you before you were successful. Of course, this writer explained, you can know that they had been real friends only when they come through for you with a mutually advantageous deal later. The magazine's boldest exploration of the business theory of friendship came in 1933 when Courtney Ryley Cooper asked, "Who Are Your Friends?" Cooper dispensed with any sentimentality in his blunt calculations of his friends' cash value: "In my wanderings I've learned that it's not how long you've known your friends that counts; it's how much you've done for each other." Whereas most writers tackling this issue tried to stake some middle ground, yearning to locate a kernel of stable feeling in the swirling midst of business relations, Cooper simply articulated a straightforward market-based approach to friendship. Going beyond the traditionally approved evaluation of the relative social equality of two people, he advocated the sheer calculation of the immediate short-term worth of any relationship. Cooper was interested in pure exchange value: "Friendship, to my mind, is the oldest form of barter and trade. Few persons make use of it. And most persons who think they have friends are merely wasting their perfectly good time with a bunch of bridge partners."[21]

The Business Friendships of George Babbitt

In order to illustrate the complex power of business friendship, I want to discuss those of George Babbitt, the main character in Sinclair Lewis's novel *Babbitt*. By 1922, Lewis could divide the friendships of this archetypal mid-level businessman into three categories. Perhaps Babbitt's deepest friendship was with Paul Riesling. Babbitt's love for Riesling began at college, and it held a nostalgic purity that had little support in the town of Zenith. Riesling had the heart of an artist—sensitive, impulsive, and unhappy with his life of compromise and getting along. His orientation toward life was in conflict with the world of deals and bonhomie that structured the majority of relationships in

Zenith. Like all of Babbitt's most powerful feelings, his love for Riesling was sentimental—it survived to the extent that it approximated an ideal separate from his daily life.

Yet Riesling could see through Babbitt's surface morality. He would ridicule Babbitt's belief that "it's the duty of responsible business men to be strictly moral," wondering if beneath that need to fit into the local political economy lived someone "essentially immoral." Furthermore, Riesling speculated that the source of this essential immorality could be found in the competitive structures of modern business: "All we do is cut each other's throats and make the public pay for it." Babbitt's horrified response, "You're pretty darn near talking socialism!" is tempered immediately by the two men hatching a plan to get away by themselves. They imagine that if they could get alone in the country, away from their families and their businesses, alone in the sentimental purity of a commercial nature camp, they could restore their souls. The trip provides a brief respite for Riesling's torment, but it changes nothing in his life. When his sense of his world fully disintegrates, he shoots his wife in the shoulder and goes to jail. From there, he writes Babbitt empty gray notes almost every week, but he effectively disappears from the novel.[22]

Babbitt's second set of friendships, a brief flirtation with Tanis Judique and "the Bunch," is presented as a fierce expression of the death drive, a longing for danger, fueled by alcohol, perhaps driven by the loss of Riesling, in many ways enacting an extreme and empty version of Riesling's way of relating to the world. Whereas Paul Riesling lived an unhappy life of compromise and contradiction, the Bunch live wholly outside the morality imposed by business relationships. In fact, Lewis's powers as a novelist are strained by the effort to describe this other orientation toward life. Evincing little sympathy for the group, he describes them as "the Midnight People, who drink and dance and rattle and are ever afraid to be silent." Unlike Riesling, they seem incapable of producing anything artistic or creative. Their disassociation from the daytime world of business leaves them too disconnected, too loosened from stabilizing ties, and, therefore, too demanding of Babbitt when he begins to come around. Under their influence,

Babbitt seems "borne on a current of desire and bad whisky and all the complications of new acquaintances, those furious new intimates who demand so much more attention than old friends."[23] Although at first they represent a welcome freedom from social constraints, these people mean nothing to Babbitt. When he finally disposes of Tanis Judique, he proclaims his freedom by describing the structures that connect him to the daytime world of Zenith: "Good Lord, do you realize I've got things to do in this world? I've got a business to attend to and, you might not believe it, but I've got a wife and kids that I'm awful fond of!" Once out her door, he sighs, "Thank God that's over! . . . I'm free!"[24]

Babbitt's most lasting friendships—if not his deepest emotional connections—are with the group of fellow businessmen who call themselves "the Roughnecks." The lives of these men are linked together through business deals, church and club memberships, political leanings, and tastes in food, drink, tobacco, cars, and houses. Lewis depicts a sort of emptiness about these relationships; he illustrates their fragility and their susceptibility to a sort of totalitarian enforcement of banal mediocrity. For example, Vergil Gunch is the local coal dealer. He is also the president of the Booster's Club and an "Esteemed Leading Knight in the Benevolent and Protective Order of Elks." He has hosted poker parties for the Roughnecks and been invited to dinner parties at each of their homes. By the end of the narrative, Gunch enforces Babbitt's turn away from the Bunch and back toward the world of business—its associations, its politics, and its morality. He invites, cajoles, and then insists that Babbitt join the Good Citizens' League. This group has "some . . . ostensible purposes," such as promoting parks, and it has "a social aspect . . . hav[ing] dances and so on." But its main purpose is to "make a conscious effort" to prevent "parlor socialists" from "working underground again." The chief strategy of the Good Citizens' League is to "apply this social boycott business" to anyone who disagrees with the league's basic probusiness positions.[25] Babbitt rebuffs the organization initially, but dreadful material and psychological consequences swiftly follow his attempt to counter their political economic hegemony. In his efforts to describe the rigid limits circumscribing Babbitt's local world along with Gunch's role as a pivotal node in the intersecting networks of business and private life, Lewis gives us a clear picture of the pattern of affective overdetermination operating in and through Babbitt.

Networks of power and affect connect the personal opinions of Babbitt's friends to the operations of his real-estate office, the health of his wife, and his own sense of well-being. These networks are materialized in institutions like the Good Citizens' League, but also in those such as the Zenith Athletic Club, where the same men gather to reinforce and, indeed, celebrate their connectedness over lunch and a game of duckpins. The interpersonal connections among these men are woven together from material, emotional, and ideological threads. Early in the book, Babbitt lectures his son on "the spiritual and mental side of American supremacy." "Our deepest and truest wealth" he says, lies in the values of "Efficiency, and Rotarianism, and Prohibition, and Democracy."[26] Later, Babbitt's public address to the Zenith Real Estate Board declaims: "the ideal of American manhood and culture. . . . [A] God-fearing, hustling, successful, two-fisted Regular Guy, who belongs to some church with pep and piety to it, who belongs to the Boosters or the Rotarians or the Kiwanis, to the Elks or Moose or Red Men or Knights of Columbus or any one of a score of organizations of good, jolly, kidding, laughing, sweating, upstanding, lend-a-handing Royal Good Fellows."[27]

These are powerful connections. Babbitt is not joking; nor is he speaking stupidly. When the two-fisted Regular Guys of the Athletic Club no longer recognize him, Babbitt feels this loss of public esteem and social connection intensely. He hears whispers. He worries constantly even as he blusters about his daily routines, claiming not to need their good opinion. Gunch and the rest of these men are not just his neighbors and business associates, but also his friends. When they turn their backs on him, it hurts. It hurts psychologically, and it costs him financially. His business drops off; his most valued employee leaves him for a competitor. Near the end of the book, when Gunch gently reinvites Babbitt to join the Good Citizens' League, he is overcome with emotion, "tearful with joy."[28] Perhaps Lewis wants us to see these tears as evidence of Babbitt's weakness, but they can also be read as evidence of the emotional power produced through overlapping and reinforcing business connections. This is the experience of business friendship.[29]

The Disciplinary Work of Business Associations

The never fully articulated business theory of friendship worked to contain the potential emotional disruption that vectors of affect could produce in a market society shaped by large-scale business organizations. In 1936, the national magazine of the Rotarian Society acknowledged that friendship was an unavoidable outgrowth of men working together: "No matter how much rivalry business may create," it necessarily resulted in "congenial tastes . . . pleasures enjoyed . . . hardships endured together." While the emotional ties that grew out of such shared experiences might be inevitable, their disruptive (that is, affiliative) effects could be best mitigated through participation in such organizations as Rotary Clubs themselves. This was clearly the lesson of *Babbitt*, but the strategy was widely followed as corporate capitalism consolidated in the first few decades of the twentieth century. "The Modern Master Printer is usually an active member of a business association of his craft," announced Robert Salade in the trade journal *American Printer*. In addition, "he belongs to the local Chamber of Commerce, and to other worthwhile associations of his town." The common understanding of the category of businessman during this period implied a man not only with some decision-making responsibility, but also with multiple memberships in associations like the Rotarians or the Elks and, even more important, in local chambers of commerce and trade associations. Although spread widely across the national economy by 1912, trade associations were most important for industries that were not dominated by a few large firms and which, therefore, had need for institutional means of sharing information and limiting competition. According to business historian Thomas Cochran, "personal factors and trade connections" were "dominant factors" in the success of small firms, which relied on trade associations to learn about new production techniques, new distribution schemes, and opportunities to expand their businesses. Trade associations were structurally quite similar to the social organizations to which the same group of men belonged. Both types of organizations institutionalized associational solutions to the conflicts of business and friendship, creating legitimate outlets for affiliation while maintaining the positive value of competition.[30]

The National Association of Greeting Card Manufacturers was founded in 1913. Among its early leaders were Sidney J. Burgoyne and Howard E. Betelle, who directed companies in Philadelphia; and A. M. Davis, Ernest Dudley Chase, and Fred W. Rust, who led firms that were based in Boston. Fearful of reproducing the chaotic competition of the post card industry, early greeting card manufacturers had quickly established their own trade association in order to share information and standardize prices. Pricing policies of member firms suggest that the organization was quite effective at coordinating prices. Whether your Christmas cards for 1915 were printed by Rust Craft, Chase, Keating, Davis, Charles Elliot, or Whitney, their prices ranged uniformly from 5 cents for the cheapest cards to $1 for the most expensive. Publishers who had made the transition from the post card business to full-time greeting card production had no intention of enduring the "cut throat practices" that had driven so many publishers into bankruptcy.[31]

The association was based on the East Coast and was most effective at organizing firms in that part of the country. It found its national ambitions initially more difficult to follow through on. In 1918, it initiated a "publicity committee," the goals of which were to promote the interests of all its members by coordinating a national advertising campaign advocating for greeting card use in general. The idea was that this campaign would save the association's members advertising expenses as they pooled their resources. The publicity committee wrote to Paul Volland in Chicago, acknowledging his firm's $2,000 "subscription" to the fund. Volland was always an aggressive marketer. For the past several years, he had placed seasonal ads promoting his cards in local newspapers in Seattle, Kansas City, St. Paul, St. Louis, Indianapolis, Pittsburgh, Washington, New York, Boston, and other cities. Even after subscribing to the publicity committee, he continued to hire an independent advertising agency that placed ads for his goods in such national periodicals as the *Pictorial Review* and the *Woman's Home Companion*. Volland was not content simply to cooperate with the national trade association; he saw the value of placing his own competing ads.[32]

Paul Volland and the Cost of Elegance

Paul Volland was born in Germany but came to the United States in his youth. He trained to be an engraver and, by 1909, was publishing Christmas cards, children's books, framed mottoes, and post cards. By the time of his death, he was a member of the Chicago Athletic Club, the South Shore Country Club, the Chicago Yacht Club, the Forty Club, and various book organizations. His company paid regular membership fees to the Chicago Chamber of Commerce. Volland was a modern businessman, a member of all the proper associations. One of his first national advertisements appeared in *American Stationer* in March 1910. In this multipage pullout ad, Volland's company adopted the strategy of emphasizing its "distinctive and artistic publications." In addition to promoting the company's books and post cards (retailing at the relatively high rate of 5 cents each), the ad highlighted a special line of wedding invitations, birth announcements, and birthday cards:

> The ten most beautiful tokens of friendship and remembrance we have ever offered. . . . Each gold Beveled Folder bears a specially written sentiment in Prose or Poetry, of the "Personal Message" kind that characterizes the Volland line. The lettering is specially designed and the decorations are the best ever made in our shop. Title and all are done in colors by hand in the most artistic manner imaginable. As a last token of elegance, each folder is tied with a satin ribbon, harmonizing with the color scheme of the design and enclosed in an envelope to match.

The ad was strikingly expensive; its size, special paper, and color printing testified to the expense. The evident cost of the ad reinforced the content's emphasis on the overlapping signifiers of quality and extravagant production that Volland wanted to associate with his cards.

Beveled cards looked back to the tradition of visiting cards, which carried a residual class meaning, while the artistic manner of the lettering, the golden edges, and the satin ribbons contributed overt references to cost that signified elegance for some and gaucherie for others. Volland was among the first of the twentieth-century greeting card companies to combine longer sentiments with hand-lettered and delicately colored designs. The softly blended coloring of one of its valentines, from 1913, complements its slight twist of the iambic (plate 13); together they work with the sentiment's verbal pun to convey an image of modern youthful vigor:

> My valentine, joy will be mine,
> if you'll my gardener be—
> Make rose-decked ways of all my days.
> And raise two lips for me![33]

By 1918, Volland had built an intriguing organization in Chicago. He took the opposite approach from Whitney, apparently owning very little of the capital equipment used to manufacture greeting cards. Most of the company's production was actually done by contract. Volland hired printing work done, cutting work done, beveling and edging done. The company's engraving, stamping, and embossing were all done off the premises. He contracted with binderies for his book-publishing efforts. He bought the highest quality paper for his top line of cards from Eaton, Crane, and Pike, having it shipped from Massachusetts until the company built a distribution center in Chicago. Internally, Volland's offices directed the design decisions, hired the artists and sentiment writers, and chose the combinations of effects and production techniques that collaborated in the materialization of the cards. They also handled the marketing and the accounting. They completed the assembly process, applying the satin ribbons and glitter, sorting the cards and envelopes into packages, and ensuring that no damaged goods were shipped.[34]

Volland himself hired most of the illustrators and writers, overseeing the artistic factors that went into his cards. He hired independent artists and letterers on a piecework basis from the growing Chicago arts community, paying letterers by the line and illustrators by the design. Whereas New York and Boston firms had to compete with one another for art talent, Volland had a much more open field to chose from. Accounting files in the P. F. Volland Company Archives at the Chicago Public Library contain numerous letters from freelance artists, requesting payment for the work they had completed for him. Whereas paper companies and printing firms could count on their accounts being settled quickly, the design and sentiment talent were often the last to be paid. Mrs. C. L. Kohler billed Volland for three drawings in October 1917. After a few months, he paid her for one of them. Maginal Wright Enright designed valentines and illustrated children's books for Volland. Her bills would often go unpaid for six months or more. Edward Poucher was forced to send a telegram following up on several letters he had written begging Volland to pay him for completed Christmas card work. The urgency of the request came from the fact that he was getting married soon and needed the cash. In an editorial commenting on the circumstances of his eventual murder, the *Chicago Tribune* said, "Mr. Volland, we understand, had had trouble before with artists and writers with whom he had made contracts."[35]

Indeed, Volland's most serious dispute over payment for artistic content cost him his life. On May 5, 1919, Vera Trepagnier entered the outer offices of the Volland Company. She approached one of the few secretaries working through the lunch hour and introduced herself as Mrs. Martin, saying, "I want to see Mr. Volland on business." Trepagnier was a sixty-year-old widow from New Orleans who had met Volland in New York two years earlier. At that meeting, she had shown Volland a family heirloom, a miniature of George Washington painted by one of the nation's most important history painters, John Trumball. Trepagnier was trying to sell the painting to put a relative through college, and Volland had been recommended to her as a potential buyer. At the meeting, Volland apparently sold Trepagnier on a different plan whereby she would retain ownership of the painting while he gained the rights to sell reproductions of it. "'It is a wonderful painting,' he told me," Trepagnier told the Chicago police later that May afternoon. "'Give it to me and I will give you $5,000 in royalties. We can sell 150,000 copies a year.'"

For the next two years, Volland ignored Trepagnier's letters as she tried to collect on her understanding of the deal. After months of frustration, she consulted a lawyer, who told her that Volland had drawn up a contract that was completely in his favor. She had failed to read the agreement carefully before signing it and had no legal recourse. The last letter she received from Volland told her that the reproductions of the painting had failed commercially. The company had sold only 174 copies. Volland offered to return the miniature to her if she would pay for the costs of the unsold reproductions, which Volland estimated at exactly $174. Trepagnier determined to visit Volland and to force him to return the heirloom. After she was announced as Mrs. Martin that afternoon, Volland came out to meet her. When he saw who it was, he said, "Oh, it's you," turned his back, and reentered his office. Trepagnier followed him and, once inside, pulled a revolver out of her purse. She told the police that she had wanted only to scare Volland. He, of course, did not scare easily. When he reached out to take the gun away from her, it went off. Volland died almost instantly. "I never meant to kill him," she said. "I hate to hurt anybody—but I waited two years and that's an awful long time." Whether or not she meant to hurt him, Trepagnier could not understand that in a social realm structured by adversarial relations mitigated only by contractual obligations, Volland had no legal responsibility toward her. His theft of her heirloom, an image of national unity that she had relied on to put a relative through college, had been legitimated by the contract she had signed.[36]

Producing Cynical Sentiment

Such was the viewpoint put forth by one of Volland's editors, Joseph P. McEvoy. Upholding the company version of the story when interviewed by the *Chicago Tribune*, McEvoy insisted that Trepagnier had received $500 in advance royalties and that it was she who owed Volland money.[37] As an editor on the company payroll, McEvoy was treated better than most artistic contributors to Volland's productions. He wrote a book of humorous verse for the company exemplifying the exaggeration of the cynical and the sentimental that occurs when the feelings and values constructed in and through business transactions are reduced wholly to economic calculations.

Slams of Life: With Malice for All, and Charity Toward None, was published in 1919. As an attempt at satire, the book fails to sustain a critical viewpoint. But it functions quite well as a document of the cheap cynicism that seemed to haunt those who produced culture on demand for commercial purposes in the first half of the twentieth century. Several of the poems focus on sentimental images of McEvoy's daughter. But the bulk of the verses attack the contradictory intersection of commerce and feeling with the bluntest of instruments. With McEvoy's connections to the Christmas card industry, it should not be surprising that he would write several poems about the tensions associated with that day. "Lines on the Real Christmas Spirit" describes the sudden display of good cheer and deferential behavior on the part of those who regularly provided McEvoy's family with services. Within the last short week or so,

> The world has changed, I'd have you know;
> The maid is always here on time,
> Her work is neat, her eats sublime.

As he contemplates why "The elevator man is kind. / The office boy has learned to mind," McEvoy theorizes a simple and selfish material cunning on the part of his employees, while reserving the final capriciousness for himself and illustrating with care his ultimate position of power and authority:

> Oh, why are they so pleasant,
> And serve me with a thrill?
> They think they'll get a present,
> A lovely Christmas present—
> They're sure they'll get a present—
> And they will.
> (Maybe.)[38]

There is no question of mutual exchange here. Neither the maid nor the elevator man nor the office boy has the means or the reason to give McEvoy presents. This gift exchange is almost feudal in its recapitulation of the master enjoying, however briefly, the proper attitude of his servants. I do not mean to attack McEvoy or to imply a particularly cruel insensitivity on his part. Rather, I only mean to show how constrained and limited was his thinking about the network of social obligations or the intertwining of the material and the emotional that the day's celebrations call forth. The men who were developing and building this industry in the first few decades of the twentieth century simply were not thinking about the cultural significance of their work.

Nevertheless, McEvoy thought a lot about the conditions of working within the greeting card business. In his 1928 epistolary novel, *Show Girl*, McEvoy again took on the contradictions he perceived to follow from the combination of sentiment and commerce. The book turns a jaundiced eye on the New York stage, muckraking journalism, finance, and politics, in addition to the conditions of producing and selling preprinted sentiments. Although his satirical aim in the novel was very similar to that of *Slams of Life*, resulting in a similar cheap cynicism, McEvoy's descriptions of writing, producing, and selling greeting cards demonstrate a real sympathy for the men who were making a living in the industry. In *Show Girl*, Denny Kerrigan is a salesman for the Gleason Greeting Card Company, with most of southern Illinois and all of Indiana as his territory. Denny is in love with the show girl Dixie Duggan, a character much like that of Lorelei Lee in Anita Loos's 1925 novel *Gentlemen Prefer Blondes*. While working the stage in Chicago, Dixie enjoys seeing Denny. But he wants her to give up the stage and join him in a life modeled on those represented in the greeting cards that he sells. This life has no appeal whatsoever for Dixie, who soon moves to New York. There she finds herself courted by three male stereotypes: the rich and corrupt older stockbroker; the passionate Latin dancer; and the clever, occasionally sneaky, but basically good-hearted Irish writer. The bulk of the novel is made up of letters and telegrams sent to and from Dixie.[39]

Throughout the novel, Denny is presented as a bit of a fool. He believes in true love and regularly quotes lines from Gleason's cards in his letters:

> Here I've been going along from town to town selling Greeting Cards for All Occasions, trying to make an honest living, working hard toward the day when I can offer you my hand and my heart and an honest home where I could come home to a nice little wife who would love me devotedly and would appreciate a good home, and maybe a little house with a garden by the side of the road, and, by the way, that's one of our best sellers—9M6o, The House By the Side of the Road, You probably remember how it goes.[40]

A first-rate salesman, Denny has memorized the retail price, product type, and catalogue numbers, along with much of the verse of his entire line. Most of his days are spent on the road, lugging "four hand trunks of valentines and mother mottoes and God Bless Our Homes," and sweet-talking the "lady buyers" who stock the shelves of places like "Ye Olde Gifte Shoppe."[41] He is happy that the company has recently hired a new head of Creative, someone named Levinson who understands the importance of religious Easter cards. Several of his letters to Dixie explain that flirting with the lady buyers and taking them to the movies is only part of his job. He has to make his clients feel special in order for them to understand the real value of Gleason's cards. Denny Kerrigan is depicted as a comic figure to the extent that he is unsuccessful at separating his feelings from his work.

Although he has been a very productive salesman, Denny's sales start to decline as he suffers from Dixie's absence. The district sales manager notices this and arranges for a meeting with Mr. Gleason, the founding patriarch of the company. Probably most closely modeled on George Buzza, to whom McEvoy was selling thousands of dollars' worth of verse per year, Gleason proclaims a hard-hearted business rationality while he reveals precisely the sentimental disconnection that structured the greeting card industry. He lectures Denny, asserting that he ought not to let his love life interfere with his valentine selling. "I don't see any reason why we should let sentiment interfere with our business. Sentiment is all right on cards, to be sold in large quantities at a profit, that's all. Otherwise it's just a damn nuisance. I know. I used to be sentimental. Then I went into this business and it took all the sentiment out of me." Or so he says. But Gleason is not free of sentiment. He simply has no way of connecting his feelings with his work. His vision of the real Christmas spirit conveys a nostalgia for feelings of security and abundance that have no place in business. "You know, Christmas is really something pretty fine, the spirit of Christmas I mean. Christmas isn't just a day to give a lot of things away . . . I mean . . . these damn sentiments! They keep coming up in my mind." Gleason's idea of the spirit of Christmas draws from his youth—the last time he can remember enjoying the holiday. His vision of the day reflects the viewpoint of a child; it is suffused with delight, joy, abundance, and the secure certainty that his world is safe. It conveys a set of values and meanings that have been stripped from his everyday life. Indeed, he asks Denny rhetorically, what does Christmas mean now?[42]

> It means that eighteen months before it comes off, I'm going to worry whether some other outfit is going to get out a line with tissue-lined envelopes for five cents retail, and how many of the old dies we can hold over and stamp on new stock, and are we going to get any more of that Italian hand made paper. And one year before, I'm worrying all about the sample line getting out on time, and six months before, how orders are coming in and three months before, how re-orders are coming in. And about Christmas, when all should be peace on earth and good will to men, I've forgotten all about angels and camels and Wise Men and I'm wondering what the hell's the matter with collections. God, what a business.[43]

In Gleason's daily life, security, abundance, joy, and delight are driven out by concerns over price competition, questions about the market viability of some of the previous year's stock, anxieties about the availability of high-quality materials, the strength of the demand for his products, and the likelihood that his customers will pay for their goods. But Gleason's products, in line with those of his competitors, are based on a nostalgic memory of the season; they reproduce the values and meanings that Gleason's business seems not to allow. His Christmas cards, therefore, are precisely sentimental agents reinforcing the very common division between production and consumption, between business and feeling. In Gleason's world, an ideological divide has been constructed between the intensely intellectual pleasures of production—successful competition, managing the complex mechanics of mass production, international trade in materials, and the organization of national distribution—and the bodily and emotional pleasures of enjoyment and abundance. This classic, if critically disabling, division is commonly articulated with social divisions along lines of gender, race, and class, and greeting cards reproduce these standard associations.

For McEvoy, as well as for many other writers who described this division between bodily enjoyment and mass production, the logic of that split was so ideologically powerful as to seem natural. Production was masculine; capitalist relations were competitive; the race went to the swift, and it was serious business. There was no room for joy in any of it. Joy, therefore, was stripped of any capacity it might have either to justify or to criticize the developing corporate political economy. With enjoyment and pleasurable engagement eliminated from the possible goals of work in the greeting card industry, a powerful cynicism took hold. A private Christmas card, illustrated and written by A. M. Davis to send to his colleagues in the greeting card industry for the 1929 season, suggests something of the physical disgust some of them felt about their work. Davis's card shows two outhouses standing next to each other in a snow-covered field (figure 3.2). A hand, holding a few sheets of paper, reaches out from one outhouse toward the window of the other. The caption reads, "The Season's Greetings—from one 'Specialist' to another!" From one specialist in the mass production of feeling to another, the paper is passed and ideas are shared for all that they are worth.[44]

A Feeling for Business

In January 1930, John Dewey published the first of several articles in the *New Republic* the goal of which was to describe the current conditions of economic production and analyze the crisis of subjectivity or

Figure 3.2
A. M. Davis Christmas
card: "From One
'Specialist' to Another!"
(Norcross Greeting Card
Collection, Archives
Center, National Museum
of American History,
Behring Center,
Smithsonian Institution)

individualism that these conditions were engendering. Dewey wanted to think through the social, cultural, and psychological implications of the coming to dominance of corporate structures that were built on the technique of mass production for a national market. He was developing a nonreductive yet materialist theory of subjectivity that attempted to account for a profound contradiction that he saw resulting from an increasing tendency toward collective means of production amid a residual ideology of autonomous individualism. Dewey recognized that "individuals who are not bound together in associations, whether domestic, economic, political, artistic, or educational, are monstrosities. It is absurd to suppose that the ties which hold them together are merely external and do not react into mentality and character, producing the framework of personal disposition."[45]

As he put it, "The influence business corporations exercise in determining present industrial and economic activities is both a cause and a symbol of the tendency to combination in all phases of life. Associations tightly or loosely organized more and more define the opportunities, the choices and the actions of individuals."[46] But this influence is not a direct linear relationship of force. It is more in line with Raymond Williams's definition of determination—the setting of limits and the exerting of pressures. Dewey was thinking through the determining effects of large business organizations on the opportunities, choices, and actions of individuals, arguing that these determining factors were operating independently of the wills of specific persons: "Personal motives hardly count as productive causes in comparison with impersonal forces." For Dewey, the most important of these forces were "mass production and mass distribution." Having "created a common market, the parts of which are held together by intercommunication and interdependence," mass production and distribution had established their financial and managerial imperatives. "Aggregated capital and concentrated control are the contemporary responses," Dewey concluded.[47] Large business organizations enabled greater standardization of methods and greater division of labor, both of which led to greater efficiencies. Within these large interlocking productive systems, it was quite difficult to change any process once it had begun. Thomas Cochran put it quite neatly: "The very basis of mass production was the commitment of vast amounts of time and money to a particular way of doing a job." Careful planning, therefore, was a necessity. The systematic requirements of fordist production produced a need for association, for the coordinated activities of a large number of individuals.[48]

One might think that Dewey was talking about only those people who worked for the largest corporations where fordist pressures were the most powerfully evident. But, like the largest corporations, medium-level businesses—those employing between twenty and a thousand workers—had to deal with problems of both organizational and financial efficiency. By 1929, such companies employed more than one-half of all nonagricultural workers in the United States. These firms, too, experienced the systematic requirements of fordism, and it was the heads of these firms who became "the backbone of chambers of commerce, manufacturers' associations, and service clubs." Through its instantiation in firms and business associations, reaching into the everyday lives of millions of workers, business culture, with all its contradictions, achieved national hegemony.[49]

In Dewey's analysis, this combination of systematic requirements fostered and rewarded certain types of individuals. But a powerful contradiction had developed. The productive system demanded of its managers a particular set of skills and tastes, the ability to reduce complex interactive systems to formulas predicting advantage and loss, a limited tolerance for risk, and the capacity to keep always in the forefront of their thinking the coordinated requirements of a large organization. The large corporation and the medium-size firm demanded individuals who could think collectively. In 1927, business professor Erwin Schell described this ability as "group consciousness." The executive, he argued, "must have a capacity for group awareness which exceeds that possessed by those whom he leads."[50] Yet the rewards for organizational planning and intricately coordinated production were distributed not collectively, but individually. Dewey thought that this disconnection between individual motives and corporate goals produced chaotic sensibilities that could not function properly. As he put it, "An economic individualism of motives and aims underlies our present corporate mechanisms, and undoes the individual."[51] Dewey's point was that as long as business culture maintained this basic contradiction, it would continue to produce not only crises such as the Wall Street crash of 1929, but also massive inequalities in the intellectual and cultural benefits of participating in the economic system. He was trying to encourage a greater engagement with collectivist theories of subjectivity in order to promote greater equality. While I am deeply sympathetic to that goal, my interest in raising Dewey's critique heads in a slightly different direction. I would not go so far as Dewey to say that the men working in the greeting card industry—by the 1920s, an established subset of the publishing industry made up mostly of medium-size firms—were so fraught with contradiction that they were "undone" as individuals. Instead, I would argue that they found a way to deal with the contradictions that Dewey outlined, and that the solutions they developed not only help elucidate the basic symbolic strategies of modern greeting cards but also go a long way toward explaining the immense success of this industry.

The emphasis on intricate long-range planning, minimal risk-taking, and calculation that was rewarded by the material conditions of large-scale mass production–based business organizations could simply have stripped from its managers all feeling, leaving them with no sentiment whatsoever, producing the stereotypical view of the unfeeling monstrous executive. But that is not what happened. These executives felt the contradictions they were living; they experienced them with all the depth of any human encounter.

The vacuity of the claim that business held no place for feeling was evident to any manager and white-collar employee. Although managers were expected to demonstrate "control of emotions," they also were expected to possess "refinement" and "general culture." While they had to have "reasoning ability," "industry," "ambition," and "concentration," they also were supposed to display "unselfishness, kindness, cheerfulness, tact, loyalty." Thousands of words were published on the advantages of and the problems caused by the phenomenon of friendship in business or on the usefulness of business metaphors for evaluating potential friends. Once firms grew beyond the productive capacity of a single family or a close set of associates, they had to cultivate the loyalty of their employees. Thus feelings of affiliation and collective belonging were promulgated within the companies. As the historian Angel Kwolek-Folland has shown, throughout the first few decades of the twentieth century, companies worked to develop a sense of "corporate domesticity," stretching the similarities between large firms and extended families through such activities as company picnics and sponsored conventions. Indeed, the concept of the corporate wife, the woman who organized social events as well as her own public presence with an eye toward her husband's advancement through the firm, indicates the interpenetration of business and family for many.[52]

Managers also had to develop the capacity to understand and evaluate the personal needs of their employees, reacting to these needs in what could be perceived as a fair fashion. Although entire personnel departments developed to handle these situations, supervisors and managers bore the initial brunt of ensuring "just treatment of workers" and promoting "contentment among workers and their families," among other duties. Similarly, markets produce particular sensitivities. Managers often had to sense a transformation in the market before they could fully articulate it. Salesmen had to develop accurate intuitions about their customers, learning how to "tell a man's inside by looking at his outside." But still, a powerful belief remained that the business world was not a place for feelings; instead, it was supposed to be a place for tough, calculating competitors who were able to "maintain and control the organization at maximum efficiency." Early in the twentieth century, Thorstein Veblen articulated the dominant view:

"The all-dominating issue in business is the question of gain and loss. . . . The business man judges of events from the standpoint of ownership, and ownership runs in terms of money." The need for calculation overrode any sentimental urge.[53]

The Materialization of Displaced Sentiment

What took place, then, in the midst of these contradictions—contradictions that Dewey identified as primarily a set of tensions between collective organization and individual rewards—was a displacement of the expression of feelings of affiliation into a safe haven, a sentimental arena outside the ideologically constrained business world. As these feelings were compartmentalized, abstracted from the complexity of their real-world engagements, they were separated from the contexts in which they were produced and which were their proximate cause and object. Once displaced, with the feelings abstracted from the real, their expression took the form of cliché. Clichés enable a simultaneous announcement of and disavowal of the feelings that they express. Insofar as they are recognizably the words of others, clichés maintain a prophylactic covering around the feelings they indexically point toward. The appeal of clichés lies precisely in their capacity to keep those feelings safe from the complexities and contradictions of modern business life. Although McEvoy's mannequin, Gleason, could no longer recognize the feelings operating in his own world, he maintained a sense of sentiment, a longing for feeling. The men who worked for the major greeting card companies shared this disconnected longing. In his autobiography, Hall linked the growth in the industry during the 1910s to the recognition that many of the cards' users were "those who tend to disguise their feelings." I am not making an argument about the inauthentic nature of the feelings conveyed either on or by greeting cards. My point is that the experience of emotional connection within modern business culture resulted in the real need for abstract, highly regularized, and familiar formulas of commercially available emotional expression. The greeting card industry expanded so rapidly between 1910 and 1930 because of the intensity of the tremors that resulted from the distillation of emotions from the corporate associations that characterized modern business culture. The ambitious, aspiring white men who collaborated in the development of the modern greeting card industry—such as Paul Volland, Joseph P. McEvoy, Ernest Dudley Chase, A. M. Davis, Fred Rust, Arthur Norcross, and Joyce Hall—exploited emotionally expressive capacities that were caught up necessarily in a displaced and condensed semiotic of clichés.[54]

Design and Sentiment in the Modern Greeting Card Industry

These men had to begin by feeling their way. Like most of the early greeting card producers, Ernest Chase began by writing his own sentiments. His Christmas cards for the 1912 season were charmingly idiosyncratic. Eschewing the influence of pictorial or holiday post cards, his pen-and-ink drawings were relatively crude, and his sentiments were written to accompany particular gifts. For example one 5-cent card read:

> Best wishes come with these cigars
> For Christmas cheer and pleasure
> May every puff bring happiness
> And memories to treasure.

Chase composed many such verses to accompany handkerchiefs, ties, bits of crochet, and books, among other gifts. While he sold enough of these to continue in business, his cards were too directly reliant on the sales of another product; his verses did not try to establish an independent function of their own. A. M. Davis, too, began by writing most of his own verses. They varied little from the traditional "Wishing You a Merry Christmas and a Happy New Year." One of Davis's more regular retail outlets was a gift shop in Springfield, Illinois, operated by Robert Lord. In 1915, Lord suggested to Davis that he might attract more customers with sentiments that were "more personal." Perhaps he was passing on a bit of local knowledge or a marketing phrase he had picked up from Volland's representatives. Wherever it came from, Lord's idea was to expand the vocabulary of all greeting cards, and his work helped establish the generative capacity of the condensed language of emotional displacement required by the business. These first verses sold well for Davis, and he engaged Lord as a regular source of commercial sentiments.[55]

Lord's most successful card carried only a slight expansion of Davis's traditional Christmas greeting. It is worth looking at carefully to begin to understand the highly condensed, self-reflexive world of greeting card verses. In full, it reads:

> It's an old, old wish
> On a tiny little card;
> It's only Merry Christmas,
> But I wish it awful hard.

Lord's "more personal" response to the continual repetition of the same holiday slogan on Davis's cards begins by acknowledging that he has nothing new to say. But he does say it in a different way. The first thing this verse does is to place itself in a tradition of holiday wishes on cards. A brilliant move, this tiny, self-reflexive gesture legitimizes simultaneously the genre of Christmas cards and this particular verse's place in that genre. Once that gesture is completed, once the sending of Christmas cards is recognized as an appropriate and valued holiday activity, all that remains is to repeat the traditional message with sufficient earnest sincerity to complement both its sender and its receiver. The dropped adverbial marker in "awful hard" testifies successfully to the missive's urgency. Davis knew this was a winner when he saw it; he paid Lord $400 for those twenty words. *American Magazine* celebrated the transaction, declaring that Lord got "more per word than Kipling." A lightly decorated vellum card with that verse engraved in black sold 350,000 copies in its first season. Within a year, Lord had sold his shop and become a full-time greeting card writer.[56]

Helen Lovejoy McCarthy was one of the first nationally recognized female authors of modern greeting card sentiment. An early contract with Rust Craft paid her a royalty for each card sold. But her biggest success, "A Greeting to You," sold sufficiently well that the company insisted on paying her on a per-line basis. This sentiment, too, threads a very simple, very abstract recognition of the sender into the fabric of the practice of card exchange. It focuses overtly on the kindness of the receiver, but by virtue of appearing on a card presented as a gift, cleverly links the virtues attributed to the receiver back to the sender of the card. The relationship between the two becomes a relationship of kindness marked by gift exchange, reinforcing the sending of cards as precisely the action of kind individuals:

> So much have you given to others
> To make life seem worth while,
> So much of real kindness and service,
> Your helping hand and smile,
> That many a one this Easter
> Would join with me and say,
> "The best that life can offer
> I wish for you today."

The sentiment expresses no direct connection with the holiday or with the theme of renewal common to the season. In fact, the name of any holiday could be substituted, rendering the sentiment useful for all the year, "a type," in the words of Chase, "of special value to the publisher." The verse itself is "gratifying to both the sender and receiver," as it compliments both on their willingness to give.[57] With the card functioning as the gift, it self-reflexively emphasizes the meaning of gifts themselves. The words reference the kind service that gifts offer and the power they have to cement social connections. As McCarthy elaborates the self-reflexive semantics of the greeting card, the sentiment enunciates a condensed reinforcement of the very practice of sending cards.

Soon after Volland's murder, McEvoy became another of the few nationally recognized sentiment writers, earning an average of $10,000 annually from this work. In 1922, McEvoy was hired by the George Buzza Company to write exclusively for it. Centered in Minneapolis, Buzza was another firm that was growing rapidly, joining the national trade association, and competing most directly for the midwestern market, which also was targeted by Hall Brothers. McEvoy's talent for composing sentimental clichés was matched by that of Edgar Guest,

who wrote perhaps the most expensive greeting card verse of this period. Buzza and Hall Brothers fought hard to gain the services of Guest,
who was popularly known as the "Just Folks Poet." His work appeared
in national magazines and newspapers, and a collection of his verse, including "A Friend's Greeting," had been published by Reilly & Lee. In
1921, the head of that publishing company made an appointment with
Joyce Hall to discuss that particular verse. Across the Midwest, Hall
Brothers greeting cards with Guest's poem printed on them were selling by the thousands. Reilly insisted that Hall Brothers destroy every
card that it had published bearing this verse, as Reilly & Lee held the
copyright and Hall had made no legal arrangements to use the material. In his autobiography, Hall explains that he first acquired the verse
when a stranger had come into his office. The man claimed to have
composed the lines and asked how much Hall would charge him to
have a few copies printed on cards. Hall struck a deal with the mysterious stranger, obtaining the rights to reproduce the poem in exchange
for a hundred free greeting cards. Hall Brothers transformed the verse
into a Christmas card, printing it next to some poinsettias and changing the fifth line to match the season. It became the firm's best-selling
Christmas card. When Reilly confronted Hall about the use of Guest's
verse, Hall was sufficiently convinced of its market worth to offer $500
for that single verse. The going rate at the time, according to Hall, was
about $1 per line; Hall had agreed to pay Reilly (not Guest, of course)
$62.50 per line for this verse:

> I'd like to be the sort of friend that you have been to me.
> I'd like to be the help that you've been always glad to be,
> I'd like to mean as much to you each minute of the day
> As you have meant, old friend of mine, to me along the way.
> And that's why I am wishing now that I could but repay
> A portion of the gladness that you've strewn along my way,
> And could I have now just one wish, this only would it be
> I'd like to be the sort of friend that you have been to me.

As I have suggested, the popularity of "A Friend's Greeting"
demonstrates its ability to appeal to and ameliorate the anxieties pro-

duced out of the intersection of business and friendship. The poem strikes a note of contractual understanding, establishing the equal market-worth of the behavior of the two parties to the relationship. As a token of a market-based friendship, it abstracts value from any messy details of the relationship. The two parties to the friendship do not have to do the same things for each other. In fact, no specifics are mentioned at all. All that is conveyed is the desire for the perfect commensurability of the interaction. The sender simply wants to "repay" the receiver in like coin. With the sense of balance reconfirmed, friendship can exist within business without disrupting its calculations. Of course, Hall was not the only greeting card executive to see the value in Guest's writing. Within a year, the Buzza Company signed Guest to a contract obtaining the exclusive rights to his verse on greeting cards, confirming the intensity of the "friendly" competition within the industry.[58]

Personal messages—those advocated by Robert Lord, composed by writers like Helen Lovejoy McCarthy, and published by Rust Craft, Volland, and Davis in the late 1910s and early 1920s—were sentiments that emphasized the value of card exchange as a process of social recognition. Personal messages were those that successfully reinforced the capacity of cards to represent, in earnest abstraction, the persons participating in the exchange. They used clichés, generically established conventions of displaced and decontextualized feeling, to insinuate the person in the exchange of cards. With emotional eloquence reduced to a practice of mutual recognition through the exchange of cards, the expression of personal sentiment became tightly compacted, highly condensed. Abstraction did not produce airiness but density. Design factors also contributed to the construction of these "more personal" greeting cards.

In 1910, the same year that Volland advertised his new line of beveled, folded, and beribboned cards, Davis added envelopes and ribbons to his cards. Although he was calling them holiday post cards, Davis's cards, along with Volland's, helped establish the design conventions of modern greeting cards. Both companies' cards were based more closely on the visiting card tradition than on the conventions of post cards. Once these companies began selling their cards with envelopes, they no longer had to divide the backs into two halves. Like visiting cards, the front of the cards carried the entire message. They also had beveled edges and used traditional engraved lettering. The introduction of folding cards, called French fold or folders, by Rust Craft helped thicken the cards' appeal, creating different focal areas for the design and the sentiment. The front of the card illustrated the emotional connection; the sentiment was printed inside. The common addition of a bit of ribbon laced through the side or top of the card emphasized the decorative possibilities of folded cards. With an almost dialectical synthesis, reacting against the flat commonality of post cards, the design conventions of modern greeting cards established by Davis and Volland re-created some of the haptic complexity of nineteenth-century valentines and Christmas cards.

A common vocabulary of images developed as well. As early as 1914, the drawings of George Wolfe Plank exemplified established conventions of nostalgic illustration that imagined, clothed, and positioned the human figures on Christmas cards as open-mouthed children, eighteenth-century aristocrats, and nineteenth-century republican mothers. Figures like those Plank drew covered the cards of all the major companies, enabling the idealized representation of individuals, abundantly cared for, surrounded by pleasures magically acquired and innocently enjoyed:

> little, round-mouthed maidens (in hoops and pantalets) singing carols with all their might; starry skies, with one great golden star shining above a listening, snow-white world; Godey Book mothers and small daughters with shirred hoods and flying fringes and shawls and nice muffs and holly wreaths, out in the thick of an old-time Christmas blizzard; adorable little girls and boys speaking pieces to an unseen audience . . . the most modish of ladies riding by, picturesquely smothered in furs and holly and new kinds of flowers; garden sprites and an old baron with his mug of ale and a holly-wreathed boar's head on a noble platter.[59]

Plank's Christmas cards imaged humans displaced from the present, submerged in nostalgic plenty.

Quite probably the most common nonhuman image found on cards from this early period is a house with a red sloping roof. An idealized representation of the home and, therefore, of everything supposedly stripped away from business, this red-roofed vision soon found its way onto birthday cards as well as Christmas cards, eventually appearing on Mother's Day and even Father's Day cards. But it was as a design element in Christmas cards that it made its first impact. The fluid sloping surface of the home could be read as a soft yet firm glans, pushing open the yielding sky, or as a comforting mound, nurturing those within. When the roof was not red, it was covered with decorated tile or coated with snow (figure 3.3). Even in the winter, the front door was almost always open, inviting the viewer to enjoy the warm glow within (figures 3.4 and 3.5). Rarely set directly in the middle of the card, the home established a decentered focal point around which the remainder of the composition could be organized. The home could be presented in isolation, in the distance, behind fences or trees. It

Figure 3.3   Two snow-covered roofs: "Christmas Thoughts of You" and "The Season's Greetings." (Norcross Greeting Card Collection, Archives Center, National Museum of American History, Behring Center, Smithsonian Institution)

could also fill the foreground. Often visitors stood before the door or
approached the home on a road or sidewalk, as another overt gesture
toward the visiting card tradition. Visitors might arrive on foot or by
carriage, never by automobile. These conventions were adopted by all
the major greeting card companies before World War I. They constructed a visual language that simultaneously represented and displaced the home. Clearly idealized, purposively isolated from systems
of production and the noisy complications of neighbors and traffic,
often displaced backward in time, the red-roofed home was a condensed imago, a containment of and a point of dispersal for all the
imaginary power of the necessarily abstract sentiment that these businessmen could conceive. Protected by that red roof, inside those four
walls, affection could survive. And from the open door of that safe
haven, sentiment could shine from the card, enveloping the sender and
the receiver in the purchased glow of abstract feeling.[60]

WITH LOVE FOR MOTHER

My thoughts turn back on Mother's Day
No matter where I roam
For those I love best in all the world
Are You and my dear Old Home

Figure 3.5 Red-roofed house seen through open door: "With Love for Mother."
(Norcross Greeting Card Collection, Archives Center, National Museum of American
History, Behring Center, Smithsonian Institution)

This home was an example of the design element that Elizabeth
and Curtiss Sprague termed "the motif"—"the most important part of
the card." By 1926, when the Spragues published their *How to Design
Greeting Cards*, article writers for a variety of periodicals had expressed
dissatisfaction with the rapid spread of these conventions of design and
sentiment. Writing in 1923 for *American Printer*, Edward Bridgman
charged that "the so-called million dollar corporations, who have national distribution . . . produce lines of merchandise so similar to each
other that the competition among them might result in the ultimate
death of the greeting card." Whereas Bridgman saw hope for the future of the industry in the small producer, "the artist who steps out of
the beaten path," some writers saw only a "dull affair" in "the average
card." "Think of its history," cried Florence Lemmon:

It is turned out by the hundreds, to fit everybody's ideas and
needs, a stereotyped design of, perhaps, a mantelpiece with a

lighted candle at either end, flanking a gay holly wreath, or, it may be, a spray of poinsettia through which is woven "A Merry Christmas," or yet again it may be a picture of the mythical Santa Claus speeding over snow-covered hills, drawn by dashing reindeers—with little drums, balls, or steam-cars trailing behind. These are piled high on the store counters, and the late holiday shoppers rummage through the mass, mauling over the lot before a selection can be made. A few cents are passed out to the worn-out saleslady, a two-cent stamp licked unhygienically and the greeting tossed into a U.S. mail box with a gratifying sigh of relief.

A fear of the disease-ridden mob permeates this description. What is wrong with these cards is that they are produced in mass for the masses. How could any real feeling survive this process? And real feeling is the issue for Lemmon. Despite the fact that "hiding sentiment seems to be the order of the day," she asserts that during the holidays we are given permission to "open up our hearts to a more kindly world, and express this feeling of abundant happiness, by lavishing some thought on the greetings we extend to our best and nearest friends." The solution to the dilemma of mass-produced sentiment, Lemmon thought, was for the cards to become more personal. Each family ought to produce its own card, for only then will it "express the family personality."[61]

"'Decidedly Individual.' 'Now that's a clever one.' That's what we like to have people say about *our* Christmas cards. And we can have cards decidedly individual if we make them, using the patterns opposite and adapting them to our own color and design ideas." Walter Frame, writing for *Better Homes and Gardens*, made the task of creating the family's personal Christmas cards easy by presenting sample designs (which did not vary far from the most popular cards in the market) and describing how to divide the productive process among the family members: "Let each one have a single operation to perform—cutting, cementing or painting—and you'll be amazed how quickly the cards will be turned out." Thus not only the dominant styles but the dominant means of production could be reproduced at home. The Spragues, too, pointed out that "the card you buy over the counter, while often well designed and in good taste, cannot be individual," for the simple reason that "it must appeal to the multitude." Designing one's own card was not that difficult, they assured their readers. Most families could copy the designs so helpfully included with the book—designs quite similar to those found on cards across the country. But if the reader insisted on fully creating his or her own card, only a few principles had to be followed. The motif was the central design element, the visual representation of the chief sentiment to be conveyed. It would have the most definite effect on the card's receiver. Lettering, too, was important. Not only the shape of the letters themselves, but the spaces between the letters were crucial to conveying the proper feeling of balance and stability with the card. Finally, the sentiment itself must be well chosen. Since a "greeting is really a decorated sentiment . . . you will find that the thought behind the card is what will govern its design." "One card might be awkward and stilted in feeling, regardless of the charm of the design used on the card, while the other one would be spontaneous and sincere and would convey to its recipient the exact feeling you had in designing it. So be sure your words are right then go ahead and decorate them as attractively as you wish." They closed their book with a few key "things to remember," repeating their basic principles before reassuring those who did not feel quite up to all the tasks they had outlined that uncolored cards could be had from the book's publisher. The requisite touch of the personal could be applied by paint or colored pencil.[62]

What strikes me about these interventions of the personal into the commercial world of mass-produced greetings is the quickness with which the industry's own solutions were recycled as options for those consumers wanting to counter the dominance of the large firms and the blank abstraction of their products. In 1931, *American Photography* recommended that amateur photographers walk through the section of town where the "'white collar' class lives. That is the class made up of tradesmen, clerks, lawyers, doctors, and merchants with average incomes who own their own homes." If sufficiently ambitious and talented with the camera, a potential entrepreneur could do a good bit of business near the Christmas season: "All you have to do is photograph these homes." With a small bit of decoration—" It does not take much talent to sketch a flaming candle"—and a brief sentiment—

"one saying 'Merry Christmas from Our House to Your House,' or some sentiment that brings in the home element"—a quite marketable, and notably individual, Christmas card could be produced. During the 1920s, the Norcross Greeting Card Company, a firm based in New York, had already worked with local photographers in Los Angeles and other cities to develop a national market for exactly this type of individualized card.[63]

The problem of expressing the personal within the world of large-scale mass production was the foundational conundrum of the greeting card business. It was the most significant condition of possibility for the industry, and it should not be surprising that the industry faced it head-on. The disruptive capacity of the market directly confronted the disruptive capacity for affiliation produced when men and women worked together in a highly organized industry. The profoundly contradictory conditions of performance in large-scale business organizations continually reproduced a series of affective responses that were disruptive to the smooth flow of a productive process that was supposed to be like a machine. Unrestrained competitive business had produced chaos during the post card craze. In response, the early leaders of the greeting card industry had established a trade organization to regularize standards of production and pricing. With such standards in place, those investing large amounts in the machineries of mass production could feel somewhat secure. They could believe, at least, that the market evaluation of their performance would be based on the quality of the product delivered. The conflict between collective organization and individual rewards placed intense pressures on the affects produced in a business culture, displacing and condensing them, feeding them with clichés, and packing them into small, red-roofed houses displaced far from the world of production. The conventions of design and sentiment established in the first twenty years of the modern greeting card industry—the primary insistence on the function of cards in the process of social recognition, the comfortable reliance on clichés supported by an earnest insistence on their sincerity, the nostalgic illustrations of person and home, and the indirect representation of the longing for the personal—were so effective because they enunciated so clearly the structures of feeling shaped by the large-scale business organizations that were dominating productive commercial life.

In the ten years that followed the creation of the National Association of Greeting Card Manufacturers, the industry grew almost 4,000 percent. Whereas in 1913 greeting card sales totaled $1 million, by 1923 they neared $40 million. Sales would peak in 1930 and decline for a few years before bouncing back up in 1936. From approximately twelve full-time greeting card manufacturers in 1913 to hundreds of large, medium, and small firms by the late 1930s, the industry's growth was based on the recombination of successful conventions in slightly different emotional and ritual contexts. Once firms were committed to making greeting cards full time, they devoted their efforts to regularizing year-round production. As Leigh Eric Schmidt has shown, the greeting card industry collaborated in the creation of new holidays.[64] But the creation of new holidays, like the creation of new stereotypes, was simply the result of the generative capacity of the basic principles of the greeting card industry to enunciate the affects produced in a business culture. From the mid-1920s to the early 1950s, illustrators and writers working for major greeting card companies developed ways to recombine visual and verbal clichés in order to expand and elaborate ever-more abstract yet still personal greetings. They became quite proud of what they had created: a world of feeling—compartmentalized, condensed, displaced, and yet still spoken as clearly as possible—in a card.

4

Condensation, Displacement, and Masquerade

The Dream-Work of Greeting Cards

*W*e do not have to look at greeting cards to be convinced that during the first half of the twentieth century, business culture was hegemonic in the United States. But if we do look at cards produced by the major companies, we can see some of the important emotional effects of that hegemony. If the argument of chapter 3 is correct—that conditions of large-scale business produced a reliance on a particularly generative, highly condensed, and displaced set of evocative images and verbal clichés—then greeting cards of the first half of the twentieth century provide a rich text for the analysis of the dominant structures of feeling produced in and through American business. The images and the sentiments found on greeting cards from this period represent interlinked striations of power and desire, displaying the absolute imbrication of business philosophy with longings for emotional abundance. Whereas nineteenth-century valentines were objective representations of emotional eloquence and could indicate, therefore, the interior qualities necessary to function in a market society, and whereas the chromolithographed Christmas card used images of both abundance and social obligation to knit emergent racialized class fractions into social networks, the twentieth-century greeting card confronted its contradictory conditions of possibility by refusing to represent precisely the feelings it was intended to display, even as it confirmed the necessity of cards for objectifying the ephemeral abstractions of modern feeling.

Emotional relationships in a business culture that emphasizes mobility are subject to the pressures placed on them not only by objective possibilities of social and geographic mobility, but also by ambitions and desires that obtain a different source of pressure, that are relatively autonomous. While the pressures of managing and operating large-scale organizations in a highly competitive industry provided the initial conditions that provoked the reliance on abstract displaced and condensed signs of emotional affiliation, the elaboration of these images and verses articulated with already present hierarchies of power that objectively (that is, relatively autonomously) limited the possibility of mobility. That is, they linked up with the cultural differences that marked and reinforced inequalities of power. The construction of social networks in a culture dominated by large-scale business organizations involved an intricate negotiation between the powerfully reinforced desire for mobility and the equally powerful longing for stability. Temporarily constructed social networks mapped out the twisted pathways between where one came from and where one longed to go. The tensions that structured the necessary sentimental displacement of emotions out of their real conditions of lived experience—the difficulty of recognizing the complexity of the conflicts produced when affiliation met business, when class aspiration confronted kinship ties—were compounded by the tension between mobility and stability.

Elaborating Holiday Cards

Even in the nineteenth century, Christmas card printers had produced cards for other holidays. Louis Prang and his competitors published cards to be exchanged at Easter, Halloween, Thanksgiving, and Lincoln's Birthday. They also produced birthday cards, and Prang had printed an early sympathy card decorated with a lily. In general, these cards were undifferentiated by design; they used very similar images. It was quite likely that a card printed for Easter would share an image with a card printed for Christmas or that an image first seen on a Christmas card would also appear on a Halloween card. Chromolithographers saw their products as cards that were gifts to be exchanged on holidays. The specific day was more typically signaled by the caption, not by the image. The card's function of materializing social networks was more important than its role as a symbol of a specific holiday.

This tendency carried over into the twentieth-century greeting card industry. Throughout the twentieth century, Christmas remained the most important holiday for the industry, accounting for 33 to 40 percent of its annual production. Card that were not tied to a specific holiday—birthday cards, sympathy cards, birth announcements, congratulations, and the like—could be made year-round, but they amounted to less than 50 percent of the total cards produced. The Christmas season, therefore, accounted for from about 60 to almost 80 percent of the industry's holiday card sales. One of the points of origin for the development of the industry, Christmas was and remains by far the dominant holiday for card sending. Yet as the larger companies turned toward owning their own production facilities, investing considerable amounts of money in the machinery of card publishing, it made the most sense to keep those machines operating as consistently as possible. In the first third of the twentieth century, therefore, the industry concentrated on expanding the number of regular calendar days for which cards could be sent. Soon after it formed, the National Association of Greeting Card Manufacturers worked to regularize greeting card production by identifying a holiday in each month for which cards could be produced, sold, and exchanged. By 1927, the Norcross Greeting Card Company produced a series of posters dubbed the "Norcross Almanac," listing each month's card sending occasions (figure 4.1).[1]

Arthur and Jane Norcross, brother and sister, started their greeting card company in New York in 1914. They scoured bookstalls and old card shops, collecting nineteenth-century valentines, valentine writers, and Christmas cards. Their company struggled during World War I, but quickly became successful in the early 1920s. In deliberate and evident contrast to the companies that were targeting the Midwest, Norcross aimed for a more urban market and produced a line of relatively sophisticated and clever cards. Some of its cards made reference to Broadway and Hollywood stars. Many of its writers and illustrators produced ironic self-reflexive comments on their roles in the mass production of feeling. The company developed an effective line of promotional materials that adopted the verse structures of greeting cards to promote its products to retail shops. Among those materials was the "Norcross Almanac." Promoting the cards for 1927, this set of four posters detailed the holidays for which the company was producing cards: New Year's Day (January), Valentine's Day (February), St.

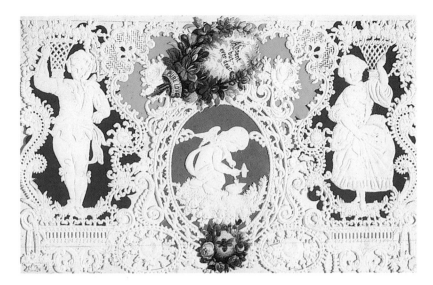

Plate 1   Esther Howland white valentine: "Absent but Ever Dear." (Norcross Greeting Card Collection, Archives Center, National Museum of American History, Behring Center, Smithsonian Institution)

Plate 2   Esther Howland gold valentine: "First Love." (Norcross Greeting Card Collection, Archives Center, National Museum of American History, Behring Center, Smithsonian Institution)

Plate 3   Prang chromolithograph of *Barefoot Boy*. (Courtesy of the Boston Public Library, Prints Division)

Plate 4 Prang chromolithograph of *Portrait of Senator Revels*. (Courtesy of the Library of Congress)

Plate 5   Dora Wheeler prize-winning Christmas card: "Good Tidings of Great Joy!" (Courtesy of the Hallmark Archives, Hallmark Cards, Inc., Kansas City, Mo.)

CHRISTMAS SCATTER MANY JOYS ABOUT YOU!

Plate 6 "Christmas Scatter Many Joys About You!" (Norcross Greeting Card Collection, Archives Center, National Museum of American History, Behring Center, Smithsonian Institution)

Plate 7 "A Hearty Christmas Greeting!" (Norcross Greeting Card Collection, Archives Center, National Museum of American History, Behring Center, Smithsonian Institution)

Plate 8 "A Merry Christmas." (Norcross Greeting Card Collection, Archives Center, National Museum of American History, Behring Center, Smithsonian Institution)

Plate 9 "Full of Mirth and Fun." (Norcross Greeting Card Collection, Archives Center, National Museum of American History, Behring Center, Smithsonian Institution)

Just over
from Japan,
Hear my jolly
little plan:
Hang me under
the mistletoe
To get a little kiss, you know.

1885.

Copyright 1885 by L. Prang & Co., Boston

Plate 10 "Just over from Japan." (Norcross Greeting Card Collection, Archives Center, National Museum of American History, Behring Center, Smithsonian Institution)

Plate 11 "A Modern Santa Claus." (Print Collection, Miriam and Ira D. Wallach Division of Art, Prints, and Photographs, The New York Public Library, Astor, Lenox, and Tilden Foundations)

Plate 12   George C. Whitney Company versions of Esther Howland–style valentines: "May Love Brighten Your Life" and "Fond Remembrance." (Courtesy, The Winterthur Library: Joseph Downs Collection of Manuscripts and Printed Ephemera)

Plate 13   P. F. Volland Company valentine: "Raise Two Lips for Me!" (Norcross Greeting Card Collection, Archives Center, National Museum of American History, Behring Center, Smithsonian Institution)

Plate 14 "Black in the Face." (Norcross Greeting Card Collection, Archives Center, National Museum of American History, Behring Center, Smithsonian Institution)

Plate 15 "I May Not Be an Angel—But—." (Norcross Greeting Card Collection, Archives Center, National Museum of American History, Behring Center, Smithsonian Institution)

Plate 16 "Hello Gorgeous!" (Norcross Greeting Card Collection, Archives Center, National Museum of American History, Behring Center, Smithsonian Institution)

Plate 17 "Christmas Greetings to My Husband." (Norcross Greeting Card Collection, Archives Center, National Museum of American History, Behring Center, Smithsonian Institution)

Plate 18 "To the Dearest Wife in All the World." (Norcross Greeting Card Collection, Archives Center, National Museum of American History, Behring Center, Smithsonian Institution)

Figure 4.1 "Norcross Almanac." (Norcross Greeting Card Collection, Archives Center, National Museum of American History, Behring Center, Smithsonian Institution)

Patrick's Day (March), Easter (April), Mother's Day (May), Father's Day (June), Independence Day (July), Friendship Day (August), Labor Day (September), Moving Day and Halloween (October), Thanksgiving (November), and Christmas (December). By 1956, the list of holidays for which cards were produced still ranged throughout the calendar year, but had been shorn of the spurious "holidays" Friendship Day and Moving Day. Labor Day and the Fourth of July were no longer considered days for card sending. Although attempts were made throughout this period to create new occasions for card use, the list of card-sending holidays remained rather stable. The major design and sentiment efforts of the industry remained focused on Christmas and Valentine's Day, with Mother's Day, Father's Day, and sympathy cards as other significantly distinctive categories of card production.[2]

Design: Identification and Displacement

From the end of World War I to the late 1950s, the basic conditions of emotional representability for mass production did not change very much. The greeting card industry focused on a concept it called sendability. This term denoted the functional effectiveness of each card. In order for a greeting card to be purchased and sent, it had to represent for its buyer some aspect of the relationship between the sender and the receiver. The buyer had to believe that the card would be meaningful for the person it was being sent to. Modern greeting cards had to construct an emotional vocabulary shared by both persons. A complex process of doubled identification had to occur for a card to be sendable. Ideally, the buyer would identify with the sentiment expressed by the card and imagine that the receiver would experience a similar but different identification. Stimulated by their own conditions of production, but also in order to provide recognizable representations of emotional relationships, modern greeting cards relied on visual stereotypes and verbal clichés. But these stereotypes and clichés should not be dismissed. They mark the understood boundaries of the social networks that sank the hegemony of American business into the heart of everyday life. If the main function of the greeting card was to establish the objectivity of an emotional relationship in a culture that emphasized mobility, the initial task of each card was to construct the possibility for social recognition without imposing too strong a set of obligations on that recognition. Too specific an image of the person seeking to establish or confirm social recognition would limit the appeal of the card—the chief concern of the industry—as well as the effectiveness of the appeal. The greeting card industry exploited the doubled ambiguity of the appeal—I claim to recognize you and you claim to recognize me, but we use these images and words of others to achieve that mutual recognition—not simply to increase the number of potential buyers for each card, but also to meet the conditions of modern life, which required mobile and flexible expressions of tentative affiliation. This strategic use of the visual and verbal language of others both confirmed the legitimacy of the feelings being enunciated and protected the users from being too closely identified with them. The strategy worked at least in part because of the conflict that arose between the need for social recognition and the need to limit mutual obligation that developed in a market society dominated by large-scale business organizations. The images on greeting cards worked through complex processes of identification and displacement.[3]

Greeting cards mediated social inequalities and constructed social networks among a constrained range of class fragments. The very use of greeting cards represented a claim to middle-class status on the part of the sender and an assumption of middle-class status for the receiver. But the precise location within that amorphous group was best left unspecified by any one card. For instance, very few direct and detailed images of white businessmen appeared on cards. Typically, these men would be shown in caricature or in silhouette. When detailed, full-frontal images of white businessmen did appear, they clearly illustrated the top boundary of the middle-class social networks constructed through card exchange. However, blackface images, hillbilly figures, American Indians, and other clearly drawn ethnic and class stereotypes marked the outer edges of the dominant and self-focused white middle classes. These stereotyped images were not used solely to signify others—those outside the social networks articulated through business relations. With what appear to be astounding acts of simultaneous identification and displacement, greeting cards of the second quarter of the twentieth century relied consistently, but not exclusively, on images of socially disempowered individuals to illustrate the sentimental feelings of those using the cards. Insofar as the exchange of greeting cards expressed a desire for the recognition of one's social position, this desire was most often illustrated with figures having relatively little social standing. In other words, whether they spoke of affiliation and love, or the connections affirmed by extended kinship and business networks, modern greeting cards tended to rely on an imagistic strategy of displacement to put these feelings in the mouths of the cute, the innocent, or racially or ethnically or class-marked others. This doubled strategy of identification and displacement was followed with remarkable consistency by the major greeting card manufacturers throughout the second quarter of the twentieth century.

The Motif

The chief image—the motif—on a greeting card is the most immediate visual associate of the emotion the card conveys. It can represent the sender or the receiver, the relationship between the two, or some aspect of the emotion itself. In chapter 3, I discussed the importance of the abstract, idealized home when used as a visual motif in the card's design. The abstract nature of this home became an issue for many card users who wanted a more concrete and individualized representation. Magazine articles advocated cards with photographs of one's own home. Some of the major firms created lines that depicted their customers' homes, using either photographs or artists' sketches to convey the individuating characteristics of the houses. One might think that this concretization of the home imago would limit its ability to function in the strategy of displacement. Yet a glance at the personal cards made by Norcross show that the photos were cropped to display only the single home. If the house was an urban town house, only the front door and its steps were displayed. Even when represented as concretely individual, then, the home on the greeting card was abstracted and idealized. This blank depiction enabled it to appear in almost any setting on the card. On cards from the 1920s and 1930s, the house often would appear outside the window of an interior shot, emphasizing its distance from the details—furniture, holiday decorations, lighting, human figures—in the foreground. I have emphasized this point because the idealized and displaced home was the nodal point in the tentative social networks constructed through card exchange. The abstract and idealized home was the ultimate fantasy scene for the enunciation of modern sentiment.

The cards for each holiday had their own common inanimate motifs. Christmas cards displayed its expected trees, candles, holly, and fireplaces; Thanksgiving, its pumpkins and corn tassels; Easter, its lilies. In each of these cases, the motif contributed a visual centering of the card along with familiar traditional symbols of the season. But often the central figure on the front of the cards was an animate body—either human or animal. Although this figure could represent the object of the sentiment—that is, the receiver of the card—it often would enact the process of speaking the sentiment and therefore point backward toward the sender. In either case, the chief function of these figures was to enunciate the emotion and, in the process, embody and articulate a shared emotional vocabulary. In the most exaggerated and clear illustration of the aspect of displacement, animals frequently took on this role (figures 4.2 and 4.3). Clearly outside the complications and conflicts of human emotional relationships, cats, dogs, bears, and birds could speak the innocent, conflict-free verses of abstract sentiment.[4]

When human figures appeared on greeting cards produced by the major companies between 1920 and 1950, they were often displaced backward in time or caricatured by means of a variety of cartooned stereotypes. Building on the forms made popular by George Wolfe Plank, valentines and Mother's Day cards from the 1920s show adult white middle-class women in nineteenth-century garb (figures 4.4–4.8). Many Christmas cards pictured visiting couples or tree-decorating parties with fantastic anachronism as eighteenth-century republicans or aristocrats (figures 4.9–4.11). Children were common figures, their presumed innocence protecting the emotions they voiced from any engagement with harsh surroundings (figures 4.12 and 4.13). Their youth, too, suggested opportunity, growth, the utopian possibility of achieved perfection that might be the ultimate American sentiment.[5]

MY MOTHER

Figure 4.4 "My Mother." (Norcross Greeting Card Collection, Archives Center, National Museum of American History, Behring Center, Smithsonian Institution)

Figure 4.5 "Valentine Greetings to My Mother." (Norcross Greeting Card Collection, Archives Center, National Museum of American History, Behring Center, Smithsonian Institution)

Figure 4.6 "To My Mother." (Norcross Greeting Card Collection, Archives Center, National Museum of American History, Behring Center, Smithsonian Institution)

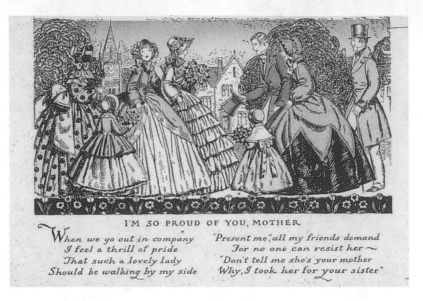

I'M SO PROUD OF YOU, MOTHER

When we go out in company   "Present me," all my friends demand
  I feel a thrill of pride   For no one can resist her ~
That such a lovely lady   "Don't tell me she's your mother
  Should be walking by my side   Why, I took her for your sister"

Figure 4.7   "I'm So Proud of You, Mother." (Norcross Greeting Card Collection, Archives Center, National Museum of American History, Behring Center, Smithsonian Institution)

Figure 4.8
"Love to a Very Dear Mother." (Norcross Greeting Card Collection, Archives Center, National Museum of American History, Behring Center, Smithsonian Institution)

Figure 4.9 "An Old Time Christmas." (Norcross Greeting Card Collection, Archives Center, National Museum of American History, Behring Center, Smithsonian Institution)

Figure 4.10 "Christmas Greetings." (Norcross Greeting Card Collection, Archives Center, National Museum of American History, Behring Center, Smithsonian Institution)

Figure 4.13
"To My Daddy."
(Norcross Greeting Card
Collection, Archives Center,
National Museum of
American History, Behring
Center, Smithsonian
Institution)

When presented in contemporary conditions, adult figures illustrating the cards were often drawn in racial, ethnic, or class caricature. Wendy Morris catalogued the ethnic imagery used by Rust Craft between 1927 and 1959. She identified twelve categories, each of which marked off a specific difference from the white middle class, which was the chief target market for these cards. Although cards could make reference to Asian Americans, Gypsies, and American Indians, these cards typically relied on a double displacement, combining a strategy of racialization with the use of animals and children to voice the longed-for emotional connection (figures 4.14–4.16). The most common non-white images that Morris found among Rust Craft cards were of black children, which illustrated 42 percent of the cards that depicted racial and ethnic others. Black children appeared on valentines, Christmas cards, Thanksgiving cards, Halloween cards, get-well cards, and birthday cards. Adult black figures, particularly the stereotypical Mammy

Figure 4.14
"Confucius Say—Hell."
(Norcross Greeting Card
Collection, Archives Center,
National Museum of
American History, Behring
Center, Smithsonian
Institution)

Figure 4.15
"It's Just the Gypsy in My
Soul." (Norcross Greeting
Card Collection, Archives
Center, National Museum of
American History, Behring
Center, Smithsonian
Institution)

and Uncle figures, were also widely used. Morris's survey of the ethnic imagery on Rust Craft cards determined that 57 percent of all non-white images were of black people. These blackface figures freely commented on their own sexuality, the bodily pleasures of consumption, and their own blackness. They typically spoke in dialect. All the classic tropes of blackface imagery are present in these cards. While Matthew Frye Jacobson identified the year 1927 and the release of the movie *The Jazz Singer* as "the end of an era in which blackface would be among the most popular forms in urban culture," Michael Rogin uncovered the extension of blackface tropes in Hollywood films of the middle part of the twentieth century. Certainly, once the presence of blackface greeting cards is acknowledged, then it becomes clear that whites' use of blackface continued for decades past the shutting off of Eastern European immigration. Although the number of new blackface cards published annually dropped after 1940, blackface cards continued to be published by the major greeting card companies throughout the early civil rights period.[6]

Why do I call these blackface cards? Two cards produced by Rust Craft explicitly label themselves as such. Published for the 1927 Christmas season, their central figures differ by gender, but both are drawn with some of the most common characteristics of blackface illustration. The female character wears a rag over her head; her large mouth and wide-open eyes shine with the made-up intensity of blackface signifying. The male character's mouth is hidden by a bullhorn protruding from his lips. Out from her open mouth and his swollen appendage speaks the same sentiment: "I'se done wished you a Merry Christmas 'til ah's black in the face" (plate 14).[7] Considering the marketing and distribution strategies used by Rust Craft, it is pretty safe to say that these cards were produced for white folks to send to one another. They narrate the conditions that promoted the continuance of blackface as a significant strategy of both identification and displacement in emotional communication. The card's sentiment makes it clear that it was the need to communicate social connection that resulted in the racial transformation of the enunciating figure. The blackface was put on for the purpose of wishing Merry Christmas as intensely as possible. The cards were relatively successful, the card with the woman selling almost fifteen thousand copies, and that with the man selling a little more than ten thousand. Why were they successful?

Of course, we cannot know for sure. With thousands of people buying these cards in potentially hundreds of different circumstances, we cannot hope to catalogue completely the reasons for their purchase. But for my immediate purposes, I want to link these cards into the tradition of blackface sentiment that they overtly referenced. During the late nineteenth and early twentieth centuries, a vocabulary of blackface images, drawn directly from the stereotypes promulgated through minstrel shows, appeared on sheet music, trade cards, Christmas cards, valentines, newspaper comics, and magazine advertisements. Scholars from Alexander Saxton to Robert Toll to Eric Lott to Michael Rogin to William Lhamon have mapped out the uses of blackface as a signifying strategy for the construction of whiteness. These scholars agree that blackface was useful for marginal whites—from the Irish in the mid-nineteenth century to the Jews in the early twentieth—when their own standing as whites was questionable. These interpretations of blackface share the view that the form was most useful in constructing a boundary where boundaries were unclear. For the Irish of the 1840s, as for the Jews of the 1920s, blackface was a strategy of othering that marked those wearing the blackface mask as white. Blackface comic valentines of the nineteenth century were unambiguous in their relentless division of black from white. And when Louis Prang published his "Modern Santa Claus" card in 1881, he was drawing on this tradition even as he tried to counter it. I suggest that the persistence of blackface imagery in modern greeting cards, beyond the consolidation of whiteness as a category of immigration, indicates that the displacement strategy embodied in these images had become an important part of a deflected process of identification that was necessary for the work of greeting cards.[8]

To the extent that we can focus on the displacement work of the cards, it must be acknowledged that blackface greeting cards of the twentieth century did reinforce the exclusion of African Americans from the white middle class. They did reproduce caricatures that, through their humiliating demarcations of difference from the established norms of business ideology, suggested that black Americans could never join the dominant group in American society. Many of the blackface cards pictured these figures as barefoot, in ragged clothes, with underwear showing and mouths open wide. But the fact that these figures were used, that they functioned as effective images on the objects that were exchanged to construct emotional connections and build social networks among white middle-class adults, says something very important about the processes of identification, the racialization of feeling, the strictures that business ideology placed on the expression of emotion, and the possibilities for escaping those strictures as they were imagined by white users of greeting cards. Blackface greeting cards no doubt built on the cultural work of "black and white melodrama" identified by Linda Williamson. But the "excess of sensation and sentiment" found on blackface greeting cards was not designed to provoke sympathy for virtuous victims or horror at vicious animalistic behaviors. Rather, the blackface and what could be imagined by whites to be true of black culture were used by some middle-class whites to enunciate emotional joy, physical pleasure, and social connection, values that were difficult for this group to articulate directly.[9]

R. F. Outcault's blackface valentines from the turn of the nineteenth century helped establish this practice. Outcault was a technical illustrator who drew comics for the penny press in New York. According to historian Ian Gordon, "Between 1895 and 1896 [Outcault's character] the Yellow Kid defined the artistic and commercial dimensions of comic strips." Outcault began drawing blackface comic-strip characters in 1898. By 1900, he had created a character, Pore Lil Mose, who became as popular as the Yellow Kid. Mose enacted all the stereotypes inherited from the tradition of blackface minstrelsy. He was childish, impulsive, innocent, and seemingly stupid. But Mose also had a certain wisdom, an insight into what mattered in the growing urban environments like New York City. In 1904, Outcault drew a valentine for the Raphael Tuck Company that continued this doubled vision of blackface. Two black children embrace, the boy's arms wrapped around the young girl. In line with the visual conventions of blackface, their mouths are open and the whites of their eyes shine. The verse calls attention to these eyes as it introduces another trope of blackface valentines: the clinging melon vine (figure 4.17). Yet Outcault's valentine is clearly different from the strain of comic valentines of the nineteenth century that continued into the comic post cards of the twentieth century. That line of cards was expressly designed to produce humiliating, demeaning images of African Americans for circulation among whites. That tradition also continued well into the twentieth century. But the differences between the two strains are evident. Whereas comic post cards continued to depict African Americans as stupid, pursuing physical pleasure even in the face of life-threatening danger, Outcault's valentine is expressive and joyful. The tradition of blackface greeting cards that followed Outcault's example did continue to reinforce images of African Americans as childish, intellectually limited, and interested in physical pleasure above all else. But they were also shown as sincere, earnest, caring, and nurturing—not only duplicating the submissive virtues associated with the stereotype of Uncle Tom, but also embodying the positive values that business ide-

Figure 4.17
"Clinging Melon Vine."
(Domestic Life Collection,
Archives Center, National
Museum of American
History, Behring Center,
Smithsonian Institution)

ology displaced onto all the powerless figures that graced the front of greeting cards. Blackface was one of the masks that fractions of the white middle class wore when they wanted to achieve social recognition. Blackface embodied the double strategy of displacement and identification that enabled emotional communication and the materialization of social networks among this group.[10]

But it was also something else. Spotted among the objects belonging to an old black couple thrown out onto the street in the eviction scene in Ralph Ellison's *Invisible Man* are two cards—one is "an ornate greeting card with the message 'Grandma, I love you' in childish scrawl"; the other has "a picture of what looked like a white man in black-face seated in the door of a cabin strumming a banjo." The invisible man does not tell us what is on the front of the ornate greeting card, but he does describe his profound emotional reaction to the discarded junk. Symbols of African-American history along with the cheap souvenirs of sentiment "throbbed within me with more meaning than there should have been. . . . Why were they causing me discomfort so far beyond their intrinsic meaning as objects?"[11] The affect attached to this ephemera, the discomfort and pain the invisible man feels, provoke him to a spontaneous public speech that stimulates the watching crowd, driving them to save the old couple's belongings and carry them back into the apartment. This collection of objects—the cards and the rabbit's foot and the freedman's papers and the torn newspaper story about Marcus Garvey and the old breast pump and the baby shoe—all carry tremendous affective power sufficient to provoke a moment of political eloquence and civil disobedience. How odd is it that among those objects are a greeting card and at least one card with blackface imagery? Were blackface cards that were produced by white-owned companies purchased and sent by African Americans? Were they invested with powerful feelings by those who used them? And if so, would that historical fact disrupt my argument?

This is difficult territory. Evidence is very sketchy. Archives that retain used greeting cards rarely keep track of who sent them or who received them—unless they were historically significant figures. Of course, African Americans used greeting cards. Drugstores ran ads for greeting cards every holiday season in the *Chicago Defender*, the *Kansas City Call*, and other black newspapers. In 1926 the *Defender* reminded its younger readers to "Remember to Send Greeting Cards." The black middle class was subject to many of the same historical forces that were reshaping social networks among members of the white middle class. But relatively autonomous developments, such as the effects of the first phase of the Great Migration, along with the myriad pressures (ranging from social exclusion to physical violence) exerted by racist whites, also contributed to the reshaping of social networks. The spreading use of greeting cards by African Americans, I argue, followed a path similar yet not identical to that of the white middle class. As the historian Kevin Gaines has argued, while working to promulgate a pos-

itive understanding of black culture during the first half of the twentieth century, northern black elites regularly opposed their sense of this
civilization to the minstrel stereotypes that had been firmly ensconced
in the white imagination: "Uplift ideology assented to the racist formulation of the Negro problem by projecting on to other blacks dominant images of racialized pathology." In fact, throughout the early
twentieth century, a "confrontation with the centrality of minstrelsy"
was crucial to the formation of both "black and white middle-class subjectivities." As the black middle class developed, its members spread
across the country, seeking employment opportunities and social networks within harsh social circumstances and conditions of extreme
economic instability. These conditions reinforced the power of business culture when it did take hold. For example, E. Franklin Frazier
has argued that when black-owned banks failed, the proximate cause
was lack of knowledge of banking principles. There was little safety net
or opportunity to learn as one went along when commercial circumstances offered initial managerial possibilities. When fully instituted,
therefore, the force of business culture was substantial, resulting in a
powerful emphasis on "piety, thrift, and respectability." Among differently racialized groups, greeting cards were sent and received as a
means of objectifying the ephemeral social networks that were under
construction by those whose emotional lives were shaped by business
culture.[12]

The first African-American sorority, Alpha Kappa Alpha, designed,
published, and sold a Christmas card as a fund-raiser in the 1920s.
Langston Hughes, Aaron Douglas, W. C. Handy, and W. E. B. Du
Bois had cards made especially for them, often using their own designs
or verse. But it is very difficult to trace the use of greeting cards among
less lauded individuals. Jeanette Temple Daindridge was an artist and
educator who taught for a while at Barber-Scotia College, a historically black institution. While employed there, she designed several
Christmas cards to be sold to alumni to raise funds for the college. The
designs ranged from silhouettes of the Wise Men and their camels to
architectural details from the school's campus. Among her sketches,
though, are blackface images that could have been designed for greeting cards or post card publication. The cards saved by Leigh Walton,

a journalist and civic leader, tended to have no human figures on them. This was true for the cards saved by Hosea Hudson as well. Nevertheless, for the valentine season of 1931, the *Philadelphia Tribune* promoted the cards that I have called blackface to its African-American middle-class readership. "The Negroid theme is more pronounced than ever before in the current Valentines," the article declared. "Shiny-faced black characters, on Valentine cards, wheedle, 'Baby yo' sho does play havoc with my blood pressure.'" Subtitled "Mah Love Am Deeper than the Ocean, Lemme Pour It in Yah Ear," the article cites dealers asserting that the most popular cards among their customers were those versed in dialect. The general tone of the piece is positive. It seems clear that for some parts of the black middle class in the period between the wars, blackface cards, displaying these exaggerated images and using dialect, were acceptable tools for emotional communication and social network building (figures 4.18 and 4.19).[13]

How could this be? I suggest that similar strategies of identification and displacement were in operation among the black middle class as among the white middle class. I am not arguing that this was a process of emulation, where middle-class blacks consciously adopted the strategic use of blackface characters that was working for whites. Rather, I am arguing that identification and displacement is a fundamental, if complex, strategy in modern greeting card practice, drawing its strength from the constrictions of business culture that worked across racial lines. This signifying strategy marks the outer boundaries of the middle class at the same time that it relies on those outside this class to embody the desires for emotional joy, physical pleasure, and social connection among a group that defines itself by the exclusion of these values. Remember that the bulk of the blackface images on the Rust Craft sample were images of black children. In that case, youthful innocence contributes to the card's ability to enunciate affiliation. But even the adult blackface figures were defined as such precisely by their difference from the black middle class. Look again at the two Rust Craft cards with which I began this discussion. The male figure is overdressed in mock finery; the female figure is dressed in peasant garb. They are clearly marked as outside the professional service-oriented black middle class. The predominance of dialect on all these

Figure 4.18
"Ah's a Neckin' Nigga."
(Norcross Greeting Card
Collection, Archives
Center, National Museum
of American History,
Behring Center,
Smithsonian Institution)

Figure 4.19
"Ah Ain't No Loafa on a
Sofa!" (Norcross Greeting
Card Collection, Archives
Center, National Museum
of American History,
Behring Center,
Smithsonian Institution)

cards is also an indicator that those speaking on the cards were outside the professional class. To the extent that middle-class African Americans purchased and sent blackface greeting cards produced by the major white-owned firms, they were participating in the dominant strategies of identification and displacement that enabled the enunciation of mass feeling.

Some white-owned firms gradually became aware of the black middle class's potential as a market for greeting cards. Soon after World War II, both the P. F. Volland Company in Chicago and the Norcross Greeting Card Company in New York published cards that were unambiguously aimed at African Americans. Volland's "De Days of Slavery's Gone, 'tis true," from 1949, relied on a cute bear cub to enunciate its valentine wish. From 1948 through the 1950s, Norcross created a line of cards that featured a respectably dressed young black girl who did not emphasize her physicality, but displayed her demure innocence as she declared a simple "Hello, Honey Chile," "You's the nicest kind of friend," or "Wish ah Could Lay Eyes on You" (figures 4.20 and 4.21). These large white-owned firms may have recognized the presence of a large African-American middle class in New York and Chicago. But just as likely, they were responding to the efforts of black-owned firms to cultivate this market. This period saw the first black-owned greeting card companies publishing their own lines of cards. While well-off black families had long been able to commission their own Christmas cards, avoiding thereby the problem of white-created images of black folks, it was not until after World War II that the combination of sufficient capital and sufficient market demand resulted in black-owned firms. By that point, Color-Tone Originals, from Mount Vernon, New York; Bronze Craft, centered in Chicago; and other companies were producing cards that still used the strategy of identification and displacement to produce sendable cards, but clearly signaled their "difference." Tawny Tint, a company based in Lake Placid, New York, created a promotional flyer in 1953 that spelled out its mission. Structured as "An Open Letter" to Santa, the flyer asked for "a set of those Tawny Tint cards, so next Christmas I won't need to search for cards that are 'different' . . . a copy of Langston Hughes' 'First Book of Negroes' . . . a subscription to *Crisis* magazine . . . a box

Figure 4.20
"Hello, Honey Chile."
(Norcross Greeting Card
Collection, Archives
Center, National Museum
of American History,
Behring Center,
Smithsonian Institution)

Figure 4.21
"You's the Nicest Kind
of Friend." (Norcross
Greeting Card Collection,
Archives Center, National
Museum of American
History, Behring Center,
Smithsonian Institution)

of that cute note-paper Color-Tone Originals put out," among other clear indicators of their specific purpose. One of Color-Tone's cards read in full: "The expression may be different but . . . the thoughts are the same . . . Merry Christmas and a Happy New Year!" Color-Tone Christmas cards relied on images of children, but the company did on occasion publish images of adult African Americans, dressed in suits and driving cars. Like many of the adult middle-class figures that appeared on white-directed cards in the 1950s, however, these adults were typically given the plump cheeks of childhood, reproducing that air of innocence so crucial to the expression of mass feeling.[14]

Morris's study of Rust Craft's cards emphasizes the company's reliance on a variety of ethnic stereotypes. The second most common type she found was the "thrifty Scot." While the ethnicity of this character was proclaimed loudly—signaled by a brogue, a plaid kilt, and plays on the word "Scot" or "Scotch" itself—the whiteness of the character was never in doubt. In fact, the chief axis of difference for this stereotype, and for a number of other characters as well, was not race but class. The thrifty Scot chose to send only a card, not a present. The thrifty Scot tried (and failed) to make his own card, since he did not want to spend even that amount. Yet he could still earnestly wish a Merry Christmas. These cards were particularly prevalent during the Great Depression, when the use of greeting cards actually expanded. Families sent cards to those who had earlier received more elaborate gifts. On one card, "Even Santa's Scotch This Year," the thrifty Scot commented on the sending family's economizing while displacing it twice—once onto the Scot and once onto the figure of Santa Claus, the abstract image of modern productivity and abundance (figure 4.22).[15]

During the 1940s, the period when Rust Craft's use of blackface images dropped, Norcross also cut down its production of blackface cards. A different articulation of identification and displacement resulted in several images of white working-class women. One hillbilly figure always appeared barefoot, often with a shotgun and a whiskey jug. Another figure always wore her nightgown and was accompanied by a lighted candle. One of the more popular characters the company created during the 1940s was "Lanky Lil" (figure 4.23). From 1942 through 1947, Lil forthrightly asked soldiers, sailors, and civilians if

they wanted her. She was often quite aggressive, asserting, "I've got what it takes, valentine. If you can take it." Lanky Lil insisted that she was no cover girl but could still be a pin-up gal. Her long braids swung out behind her head; her short skirt rose over her lace-bottom bloomers, showing off legs as skinny as her braids. Not surprisingly, by 1947, Lanky Lil was married, searching for "a new slant to this valentine business" to send to her husband.[16]

Another popular character, "Suzie Q," was not a traditional pin-up either. But where Lanky Lil was skinny, Suzie Q was plump. Throughout the 1940s, Suzie Q appeared as a rather precocious child. The sentiment on one early card read: "I may look demure and awfully pure— but that ain't nothin' that love can't cure." In card after card, Suzie Q exploited the possibilities for displacement and identification that a childish face offered to feminine sexuality. For Christmas of 1940, she is seen decorating her tree in her underwear while lifting a candy cane to her mouth. Inside, the sentiment reads:

> Do exactly as you please,
> Don't suppress a yen,
> It will be a whole long year,
> Till Christmas Comes Again.

Of course, inside the card, the candy cane is fully inserted into her mouth. In 1944, Suzie Q's proclivities expanded. Bent over a table, with a sphincter-like halo glowing above her head, she shouts: "Listen, Valentine!" As the exclamation point directs attention to the rear of her lifting skirt, she proclaims: "I may not be an angel—But—" (plate 15). Inside the card, the verse continues, "What I lack in halo and wings, / I more than make up in other things." Unlike Lanky Lil, Suzie Q never seemed to get married. In a card for the 1948 season, she was working in an office, dropping "Just a line on the boss' time" and still satisfying her oral tendencies through a bent straw leading from her mouth into a foamy soda (figure 4.24). Suzie Q's playful sexuality quite probably appealed to more than straight female buyers. It may even have been intended to do so. In the late 1930s, Norcross had developed a character who may or may not have been a working-class woman, but

Figure 4.24
"Just a Line on the Boss'
Time." (Norcross
Greeting Card Collection,
Archives Center, National
Museum of American
History, Behring Center,
Smithsonian Institution)

who simultaneously sported a mustache and an hourglass figure. The sentiments that accompanied this character always had the phrase "gay deceiver" worked into them. With the character leaning against a phone, the sentiment on a card from 1938 reads: "Although I know you're a gay deceiver, / how my ear does cling to that old receiver." A card from 1939 featuring the same character read, "You're a gay deceiver and not to be trusted, / Little you care 'bout the hearts you have busted" (plate 16).[17]

The Masquerade of Business Culture

The simultaneous operation of displacement and identification is the defining characteristic of the masquerade, as outlined by Joan Riviere in 1929. Notoriously, Riviere was not talking about cross dressing or queer sexuality of any sort. Rather, she was theorizing about basic straight femininity. "My suggestion is not," she insisted, "that there is any such difference" between womanliness and the masquerade. "Whether radical or superficial, they are the same thing."[18] Up to this point, I have been focusing on cards in which the process of displacement is evident while arguing that identification was also occurring in the simultaneous double movement of greeting cards. I still believe that this is the most common pattern—displacement is emphasized in order to allow identification to occur. But that pattern does not account for the cards that did picture the dominant middle class of business culture. Many Christmas cards, valentines, and, especially, Mother's and Father's Day cards did display those who enjoyed the fruits of the productive system. Not always, but most often shown in the abstract and idealized home, these figures were represented with all the accoutrements of their positions. With these ideal images clearly depicted, one might expect a rather simple process of identification to have been taking place. Beautiful, comfortable women in nice surroundings could seem to speak directly for the senders of these cards. Powerful-looking, well-dressed men might seem to represent rather immediately the object of desire. Quite probably these cards did speak their love as directly and clearly as it could be spoken. But if we look at them closely, we will see that they, too, convey the disruptions that accompany desire, and that the expression of love and affiliation is still displaced even if the illustration wears a perfect masquerade, one consistent with the imperatives of business culture.

I want to begin with an astonishingly clear depiction of the masquerade of business culture. For the 1943 valentine season, Norcross created the card shown in figure 4.25. In contrast to many of the cards examined so far, its outside images the receiver of the message, not the sender. A seemingly innocuous image, the wife sits with her legs crossed, leaning on a table and chatting on the phone. She is not displaced in time. With a bland attractiveness, her hair, dress, and shoes, as well as the phone, make her out to be thoroughly modern. Her expression suggests that she is paying eager, thoughtful attention to the voice at the other end. We have a sense of what the message is, as it is spoken by the caption: "A Big 'Hello' for My Wife on Valentine's Day."[19] When the card opens, the giant head of a white businessman unfolds, rising up over the top of the card, completely dominating the scene (figure 4.26). His face is presented with remarkable detail. The

Figure 4.25
"A Big 'Hello' for My Wife on Valentine's Day." (Norcross Greeting Card Collection, Archives Center, National Museum of American History, Behring Center, Smithsonian Institution)

neat part in his hair along with his suit and tie testify to his success, as does the sentiment, with its clear indication that his home has a private telephone line. On the surface, this card exclaims that the businessman wants "folks far and near" to know that "My Wife's my Valentine!" But let us stop for a minute to see what is pictured in this card. First, the husband has to call his wife on the phone to deliver the valentine message. He is not at home; he is not pictured with her. The first displacement, which might be no displacement at all, but merely the reality, is to situate him at the office, too busy to come home to wish her a happy Valentine's Day in person. At least, he seems to be calling her from the office, but no office is depicted, so she really does not know where he is calling from. But she is grateful for the "Big 'Hello'" nonetheless. Second, the initial wish that the card enunciates seeks to cover over his absence, to make him as present as possible by exaggerating his size and his power to compensate for his absence. This is precisely the way in which the masquerade works—in order for the card

Figure 4.26 "A Big 'Hello' for My Wife on Valentine's Day." (Norcross Greeting Card Collection, Archives Center, National Museum of American History, Behring Center, Smithsonian Institution)

to make sense, his power must become the focus of the relationship. Once the husband is presented as gigantic and powerful, his absence is explained; his business responsibilities keep him away. The identification that initially seemed so straightforward in this card is really an identification with the masquerade of business culture, with the valuation of production over feeling. For there to be love like this, his performance of manliness must proceed in line with the masquerade.

Let us assume that, for those who bought and sent it, this card faithfully enunciated the objective conditions of their relationship. Let us assume that there is no difference between what the card imaged and what the users imagined to be true. The card claims that the sentimental quality of their marriage can be best declared with a card that imagines itself as a phone call. The widespread prevalence of telephones and other communication technologies on greeting cards suggests an anxiety about the card as a form of emotional communication. Cards are initially sent privately, in envelopes. But they are also created for display. Their objectifying publicizing function competes with the privacy typically demanded for emotional communication. This card thematizes this conflict between the private quality of the relationship and the desire to publicize it, by displacing the objectifying function of the card onto the (im)possibility of neighbors' listening in on the call. Doing so, it calls attention to one of the critical contradictions in Western love that greeting cards address. The lovely fiction of the happy heterosexual couple plays a key role in holding together the social order. This card reminds anyone who views it that there is a public responsibility attached to having a happy marriage. And it raises the possibility that the card could be sent out of obligation, not from spontaneous desire. This possibility is underlined by the capitalization of "WIFE," as though it were an earnestly shouted answer to the unasked question, "Who *is* his valentine?" But look at the businessman's face. These issues do not bother him. These anxieties are not felt. He is powerful, happy, confident in his ability to stand above any messy emotional difficulties that might arise were he to publicly proclaim his affection. As this card so powerfully demonstrates, in the world of greeting cards it is possible to invert the gendered meaning of Riviere's classic formulation. In greeting cards, as in business culture, there is no difference between manliness and the masquerade. Manliness is the effective performance of masculinity.[20]

Rarely did the white businessman appear so fully displayed in greeting cards. But the common racial and class displacements were not wise strategies for enunciating the affiliations celebrated on Mother's Day and Father's Day. As we have seen, Mother's Day cards often relied on displacements in time. In fact, Mother's Day carried an implicit nostalgia that evoked times past even when contemporary images were used. Mother's Day sentiments almost always referred to things that Mother had done in the past, the love she had given. For those buying and sending Mother's Day cards, Mother's day was done; her moment of affectionate power was over. Father's Day cards, however, did not project Father's work into the past. Although some early Father's Day cards from Rust Craft imaged fantasies of elegant men at bookish leisure, most cards dedicated to this day reveled in the masquerade of manliness in a business culture. From the first Father's Day card it produced, Norcross created some of the most straightforward representations of the contradictions of emotional affiliation in a business culture. The company's inventive solution to the problem of simultaneous displacement and identification in Father's Day cards was to show the father—the white businessman—in profile, in silhouette, from the rear, or with only part of his face showing. This image could be anyone or no one. It could convey the necessary specificity of race and class, without individuating too clearly the object of affection.

Norcross's first Father's Day card, produced in 1929, shows a silhouette of Dad, sitting in his chair, reading and smoking. The caption, "To My Best Pal—Dad," suggests straightforward affiliation (figure 4.27). But a careful look at the card disturbs this impression. Dad's chair sits in front of the window, and just outside that window

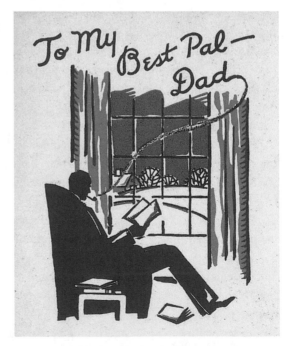

Figure 4.27
"To My Best Pal—Dad."
(Norcross Greeting Card
Collection, Archives
Center, National Museum
of American History,
Behring Center,
Smithsonian Institution)

is a snow-covered, sloping-roofed home. The sentiment inside the card reads:

> You've a way of understanding,
> Of always playing square,
> And as a pal, believe me, Dad—
> You've always been right there.

The power of this wish is contrasted with both the silhouetted figure and the image of the idealized home outside the window. Regardless of where Dad actually is sitting, the ideal home is shown to be elsewhere; Dad is not "right there."

The following year, things had not improved at all. On a card addressed "To the Best Father in the World," the businessman cannot turn around to face his children; rather, he keeps his back to them as he stares into the fire (figure 4.28). In 1932, Dad is back in his chair,

TO THE BEST FATHER IN THE WORLD

Figure 4.28
"To the Best Father in the World." (Norcross Greeting Card Collection, Archives Center, National Museum of American History, Behring Center, Smithsonian Institution)

Figure 4.29
"To Dad on His Day."
(Norcross Greeting Card
Collection, Archives
Center, National Museum
of American History,
Behring Center,
Smithsonian Institution)

smoking and reading (figure 4.29). Again, the ideal home is imagined to be outside the window. But at least this time, Dad is taking the trouble to read the card that was sent to him. The cover of the text in his hand reads: "Love to Father." The sentiment inside the card repeats some basic tropes from an earlier card:

> There is a certain someone
> Who's always just and fair
> A ready, steady comrade
> A friend who's on the square
> He has a way about him
> That makes everybody glad
> Life's brighter and it's more worth while
> Because of you, dear Dad!

The repetition of "square" from the earlier card and the addition of the rhyming "fair" suggest again a contractual understanding of emotional relationships, as well as the difficulty of imagining feelings toward Dad in any language apart from that of exchange. The following year, Father is back at work (figure 4.30). If his children are to send him "a very special greeting," then they have to send it to him at the office. The home again sits as an imagined and impossible ideal on the top left of the image. By 1935, Mother seems to have worked up the courage to interrupt the businessman's reading—at least on Father's Day (figure 4.31). We are almost allowed to see his face in this card, were it not for her hands covering his eyes. As she asks her playful question, "Well—guess who!" we can only wonder if he knows the answer. The real abstraction of the father, his absence from the ideal home, was so taken for granted by the manufacturers of greeting cards that, by 1941, even Christmas cards pictured him as absent (plate 17). The performance of masculinity was brought off simply through the representation of some of his characteristic belongings: his chair by the fire, his hat, his gloves, his newspaper, and his dog.[21]

Figure 4.30
"Here's a Very Special Greeting." (Norcross Greeting Card Collection, Archives Center, National Museum of American History, Behring Center, Smithsonian Institution)

To MY HUBBY
on FATHER'S DAY
with love
from

WELL—
guess who!

Evan Connell's brilliant fictional evocation of this absence, *Mrs. Bridge*, relies on many of the same tropes to describe the masculine masquerade of business culture and its effects. The novel is set at the eve of World War II. Mr. Bridge is a very successful lawyer, and the family lives in the Country Club district of Kansas City. Mrs. Bridge's life is taken up with worrying about her children, two girls and a boy, and enduring enforced social encounters with women who are either odd, arty, and disheveled or competitively perfect in their finely wrought manners. From the beginning of their marriage, Mr. Bridge had developed the habit of working late at night and throughout the weekend, arriving home harassed and angry, distracted by cases he could not forget. He is known by his Chrysler, his briefcase, and his hat. Mrs. Bridge had hoped that with the arrival of financial security, Mr. Bridge would spend more time at home. Before their children are grown, she has given up that hope. He does show his love by lavishing expensive gifts on her: a Lincoln, an ermine wrap, and a trip to Europe.

Occasionally, Mrs. Bridge finds herself swamped by feelings that she has no words for. At those moments, she longs for Mr. Bridge's presence. But when he does arrive, they stare at each other blankly, or his pent-up irritation spews out unexpectedly. Nothing really happens in the book. Rather, its emotive power derives from the absence of action, the absence of affective experience, the confusion of everyday life, all driven by a powerful undercurrent of feeling that remains continually unspoken.[22]

A decade after the publication of *Mrs. Bridge*, Connell wrote a sequel that was narrated from the perspective of the husband. Not as successful as the first volume, *Mr. Bridge* renders explicit what the first purely evoked. It begins,

> Often he thought: My life did not begin until I knew her. She would like to hear this, he was sure, but he did not know how to tell her. In the extremity of passion he cried out in a frantic voice: "I love you!" yet even these words were unsatisfactory. He wished for something else to say. He needed to let her know how deeply he felt her presence while they were lying together during the night, as well as each morning when they awoke and in the evening when he came home. However, he could think of nothing appropriate. . . . After all, he was an attorney and not a poet.[23]

When reading this, one wishes for the evocative and objectifying power of a greeting card. If Mr. Bridge had gone to the store to purchase a valentine for his wife, he most probably would have bought one like the card that Norcross produced in 1945 (plate 18). From the company's most expensive line of valentines for that year, "To the Dearest Wife in All the World" relies on the most common design motif of all for its ability to evoke displaced identification. Flowers, the fragile and temporary reproductive organs of plants, have long signified the beautiful abstraction of love from the messy complications of life. On this card, blue lilies of the valley surround purple orchids that are set off by small drops of clear plastic intended to signal the innocence of morning dew. Strategically placed near the core of the opening of each orchid's blushing bell, the drops delicately suggest other fluids as well.

Mr. Bridge, of course, would not have noticed that—at least, not consciously. He would have been more taken by the verse inside:

> I never knew till I met you that anyone could be
> As near and dear and wonderful as you have been to me
> And when I send this valentine to you on Sweetheart's Day
> There's more love in each line, dear than I can ever say.[24]

Sentiment: The Mute Objectivity of Mass Feeling

"To the Dearest Wife in All the World" makes an astonishing claim, really. But it captures so precisely the difficulty of emotional eloquence in a business culture. The valentine itself has "more love in each line" than "I" can ever say. The feelings are there, but they remain unspoken. Apparently, they are impossible to speak. Look at the shifting authorship here. The valentine does convey the love; it has more love in each line than the sender can say. Of course. That is why the sender purchased the valentine in the first place. But the surprising aspect of this valentine sentiment is that it does not try to articulate this love. It just asserts it. Why? If the valentine is a commercial source of emotional eloquence, as I argued it was in the nineteenth century, then why does this valentine not try to describe the specific qualities of this love? It simply states that its receiver has been "near and dear and wonderful"—nothing more. Why does it not go beyond those rather bland assertions? Should it not try to say more? Why does the valentine itself refuse emotional eloquence? Or does it? Perhaps emotional eloquence takes a different form when it is sent by an attorney and not a poet. Perhaps it is worth reading this sentiment closely for what it can tell us about the forms of emotional eloquence endemic to a business culture.

Formally, the verse adopts the rhythm that is the most common among sentimental greeting cards: a ballad quatrain. The first line is a four-foot iambic line; the second is a three-foot iambic line; the third, a four-foot again; and the fourth, a three-foot. This entire structure then repeats. It is only when you scan the lines carefully that you find the error in the last line. The word "dear" creates a lump in the verse that you stumble over as you read it. Just as Robert Lord's "awful hard" constructed sincerity out of its grammatical error, so this verse conveys an earnestness that is too powerful to be constrained by prosodic rules. The rhythmic lump in the last line evokes the lump in the throat of any Mr. Bridge who would have sent it. And that is the line that proclaims precisely the absence of emotional eloquence. The lump testifies to the sincere yet inarticulate feeling that the card claims to represent.

Sometime in the 1950s, Rust Craft produced a writer's manual that laid down some general rules for greeting card composition. The section on cards sent from husband to wife is worth quoting at length:

> The husband, if he is the right kind of man and is sincerely interested in the welfare of his marriage, must know and understand the female mind. He knows that his wife wants to hear expressions of love and affection, and he also knows that she wants him to be sincere. This can be covered in the modern day and age by a good, sensible, sound expression of love and affection. Most women do not prefer the overly-expressive type of sentiment. Some of the things that can be said are, first, your happiness of being married. The second thing is a bit about the love that you feel, without being too ostentatious about it. The principle thing in regard to a sentiment for a husband to send is the sincerity with which you are writing, and the personal quality. The personal part should be tempered with a degree of restraint. In other words, not so emotional that either the husband or the wife might be embarrassed.[25]

The Norcross card "To the Dearest Wife in All the World" perfectly achieves these goals. The husband, if he is the right kind of man, knows that his wife wants to hear words of love. There is no assumption that he might want to say such words. He also knows that she wants him to be sincere, so he must figure out a way to sound sincere. But the language of emotion is not a familiar or a comfortable one for either the husband or the wife. Too much dwelling on such matters could embarrass them both. The blank assertion that she matters, that she is "near and dear and wonderful," is the best that either could want to send or receive.

Rust Craft's manual was part of the equipment that each staff writer received when he or she was hired by the company. Containing hints about where to find ideas for cards and rules about their construction, the manual states many times that "greeting cards are basically messages from one person to another. We find that our customers prefer those cards which sound the most natural. Let this be your number one rule in writing: it must sound natural!" Similarly, H. Joseph Chadwick, who had spent years writing for the Barker Card Company, insisted in his handbook: "It is important to express yourself in the down-to-earth, everyday language of the people, because that is the language the people prefer in their greeting cards." Indeed, he continued, "a card is successful if enough people can identify so completely with what it says and how it says it that they consider it *their own expression*."[26]

Although sentimental valentines could never acknowledge this problem, some humorous valentines directly addressed the impossibility of emotional eloquence. In 1936 Norcross published a valentine that proclaimed the vacuity of all such cards:

> Little shops are full of cards
> In tidy little rows
> On every shelf along the wall
> Everywhere one goes
> But not a card in any shop
> Could ever make it clear
> How wonderful it is to have
> A friend like YOU my dear!

This card sold to those who were saying that cards cannot possibly say what is meant. For the 1942 season, Norcross produced this "valentine for my son":

> The postman brings this valentine
> And someone else designed it
> But I'm the one who sends it, son
> And ALL MY LOVE'S behind it.

In 1944, a valentine for a husband proclaimed:

> I'm trying and trying
> To get a new slant
> To this Valentine business
> But Honey, I can't
> I just plain love you.

And for the 1945 season:

> Valentine! I'm the bashful type, you know.
> At speeches I ain't a hit—
> But once I get in action,
> You won't miss the words a bit!"

Clearly, the objectification of feeling in these cards did not require emotional eloquence. The words mattered, but they mattered in a different way.[27]

Perhaps the clearest examples of this mute objectivity can be found in sympathy cards. Their function and wording changed very little throughout the twentieth century. Sympathy cards mark the death of a person and assert that the social network to which that person belonged will continue to function, will still be able to circulate meanings and affects. These cards might be said to paper over the gash cut by one person's death in a particular social fabric. Yet the most common trope to be found in sympathy cards from the 1920s through the 1950s was the impossibility of words communicating the intensity and sincerity of the feelings of the sender. Norcross began publishing sympathy cards in the 1920s. A typical sentiment from 1926 said: "I know that nothing I can say will comfort you but my sympathy is sincere and heartfelt." In 1928 a card read: "It is difficult to express my sympathy for you at this time of your great sorrow but my heart goes out to you and yours." Another, from the 1930s, read: "No words can express the deep sympathy this message brings to you in your sorrow." Yet another said:

> Your loss I know is hard to bear
> No word can ease your grief
> But know that you have friends who care
> And long to bring relief.

Sympathy cards are traditionally the hardest cards to write, death being perhaps the most difficult family event to confront. But rather than strive to say the impossible, sympathy cards typically acknowledged the impossibility of language while insisting on the value of objectifying emotional connection.[28]

This mute objectivity of greeting cards was not experienced as inauthentic. A touching thank-you card from an archival collection demonstrates the saturation of this inarticulate structure of feeling. In 1943, Mildred bought a Norcross thank-you card to send to Mrs. Lennon. The outside of the card describes Mrs. Lennon as "an ANGEL," while the inside goes on to say: "Thank you very much." In her own handwriting, Mildred tried to say more, to render the mass-produced "thank you" more personal:

> There's so much I want to say to you to express my feelings. But I guess it's just one of those things I can't speak or even write about. I do though want you to understand a little of how I feel. You've been so darn swell and helpful to me in so many ways that I know I'll always value your friendship as well as that helping hand.—Golly, this all sounds so inadequate; but all I can say from the bottom of my heart is [the card's preprinted line] *Thank you very much* for everything.

Mildred's need to enunciate a very particular form of gratitude exceeded her ability to speak it. She turned, quite reasonably, to a card that said only "thank you." And when she tried to say more, despite her own feelings of inadequacy, she found that those words were simply the best.[29]

Greeting cards had to develop a language of emotional communication and social connection that could be recognized as the language natural to those who bought the cards, when the reason they bought the cards was that they had no such language of their own. The resulting vocabulary became so condensed that it would nearly implode with meaning and affect. Like workhorses of sentiment, the clichés that trod across the inside of greeting cards had to pull such emotional weight that they could not worry about looking pretty. They had a job to do. They had to absorb the multitudinous intentions of the sender and then release them with respectful sincerity when opened by the receiver.

The Use of Greeting Cards

On January 31, 1925, Clara Raddant Bleck mailed a birthday card to her sister, Edith Raddant Meggers. It read:

> To My Sister on Her Birthday:
> You are just the best ever!
> Believe me, I know it,
> And love you no matter
> How little I show it!

Clara had mailed the card from her home in Clintonville, Wisconsin, close to Shawano, the small town where she and her sister had grown up. Edith was living on Harvard Street in Washington, D.C. She had moved there in 1920, when she married. Dr. William F. Meggers had grown up in Wisconsin as well. He was born in Clintonville, on July 13, 1888. His family was among the many descendents of German immigrants who had found that the fertile farmland of Wisconsin provided a congenial new home. Meggers had received a bachelor's degree from nearby Ripon College in 1910 and had been working for the federal government's Bureau of Standards since 1914. Having earned his Ph.D. in physics from Johns Hopkins in 1917, Meggers was promoted to chief of the spectroscopy section of the National Bureau of Standards in 1920, a position he held until his retirement in 1958. As late as 1916, Edith Raddant was still living in Shawano, receiving Christmas cards from her out-of-town friends. I do not know when or how Edith and William met. Curiously, Edith seems not to have saved any valentines or other tokens from their courtship. It is possible that there were none, but it seems more likely that she destroyed them, perhaps out of a sense of privacy. But Edith did save Christmas cards and birthday cards; the Meggers Collection, therefore, documents the family's extended social network.[1] As this network developed over time, it reflected the Meggerses' class trajectory, tracing a not untypical journey from a small midwestern town of shopkeepers and teachers to a large urban center of modern bureaucratic organizations. This chapter traces patterns of greeting card use in the middle third of the twentieth century. It begins with an analysis of the social networks documented in collections like that of the Meggerses' and then moves on to discuss the marks that users make on the cards they buy, the small signals of individuation that signal a personal claim to the purchased sentiment.

Christmas Cards and Social Trajectory

The oldest cards in the Meggers Collection were sent by friends and family members living in small towns not far from Shawano. Once Edith moved to Washington, her family continued to send birthday, anniversary, and Christmas cards, relying on these mass-produced tokens of affection and affiliation to represent materially the emotional links that connected her with her family of origin and her old home in small-town Wisconsin. Given the geographical distance and, probably, the growing social distance, Clara and her mother and father did not have many opportunities to demonstrate their love for Edith. The cards, therefore, had to perform important emotional work. To a certain extent, they must have been successful, for Edith saved almost every one of them. More often than not, Edith's sister and parents would allow the printed design and sentiment to speak for them—at least to represent suggestively, if not to articulate accurately, the emotional connections between the sender and the receiver. Edith's father, for instance, never wrote anything on the cards he sent but the touching lower case signature "your father." The Meggerses' social network soon expanded to include professional colleagues of William's, local friends of Edith's, and neighbors who shared their lovely upper northwest section of the city. (After their first daughter, Betty Jean, was born, the family moved to Brandywine Street, near Chevy Chase, Maryland.) Edith saved these cards as well. The last cards in the collection arrived during World War II. They were sent by Edith and William's son, Bill, and by young friends working in new war jobs. For over twenty years, Edith had saved the cards that materialized the extension of her kinship networks beyond her immediate family and that traced the rhizomatous lines branching out into the professional world that she and William had entered.

In an important article first published in *Signs*, the anthropologist Micaela Di Leonardo identified card exchange as a central practice in the production and reproduction of kinship networks. Di Leonardo underlined two very important facts about these networks. First, their maintenance requires effort—real, if unpaid, labor. Second, these networks are not simply the passive effects of other social forces; they are not "the epiphenomena of production and reproduction." Nor are they "leisure activities, outside an economic purview." She coined the term "kinwork" to describe this labor, and placed the celebration of holidays and the exchange of cards at the center of this kinwork. The social networks that kinwork reproduce link households, negotiating and mediating power and status inequalities among the households. According to Di Leonardo, kinwork links households across family lines and seems to be relied on to a greater extent in those societies where economic production is not tightly tied to kinship networks as traditionally understood.[2]

Despite its relatively autonomous functioning, the kinwork that Di Leonardo identified in the second half of the twentieth century can be understood as a necessary response to the economic transformations that restructured dominant society in the United States during the first few decades of the twentieth century. Twentieth-century greeting card practice continued the nineteenth-century function of materializing class aspiration, but these aspirations were now channeled into social trajectories shaped by the dominance of large corporations. The transition from an economy grounded in small firms to one structured by large-scale business organizations created emergent uses for mailed cards and reinforced the basic narrative of greeting cards—the dream of emotional and material abundance achieved together through upward mobility. The dominance of business culture in the United States reinforced this narrative, placing a high value on mobility while implying always that the social trajectory would be upward. According to Alfred Chandler, Jr., "With the coming of modern business enterprise, the businessman, for the first time, could conceive of a lifetime career involving a climb up the hierarchical ladder."[3]

In his 1943 analysis of kinship structure in the United States, Talcott Parsons asserted that the open conjugal system of the isolated "family of procreation" provided a neat fit with the structure of modern industrial capitalism. "Preferential mating," as Parsons called it— that is, marriage on the basis of romantic love—links two previously unrelated families that are joined only in this one instance. This mating strategy has the effect of constructing a relatively open, multilineal system. By freeing itself from elongated kinship structures and by abandoning the hierarchical expectations that had accompanied the older institutional functions of the family (education, production, and care of the aged, sick, and poor), the conjugal family structure "interferes least with the functional needs of the occupational system." Two main effects followed from this kinship system. First, it encouraged an outward and open orientation among the members of each conjugal family. This outward orientation enforced a certain adaptability and responsiveness to external social forces. Second, each relatively small "nuclear" family derived its status—its class positioning—not from its place in a traditionally understood extended kinship structure but from the status ascribed to the occupations of the individual family members. "The conjugal unit can be mobile in status independently of the other kinship ties of its members," Parsons argued. Thus any drive for status recognition found its most available object in what Parsons called "the occupational structure." In the United States, then, during the first half of the twentieth century, the social status of a particular family was most directly determined by the work success or failure of its individual members, and any career ambitions were powerfully affected by the need for status recognition that would not be met elsewhere. Conjugal families within the professional managerial class became mobile units that could be placed according to the needs of the fastest growing sectors of the economic system.[4]

Notoriously, Parsons was interested in describing the stability and coherence of the social system operating in the United States. The flexibility that he saw in the kinship system enabled crucial moments of adaptation to the demands of the economic system, ensuring its fundamental stability. It is, of course, possible to see this social flexibility in another light. If a kinship network is a chain of loosely linked units, each of which seeks its status recognition and, therefore, its social legitimacy through the position of its members in the "occupational system," then kinship networks are profoundly shaped by the class trajectories of individuals that have been fashioned by the relatively unforgiving demands of the economic structure. As men worked their way through the large business and bureaucratic structures that determined economic life, women wove the lacelike connections between household units out of holidays, shared recipes, and greeting cards. These networks were often ripped apart and then reknit among new families, in new neighborhoods and towns, creating patterns more capable of reflecting back the social recognition appropriate to a family's current status. In other words, the networks constructed through kinwork were stitched together according to the demands of a society structured by large-scale business organizations.

Curiously, sociological studies of the family during this time period emphasized not this connection to the work world of status, competition, struggle, and conflict, but the relative isolation of the family from these influences. The new family model, the "affectionate" family, formed its bonds strictly on the basis of mutual interests and ideals, respect, and love. This affectionate family, based on a "companionate" marriage, was ideally believed to be the source of all emotional satisfactions. A "well-organized" affectionate family was "unified." Signs of this unity included "the degree to which members of the family [found] satisfaction for their interests within the family group . . . provide[d] its own amusements and intellectual stimulation . . . care[d] financially for its own members, and . . . provide[d] for mutual response relationships." In the viewpoint proffered by these studies, the well-organized family was as independent of its cultural and socioeconomic context as one could conceive possible. This affectionate family was first theorized in the 1920s. According to social historian Paula Fass, the sociologists of this decade "inherited the traditional view of the family as the building block of social order." In order to maintain that centrality after kinship structures had lost their institutional structural power, these monadic families "substituted emotional for productive functions. . . . Families were no longer hard, structural, economic atoms locked in the metal of society but emotional clouds formed on the basis of love and united through personality and emotional satisfaction." In 1928, the sociologist William Ogburn suggested that "even if the family doesn't produce thread and cloth and soap and medicine and food, it can still produce happiness."[5]

While the family structure that developed during this time was believed to operate independently of economic forces, to find its reason for existence not in the world of production but purely in the realm of ideals and emotions, the outlines of the "well-organized" affectionate family (the specific form of the new family structure that sociological studies argued was most likely to successfully navigate the storms of the Great Depression) were clearly based on the characteristic attributes of the families of the emergent urban professional–managerial class. This was the family model that provided a site for consumption and entertainment, where the mutual sharing of ideals and affection could supposedly provide happiness regardless of the economic context. This was precisely the family model that Parsons found interfered least with the demands of the occupational system. Rather than operating independently of economic forces, however, this social unit was clearly the immediate product of the consolidation of large-scale business organizations and a nationally integrated economy. Patterns of greeting card exchange from this period show that these "nuclear" families were not isolated, but were constantly struggling, through kinwork, to situate themselves in relationships of mutual recognition with other families that had the requisite status to enable them to bestow on one another mutual social legitimacy. That is, families, particularly women, engaged in kinwork to concretize social relationships in a relatively unstable and fluid social system structured by the competitive forces of large-scale business organizations. Greeting card use shows that families not only were not isolated from the forces of economic production, but relied on kinwork to establish networks of recognition that specifically included other families first encountered through business relations. One of the most important tasks of greeting card exchange was to legitimize and naturalize the affective and affiliative relationships produced through business transactions by including those people, for the moment or season, in an expanded, if necessarily temporary, kinship network.[6]

After William Meggers and Edith Raddant married, Edith worked hard to maintain the traditional connections back to their families in Wisconsin. Greeting cards were sent to acknowledge birthdays as well as Christmas, anniversaries as well as Easter. Their first child, Betty Jean, was born in December 1921, and she soon began receiving cards addressed to her. Clara, now "Aunt Clara," and Betty Jean's grandparents regularly mailed cards to the child. By 1926, however, after William had been head of spectroscopy for six years, a change became evident in the pattern of card use. For this year, the Meggerses received cards from Cambridge, Massachusetts; Williamsburg, Pennsylvania; Los Angeles; and Paris. The card that Ch. Fabry mailed to Doctor and Mrs. Meggers in 1926 was addressed to the Meggerses at the Bureau of Standards. Not a typical Christmas card, this picture post card displayed an image of the new optical institute of Paris—or so says the inscription written across the top of the image. The back of the card contains the holiday greeting "My best wishes for the new year—to you and your children." From Los Angeles, Albert sent an elegant flat Christmas card: "With best wishes for a Very Merry Christmas and a Happy New Year." Mr. and Mrs. Ralph Young had their names printed on the flat Christmas card they sent from Williamsburg, Pennsylvania, while Melvin and Emmie signed the card they mailed from Wittenberg, Wisconsin. The Barbers' card, sent from Ripon, Wisconsin (the home of the college that William Meggers had attended), was almost identical to the card mailed by the Renfro family from Washington, D.C. The Larsens designed their own card before mailing it from Chicago. So did the Strattons, although they may have lived close enough to hand-deliver their card, as no envelope remains. The card sent by Mr. and Mrs. Takamine has a Japanese inscription next to an image of a mountain rising over a sea. Betty Jean's cousin, Elenor, stitched the sentiment into the card she sent. Edward H. Miller's card was an embossed and decorated visiting card. Mr. and Mrs. Burt Carroll seem to have printed theirs from a linoleum block, while the Stimsons' card displays a photograph of their suburban home. Thomas

Baker's card, mailed from the Carnegie Institute of Technology, seems to have been the first folded card the Meggerses received. Of the thirty-seven cards saved from 1926, eight were clearly sent by Wisconsin relatives and friends. The remainder represented relationships developed after the Meggerses were married and living in Washington.[7] Slowly the bulk of the cards saved came to represent more and more the new relationships the family had made since the move from Wisconsin. The kinwork that Edith engaged in so carefully was gradually being devoted to families not connected through traditional kinship structures, but through business relations and suburban life.

The social trajectory mapped out by the Meggerses' Christmas cards was not atypical of the white, professional, managerial class during the second quarter of the twentieth century. W. Lloyd Warner's study of corporate executives, completed in 1952, showed that "at the high managerial levels . . . recruitment of business leaders from the bottom is taking place now and seems to be increasing." In addition, the rate of geographical mobility was high. Only 40 percent of the executives Warner interviewed remained in the same state in which they had been born, and many of those who stayed in-state had moved from their place of birth to a larger community. According to Warner, the "major force in their territorial mobility [was] the need to move to larger cities to conduct a business career."[8]

Even families that remained in the same city found their social networks becoming national in scope and increasingly shaped by business relations. The Christmas cards that the family of Benjamin Platt Forbes received between 1938 and 1949 were carefully saved and pasted into large scrapbooks, one for each year. Forbes was a successful candy manufacturer living in Cleveland. He had trained as an engineer and designed several machines for the efficient production of chocolate candies. In 1920 he was living in St. Joseph, Missouri, when he mailed a valentine to his mother, Mary Jane. Mary Jane Forbes seems to have been quite interested in greeting cards, as she carefully saved a collection that had been given to her by an elderly woman who lived nearby. The neighbor, Mrs. J. Reid, had saved a few valentines and Christmas cards from 1858 through the 1930s, some of which had been sent to her by her husband, a coal peddler. This collection may have sparked the Forbes family's interest in saving the evidence of its kinwork. After Ben moved back to Cleveland, he married a woman named Edith and established his successful candy-manufacturing business. Just as the Meggerses had, the Forbeses used Christmas cards to document their extensive interlocking network of family and business friends, a network that reached across the nation. Cards were sent to them from California, Connecticut, Florida, Georgia, Indiana, Maine, Massachusetts, Michigan, New Jersey, North Carolina, North Dakota, Pennsylvania, Texas, and Washington, D.C., as well as from Cleveland and other towns in Ohio. While the vast majority of their cards came from addresses in major cities, some were mailed from small towns.[9]

The Forbeses clearly took great pride in the large number of cards they received. In addition to the scrapbooks, they kept lists of cards received each year. For 1938, their list includes 107 names. By 1949, the growth of their network was documented by a scrapbook that held 191 cards. Discrepancies between the lists and the scrapbooks are quite suggestive. During 1943, the Forbeses sent 125 cards and registered receiving 110. But their scrapbook for that year contains 131 cards. What is the basis for the difference? Although the list did not remain exactly the same from year to year, it may have represented those from whom cards came more or less regularly, those for whom there was a felt need to send cards back the following year. Not every person who sent the Forbeses a card was placed on the list. In each year's scrapbook, the cards are pasted onto the pages in alphabetical order by the sender's last name. In the back of the scrapbook, pasted in behind all the cards sent by persons, can be found those cards sent by companies and associations. For 1943, this included such firms and organizations as the R. J. Prentice Company, the YMCA, and the Distribution Terminal Warehouse Company. Some of these firms are also on the list of cards received for 1943. The YMCA, the Women's Association, and the Distribution Terminal Warehouse make the list. The R. J. Prentice Company does not. While the scrapbook does register a distinction between persons and organizations, spatially separating the two categories, the presence of some firms and organizations on the list demonstrates the profound intertwining of business relations and kinship among the professional–managerial class through the exchange of

Christmas cards. For the Forbes family, the social network maintained through Christmas card exchange included business firms and community organizations as well as families.

The illustrations on the cards the Forbeses received reflect the visual imagery of the happy family they were presumed to represent. They display the basic design motifs that dominated the industry during the middle of the century. The most common images are of the single-family home. During 1939, a year when they received ninety-four cards, ten featured a close-up image of the front door and five showed the classic motif of the snow-covered roof set behind trees. Eight cards featured candles; seven showed the Three Kings; five displayed churches. Secular images outnumbered religious motifs seventy-three to twenty-one. While some of these cards were made to order, with photographs of the senders on the front and names printed inside, none went beyond the commonly accepted and commercially defined boundaries of the genre. Each of these cards served its function by gesturing almost indirectly at the season while illustrating the fragile longing for social connection.

The social units that relied on greeting cards as tools to forge networks amid the tensions of modern business in the middle third of the twentieth century did not always take the stereotypical heteronormative form of the reproductive conjugal family. Helen Sioussat was born in 1902 in Baltimore, where she lived until attending Goucher College. She left school early and began a series of short-term jobs that ranged from being the secretary to the dean of Goucher College, to traveling as a member of a Spanish adagio dance team, to working as a sales representative for Hall Brothers Greeting Card Company in Kansas City, Missouri. Little is known about her experience in these jobs, however intriguing they may have been. She married twice and divorced twice in this early period, but she remained single and childless throughout the remainder of her life. After she moved back to the East Coast in 1935 and began her long career in broadcasting, her life became better documented. By 1936, she was assistant director of the Talks and Public Affairs Department for CBS Radio, working directly under Edward R. Murrow. The following year, Murrow became the chief of CBS's foreign correspondents, and Sioussat was made the department's director.

Until her retirement in 1962, Sioussat produced and directed news shows, talk shows, and public-affairs programming for both CBS Radio and Television. Her papers are held at the archives of the National Association of Broadcasters. When I spoke with the archivists there, they expressed frustration that this centrally positioned producer of so many important radio and television broadcasts had chosen to keep so little evidence of her professional life. By far, the bulk of the collection is made up of the greeting cards she received.[10]

Sioussat's greeting cards, however, do document her professional life. As a producer of public-affairs broadcasting, she had to situate herself near the center of multiple overlapping social and informational networks. Her use of greeting cards demonstrates the blurring of lines between personal and business life in the professional–managerial class. Her cards were not simply tools for kinwork, nor were they the functional equivalents of business cards. She used her cards to initiate personal contacts among business associates, to maintain important political and business connections, and to advance both her career and her personal social standing. If she had not previously understood the professional benefits that devolved from greeting card exchange, she probably obtained a crash course while working for Hall Brothers. She grasped the principles of using cards to objectify and thereby solidify extended social networks. These principles had been elaborated in a booklet published by the Greeting Card Association in 1926, the year before Sioussat arrived in Kansas City. This publication detailed the "well-defined etiquette [that] govern[ed] the choice and the manner of sending such cards." Displaying the tropes common to all etiquette books, the booklet flattered its readers by presuming that they were familiar with "that important world of social life where move men and women of culture." These were the people for whom "the invention and perfecting of Greeting Cards [had] simplified life." According to this organization of greeting card manufacturers, these cards had become a necessity for ambitious members of the middle class because "convenience and beauty alike commend them to busy and yet friendly folk."[11]

Helen Sioussat was clearly both busy and friendly. To an undated Christmas card sent by Hope and Johnnie Hanes was added this handwritten message: "Dear Helen: I haven't forgotten how kind you were to remember me with red roses (my favorite!) when I was laid up this fall. The busiest people for some reason are always the most thoughtful." In 1941, Frances Basse urged the busy Sioussat not to worry about her as she already had "so much to handle." In addition to this correspondence with her friends, Sioussat sent greeting cards to many of the public figures she had met through her job. Occasionally they responded. Among the cards in her collection is an engraved card, postmarked January 3, 1948, that reads: "Mr. Herbert Hoover reciprocates your friendly greetings and wishes you a happy and prosperous New Year." Sometimes this initial exchange would develop into a lasting relationship. A correspondence begun in 1956 with Pat and Richard Nixon lasted for decades. During the late 1960s, even Rose Mary Woods (President Nixon's secretary) sent cards. Sioussat regularly exchanged Christmas cards with the ambassadors of Sweden, Denmark, Finland, Belgium, and the Netherlands. J. Edgar Hoover sent her cards from 1939 into the 1970s, always engraved, never with anything extra written on them. Half a dozen cards, each sent in a different year, carried the same engraved message: "Mr. and Mrs. David Sarnoff send Season's Greetings and Best Wishes for the New Year." Formal engraved cards like these continued to demonstrate the roots of the Christmas card ritual in older forms of visiting card exchange, and they typically came from powerful politicians and top executives. These cards were objects, not messages; they were used to recognize a formal social relation, not communicate an intimate connection. Cards with handwritten messages came more often from people less highly placed, but not necessarily from close friends. Often these notes conveyed gratitude for a past favor. Val and Irwin Perera wrote: "Merry Christmas and Happy New Year Helen Darling and thank you again for your kindness to me." Ed Fanscher expressed "Many thanks for your kind remembrance and for the many kind things you have done for me." In 1950 Paul Willis took the time to "say that I value and enjoy your friendship, and appreciate greatly the opportunities you make available to me from time to time." In his 1945 Christmas card, Dick promised to take her up on "the CBS invitation" when he got home the following year.[12] The Christmas cards received by Helen Sioussat represent the social networks to which she belonged, networks of mutual social recognition that encompassed family, friends, and, most significantly, business acquaintances and political contacts developed through her work in public-affairs broadcasting. She used these cards to confirm the substance of her connections. The objectifying qualities of the cards worked to solidify the otherwise ephemeral relationships produced in a society structured by the flows of modern business.

These structural demands were not limited in their effects to socially ambitious radio producers. Florence Luscomb was born in 1887 and was among the first women to graduate from the Massachusetts Institute of Technology with a degree in architecture. She traveled across the country to speak publicly in favor of woman's suffrage as a relatively young woman, and continued to advocate for liberal causes throughout her long life. Eschewing the powerful professional career that her training as an architect had made possible, Luscomb worked for the Women's International League for Peace and Freedom, the American Civil Liberties Union, and a variety of other labor, civil rights, and anti-imperialist movements almost up to the day of her death in 1980. Her papers, archived at the Schlesinger Library at the Radcliffe Institute, contain birthday cards, Easter cards, and Christmas cards that mark out her extensive social networks. Although the names of the senders are different, the cards that Luscomb received served also to solidify relationships forged in the fires of temporary alliance. Cards from W. E. B. Du Bois and Shirley Graham mingle with cards sent by young leftists who, during the 1960s, had taken inspiration from her extended career of committed activism. Longtime friends, such as Zara DuPont, searched for birthday cards with dogs on the front to send to Luscomb. One card, produced by Rust Craft in the 1950s, seemed designed especially for these social circles. The front pictures a dog holding a gavel, and the slogan says: "It won't take a Senate Investigation to find out who sent this birthday card." Inside, the same word, "Senate," printed in red, creates the pun: "I'm the one who 'Senate' and I'm damglad I did!"[13] Even as the card trivialized the Senate hearings run by Joseph McCarthy, it provided a humorous node of connection for some who quite probably felt excluded from much of mass culture. The abstracting forces that were produced by modern business and that were shaping social life did not respect political differences. Identification and displacement were necessary processes in the articulation of mass sentiment regardless of the level of education or political ideology.

These and similar collections cannot, of course, record the omissions: the cards that were not received, representing the social overtures that were not reciprocated and the scars of amputated social connections. But we can imagine that, within the empty spaces that surround even the cards pasted into the capacious Forbes family scrapbooks, one could feel the refusals and the social slights, imagined and intended, that marked the torn limits of these fragile networks. While sociologists such as Warner could celebrate the "needs of a fluid and flexible society" in which "fixed status is no longer adaptive" and "there is greater freedom for the individual and his family to move unfettered and thus be available for use in a changing world,"[14] the changing names on Christmas card lists testify to friendships lost, connections broken, lacelike networks rewoven in the shape of each year's understanding of one's social place.

Handwriting the Real Message

As the extensive Christmas card lists of the Forbes family and the more formal qualities of the Christmas cards received by Helen Sioussat indicate, Christmas card exchange took place among the most extensive and publicly symbolic social networks of which a family could claim to be a part. Other holiday cards—Easter, St. Patrick's Day, Halloween, and the like—were purchased and sent by much smaller numbers, but served very much the same social function. Birthday cards and, of course, valentines marked out a different relation; less formal, these cards typically were sent to a smaller group more closely knotted into the social lace. While the printed message often would suffice for many senders regardless of the occasion, from the earliest years of the modern greeting card industry, some card users would add their own brief notes. Before the post card craze, the Christmas cards produced by publishers such as Louis Prang were treated like gift cards. Signatures were an infrequent addition. Although the earliest valentines, as likely as not, were handwritten, copied from a quickly perused valentine writer, rarely were any lines added by the sender to a printed sentiment. The practice of adding one's own message to the printed card grew out of the merger of post cards and gift cards. Gertrude Maurer saved the holiday post cards she had received while attending the Ohio State School for the Deaf in the late 1910s. While most of the cards did carry handwritten messages, these notes rarely contained more than a brief holiday greeting and a promise to write more at a later time. This was the typical practice; post card messages tended to be brief and to follow rather narrow conventions.[15]

Early on, the producers of modern greeting cards understood the problem of the mass production of personal sentiments. While they promoted their products as a convenience, they were equally eager to proclaim their cards' personal qualities. As publishers of brief and illustrated verse that was meant to provide expressions of feeling and social connection, greeting card manufacturers felt vulnerable to the charge that they were standardizing and, therefore, depersonalizing what should be highly individual and personal communicative processes. Fighting off such accusations, manufacturers such as A. M. Davis and Paul Volland emphasized the personal nature of their cards. Norcross urged its customers to purchase the card that reflects "your personality—your own kind of Christmas card!" For these and other early greeting card producers, however, the turn to a more personal greeting card verse resulted in precisely the abstract and condensed language that came to characterize the common sentiment. Joyce Hall acknowledged that one of the functions of greeting cards was to give a voice to those who "tend to disguise their feelings." In fact, expressions of sentiment produced within a culture structured by large-scale business organizations simply could not be individual, for they ultimately had to be fungible. A sentiment that was unique and too personalized effectively limited the market for the card. The greater the eloquence of expression, the less transferable the sentiment's status. Gradually, the major greeting card producers recognized that they could not provide the quality of individuation that would answer these criticisms, but they could produce a product that acknowledged the need for and conveniently enabled individuation.[16]

During World War II, Norcross initiated a line called Service Notes. These cards were designed to send "To My Boyfriend [or husband, son, friend] in the Service." In addition to a printed sentiment typically illustrated by a picture of a long-legged lass sitting on a fence or a mailbox, these cards included a slip of rolled-up paper on which, it was assumed, the sender could write precisely those messages that no card manufacturer could authentically compose. By the mid-1950s, with the spread of offset printing, the major card manufacturers made certain that they were leaving sufficient blank space on the cards for senders to add their own words. Throughout the second half of the twentieth century, writing an additional note on the card was a normal—indeed, expected—practice. In light of this, it might be tempting to theorize a significant distinction between the words printed on the card by the manufacturer and those added by hand by the sender. Such a distinction was, in fact, one of my initial operating assumptions when I began this project. At first I believed that the handwritten message, individually composed and personally inscribed, was the mark of authenticity, the sign of the bricoleur transforming the mass-produced artifact into a true lover's discourse. The abstract displaced and condensed language of greeting cards would necessarily produce the individuating punctum of the sender's own words. Thus the sender of the card would reclaim the authorship of the expression and establish the point from which individuality and real emotional connection would triumph over trite artificiality and predigested sentiment. Indeed, examples of the clever transformation of the printed message abound. Mary Davis rewrote the final stanza of a Norcross birthday that card she sent to Florence Luscomb. The original said,

> People who make noise (not love)
> Should certainly be banned
> But folks as NICE AS YOU ARE
> Will ALWAYS be in demand.

Davis crossed out "But folks as nice as you are" and replaced it with "But Luscomb liberated," and beneath the final line added "Yea, Florence is the *PERSON* who's ALWAYS in demand!"[17]

But as even this example demonstrates, there is not a significant generic distinction between the language printed on the card and the language added by the sender. Emotional language, like all other language, is composed of generic conventions and shared tropes. I have been arguing throughout this book that the verbal and visual emotional language found on modern greeting cards is an effect of transformations in the economic structure of modern societies, most especially in the United States. I have argued that the abstract condensed and displaced language of mass feeling is actually necessary for the expression of modern sentiment in a culture structured by large-scale business organizations. Here I want to reinforce that assertion by turning to the language used by the senders of used cards as they worked to individuate their expressions.

The Popular Culture Library at Bowling Green State University in Ohio has one of the largest collections of used greeting cards in the United States. The Collection of Greeting Cards contains thousands of used cards that had been sent to commemorate birthdays, holidays, births, and deaths as well as cards with get-well wishes and welcome-home cheers. Ripped from their envelopes, stripped of postmarks, and thrown into boxes according to the holidays and events they represent, these cards provide little evidence of extensive social connection. It is nearly impossible to trace the continuities and disruptions among the networks constructed by social trajectories. But inscribed onto thousands of these cards retrieved from the emotional trash heaps of the past are the marks of individuation, the handwritten expressions of emotional eloquence, and the longing for social connection written by the senders themselves. Nothing conclusive about broad patterns can be claimed from a brief and uncontrolled survey of this material, but some suggestive observations can be recorded.

What did these senders write on their cards before mailing them and requiring them to speak? What were the most common forms of inscription that joined the printed message? Names, of course, were primary. Signatures of the sender were necessary on cards in which the names were not printed, though they were quite rare if the senders' names already appeared. Signatures were often accompanied by common closings, such as "Love always" and "Much love." Generic categories like "Happy Birthday Brother" were often individuated with proper names. But sometimes the specification in itself remained generic, such as when LaVerne Miller addressed her valentine to "Dear Friends." Brief notes modified the printed text on occasion. Dick and Pauline added to their birthday card "Wishing you many more 'Happy Birthdays,'" before they sent it to their brother, Lee. Bob wrote, "The Happiest Birthday to you, Mom!" and then added, in parentheses, "Are you a hundred years old, Mom?" He also added a joke about his mother's work load, promising to grant her a birthday wish of only one floor to scrub each day for the rest of her life.

Among the longest notes on any of the cards I found was Pauline's brief message on the back of her card to Lee that described a group dinner at a Ponderosa steak house and a bus trip to Dearborn, Michigan, in 160 words. Longer notes like that most often told news of illnesses or trips; they spoke of the weather and about children. Most were much shorter, adding simply a quick yet sincere restatement of birthday wishes or Christmas greetings or valentine promises. Norman added to the "Love Note" that Hallmark had made for him, "You are my love forever more." Coleen and Dany'ale sent their love and promised to write soon. Some users made a clear break between their own intentions and the message on the card. Eva made sure that Fred knew, "This isn't the kind of card I'd planned to send, but no time to go for the right one." But she went on to mention that she had seen him in church and that she would pray for him to have a better year this year. "Anyway—we hope you'll have a Good Day, Sept. 6th," she concluded. When Marie sent a sympathy card to another Marie, she wrote in her own hand on the page facing the printed message a different yet still common example of sympathy verse:

> We would not wish them back again
> Amid this world of care,
> For God in love has called them home,
> And we shall meet them there.
> Love, Marie

I found one used Service Note in the Collection of Greeting Cards. Written on the extra slip of paper was only "I hope that your opening will earn you a million bucks! I do love you." Examples could be multiplied, but the point is that the language added by their senders to the greeting cards in the collection very rarely differed from the abstract and condensed language that typified greeting card discourse. Individuation was achieved by the adding of names and dates and by the repeating of common greeting card phrases in the handwriting of the sender, not by varying the conventions or escaping the generic limits of greeting card language. In fact, the most common mark added by the senders (apart from the signature) was the underlining of certain words in the printed message. Bob gave a double underlining to the words "Happy Birthday" and "wonderful" on the card that he sent to his mother. Leslie and Mary underlined "He is always near" on Frederick's birthday card. Sandy and Ron emphasized "For so many nice things you do" on the valentine to their parents. Ed and Mary underlined every word of the get-well card they sent to Marcella.[18]

This is not simply a regional effect, found only among card users in Ohio. Although most of Helen Sioussat's cards have little extra writing on them, and the writing that appears on the cards from business acquaintances usually remarks on favors done or owed, the cards sent to and from family members display several of the marks common to the cards in the Collection of Greeting Cards. Helen sent many cards to her longtime companion, Aunt Bertha, her father's sister. She called Bertha "Boney-Bye" and added that nickname to the salutation on every card sent. Near the bottom of one Hallmark birthday card that Helen gave to Bertha in 1949, she had underlined the word "really" three times. On another, she underlined the word "many" three times. A valentine from 1950 has "dearest" and "bestest" underlined. The words added to a birthday card sent to her by her father and stepmother copies the form as well as the content of greeting card verse:

> I t'ink dat poetry ain't hot stuff
> Said Hatt to me in voice gruff.
> I t'ink it punk, it makes me groan;
> And so I t'ink I write my own.
>
> So, on your natal day I send
> A little token dear.

And upon your precious lips I'd press
A kiss for every year.[19]

Reading Between the Lines

While some card users took delight in demonstrating their mastery of
the forms of greeting card verse, others never appended any words beyond a generic closing and their signature. Jack and Edith, along with
their children, Irene and Richard, saved most of the birthday cards
they had sent to one another for fifteen years.[20] I do not know where
Jack, Edith, Irene, and Richard lived or how old any of them were. I
know only what is on the cards. Their best wishes and expressions of
familial love followed a very narrow set of conventions. Between 1943
and 1957, the cards they sent to one another evoked the placid and stable world of the well-organized, affectionate family. They never added
anything to the cards beyond a closing "Love" and their first names.
The Volland birthday card that Jack sent his wife, Edith, in 1943 says:

> It's the thoughts we share together
> That have brought us closer, Dear—
> It's the happiness you've given
> In a hundred ways all year;
> It's the love and understanding
> that we've known together, too,
> that bring this wish for happiness
> Right from my heart to You!

The front displays a lace umbrella with flowers drooping out from the
top. The Rust Craft card he sent in 1944 says:

> There's a place in my heart
> that no other can hold,
> For I'm keeping it always for you,
> And it's there that I treasure
> the things that you say,
> Your smiles, and the things that you do;

And I'm wishing you blessings
that will gladden your life
In the sweetest and truest of ways,
for it's always just you,
the Queen of My Heart,
Who brighten and cheer all my days.

Its front shows a queen's crown, surrounded by roses. For 1946, Jack again chose a Rust Craft card. This one features a cameo necklace surrounded by flowers. Inside it says:

To all the loving thoughts of you
I have each day all year.
I'm adding special wishes
Because your Birthday's here:
There's a special wish for gladness,
And a wish for new joys too,
In the loving "Happy Birthday"
I'm wishing, Dear, for you.

It did not seem to bother Jack that Norcross could produce different cards only a few years apart that relied on the crucial rhyme of "phrase . . . always." He gave Edith one in 1945:

All my love and my best wishes, too
Are in this little phrase
"A happy birthday dear," to you
And the best in life always

And another one in 1952:

No warmer wish was ever meant
No warmer love was ever sent
Than you will find within this phrase
That's just for you—to have always
Happy Birthday, Darling.

These cards seem to explain why Jack never added to the cards he sent to Edith. Perhaps Jack always wanted Edith to focus precisely on the phrase, not to wonder at all about the world outside the card, but simply to accept the birthday wish for what it was.

The Norcross birthday card that Edith sent to Jack in 1948 pictures a book surrounded by flowers. Its perfectly constructed sentiment reads:

> It's hard to find the words to show
> How much I love you, dear
> And how much I wish you happiness
> On all days of the year—
> But if you'll read between these lines
> You'll know in some small part
> The love and all the wishes
> For you, within my heart.

This masterpiece of greeting card verse instructs the reader to look past the printed words and between the lines to know the love that is in the sender's heart. Edith had the good sense not to try to improve on or individuate this message, but to allow Jack to fill in the gaps with his own image of her longing.

The children, Irene and Richard, followed the same strategies. The Volland card that Richard gave his mother for her birthday in 1949 playfully asks, while Mother whizzes by the door carrying her own birthday cake:

> What's going on behind your back?
> Well, Mother, this is it—
> A loving wish that your BIG DAY
> Turns out to be a HIT!

According to the card, Richard is not doing anything behind her back except for wishing for her birthday to be successful and happy.

The Gibson card that Irene sent her mother in 1951 taunts her:

> And you couldn't guess how much birthday love
> This greeting brings to you!

During these fifteen years, Jack, Edith, Irene, and Richard sent dozens of birthday cards to one another. They sent Father's Day and Mother's Day cards, too. None of these cards ever tried to perform more than this odd reflexive gesture back to the card itself. Even when asked to read between the lines, the receiver is instructed to look closely at the card, not directly at the sender's heart. The card is the objectification of the phrase; the phrase is the excuse to send the card; the phrase can never convey its full message; the card serves to cover as it enunciates the feelings it evokes. Perhaps this was what it meant to be a well-organized, affectionate family, the secure monadic center of satisfaction achieved through companionate consumption.

While the Meggerses chose not to save any valentines they may have received, Mrs. William Barker, Jr., retained those her husband gave her every year.[21] Like Jack in his missives to Edith, William did not add to the sentiments printed on the cards. For almost fifty years, from 1902 to 1951, William sent a valentine each year to his "Mrs." The Barkers lived in Troy, New York. Or at least Mrs. Barker did. Postmarks and scattered remarks on the few envelopes and post cards that remain show that some of the cards were mailed from other towns in New York; Denver, Colorado; and Fort Sill, Oklahoma. Perhaps some routine annual event kept the two apart every Valentine's Day. But it is equally likely that no such regular distancing produced the card use. The earliest valentines sent to Mrs. Barker convey the historical memory of Esther Howland's valentines as it was reproduced using the flatness of modern printing methods. The 1902 valentine shows Cupid bursting out of a lace-covered heart. Inside, the verse reads:

> Remember me! That single phrase speaks more than
> words can tell,
> More of affection's wealth conveys, when hearts
> responsive swell,
> Than breathes in passion's wildest tone or e'en the
> heartfelt sigh.
> I ask but this when thou art gone: Remember me!

Yet for all the concern evoked by the card for the memory of the sender, the card is not signed. The following year, the valentine carries no sentimental eloquence, only the short phrase "Cupid's Message" above an image of Cupid and Diana. No signature graces this card, either. The card from 1906 was mailed from Watervliet, New York, again showing no writing at all. The first hint we have that the cards may actually have been sent by William Barker appears on the two cards sent in 1907. For that year, Will (as he signed the back of one of the cards) sent two cards, clearly a matched pair. One shows a young boy above this absurdly unsentimental didactic message:

> Good morrow to you Valentine;
> Wear your hair as I do mine,
> Curled in front and straight behind,
> Good morrow to you, Valentine.

The second card shows a young girl in a very similar pose, saying:

> Good morrow to you Valentine;
> Add your sums as I do mine.
> Three & three & three are nine.
> Good morrow to you Valentine.

On the back of the card showing the boy is a handwritten message: "You can chose which one you want Will Feb 14—1907." Why would Will offer a choice between two such unromantic valentines?

I know nothing about the romantic or family life of the Barkers apart from what can be discerned from this collection. I do not know where either was born, when they were married, whether they had children, and which one died first. The only evidence of their relationship is the forty-six cards that survive in the archive (there are two undated cards, cards from seven years are missing, and two cards were sent in 1907). I do not really know why these cards were purchased and sent. While it might seem that the Barkers maintained a sentimental, loving relationship over the years, the validity of this guess is weakened (although not eliminated) by the absence of any personalizing message. These cards stand alone. Whatever work I might want them to do, they must do by themselves. What do they tell us?

As already discussed, apart from the first card, the earliest valentines carry little overt sentimentality. Some of the valentines seem more appropriate for children; others are so general that they could have been sent by anyone. The card from 1908 may not even be a valentine at all; its image shows a young woman at a writing desk, and the words simply say: "My thoughts are of thee." The card is transformed into a valentine only by the date that Will wrote on the back: "Feb. 14—1908." By the mid-1910s, however, the valentines that Will was sending had become, if not more personal, at least a degree more specific. By this point, the industry was offering greater choices, and Will's valentine selection skills seem to have improved. For 1914, Will sent a Berdan card that jokes: "To the nicest girl in the world from one who likes to be next to the nicest." A Whitney post card sent in 1916 acknowledges its commercial origins through its claim that it brings "a Love as strong and true as e'er was found in Cupid's mart." By 1921, Will had developed a taste for the cards that offered simple images of hoop-skirted and bonneted women along with verses addressed "To My Wife." The cards from both 1920 and 1921 rhyme "blue" with "you" and make reference to roses and the sun. The Rust Craft card from the latter year includes printed underlining that emphasizes the last line of the verse: "Somebody cares for you." Although Will could count on the regular availability of "to my wife" cards, the A. M. Davis card he sent in 1926 proposes "Love's Questionnaire." Inside the card are questions that Will could not seriously have meant to ask of the woman to whom he had been sending valentines for more than twenty years:

> Can you make a pan of biscuits?
> Can you tidy up a room?
> Have you ever seen a dishcloth?
> Are you handy with a broom?

Although the questions seem more appropriate for an interview for a maid, Will sent this to his Mrs. with no comment. In 1929, he chose a card with masked revelers on the front that speaks inside of a secret love:

> I've been a bit too bashful
> To make my wishes known
> May this Valentine tell you
> I want you for my own.

The bulk of the valentines that Will bought throughout the 1930s feature anachronistic images of aristocratic couples and rely on the strategy of time displacement to enable the increasingly sentimental verses inside. One explicitly foregrounds nostalgia by printing an image of "Godey's Fashions—1853" on the front. Curiously, the verse inside makes no reference at all to this illustration. Occasionally, one valentine or another seems to capture the inarticulate nature of the love that Will wanted to express. Rust Craft's 1943 card spells out Will's mute directness:

> You know I always shy away from sentimental stuff,
> Those flowery phrases always seem to me, just so much bluff!
> And that's the reason why I chose this special Valentine,
> Because it says what's in my heart in just a single line:
> I LOVE YOU DEAR!

While it might seem that Will was a complete dope about valentines, sending as many misguided missives as he did well-aimed ones, the strength of that interpretation is undercut simply by the fact that these cheap, disposable cards were saved by his wife for almost fifty years. Clearly, the manifest content of these cards—their specific images and words—were not their only important aspect. The last three cards in the collection were produced by Hall Brothers. All are addressed to "My Wife." The card sent in 1949 hides the faces of the married couple behind a fan, while the verse inside shies away from specifying the quality of the relationship. The following year's card repeats the formula that "it's asking far too much of any Valentine / to half express the love for you within this heart of mine." The final card in the collection blankly applauds:

Someone beside me
Who's always true blue,
Someone to plan for
In all that I do,
Someone to count on
Each day of my life—
This brings all my love
To my wonderful Wife!

Perhaps here, in this card selected after fifty years of practice, William Barker managed to purchase just the right sentiment. For fifty years, Will sent his wife valentines, never adding a word except once, and signing them only rarely, so that he seldom even authenticated the borrowed feelings expressed in the cards as his own. But the sentiment on this last card clearly articulates the blankness of Will's image of his Mrs. She is someone, indeed; beside him every day of his life, she is dependable, included in his plans. Perhaps this steady dependability is precisely what Will cherished most about his marriage. Perhaps it was exactly this regular consistency that inspired him throughout fifty years of marriage to send cards that convey the mute significance of their relationship, not through any emotional eloquence or specific description of their love, not even through any consistent representation of his wife or himself, but only through their sheer material objective existence—the "This" in the final card's final stanza. Perhaps this was the most radical love that one could find in a society structured by business. Pictured through these utopian figures of stability—forty-six valentines sent from one person to another—this marriage stood in stark contrast to the clever, fungible quality of most relationships, regardless of whether this dumb solidity existed anywhere beyond the plane of greeting cards.

What, Then, Do Cards Do?

Greeting cards are not simply the drab results of the commodification of desire, the transformation of love and social connection from an intimate personal relationship to an object of exchange. In their delightful ambiguity, greeting cards enact the perverse objectivity of social longing in a culture structured by large-scale business. This is what the people who used them knew: they knew that their friends and family members expected to receive cards from them; they knew that they could know who their friends were by the cards they received; they knew that not everyone would remain their friends forever, and that at some time, one or another of their old friends would no longer receive cards from them. Greeting cards did not become such a crucial social tool because of the mendacious calculation of the costs and benefits of a particular social connection or because of the hegemonic imposition of a false need. They were an organic hybrid bred from the conflicting demands of the social and the economic, nurtured in a hydroponic environment in which the traditional forms of kinship and stable status were absent, but flourishing in the hothouse atmosphere of a status competition fired by the erratic flares of large-scale business.

The virtuoso of card use was one like Edith, who could find just the right card for Jack, the card that would engage his own longing in the assemblage of desire, so that Jack could, through the projection of that longing, insert himself between the lines of the card and then find himself there, recognized. When that happened, no extra words were necessary. The card had done its work—and, significantly, had not done it too well. There was always the chance that Jack would not read between the lines. There was a chance that Jack would want more than the card could give, and whenever this was true, then Jack, any Jack, would be wanting more than Edith, any Edith, could give. For the card is only the mute bearer of a silent message. Even for the virtuoso of card use, the greeting card did not need to speak precisely. For Edith Forbes, the Christmas card was a means to inclusion on a list; the list was a means to remembering those who had to be sent cards; the circulation of cards mimicked the flow of social forces; the shifts in these flows changed the shape of the cards' circuits. Whether the card showed the red rooftop of an imaginary home, the parking lot of a business, or a candle, sleigh, or star, it said little, but simply embodied the objective need for connection. The perfect card was one that allowed the receiver to see past it; in this way, all greeting cards are blank cards, empty tokens of fungible affection. In the end, the greeting card does not speak; indeed, it insists on the absolute impossibility of speaking. It stands there, on the mantel or desktop; perhaps is pinned to the Christmas tree; or else hides in the nightstand drawer, keeping itself pure for a special one's eyes only. Either way, it says nothing. It only is, and in that state of being, it is the ephemeral token of an even more temporary event, a felt connection between people in a society structured by business.

Beyond the End of the Modern Era of Greeting Cards

*A*t the beginning of the twenty-first century, with electronic cards filling our e-mail in-boxes and Hallmark branching into cable television, the era of the modern greeting card is largely over. Which is not to say that people have ceased to use paper cards. Millions of them are still sent every day. Throughout the last quarter of the twentieth century, the annual growth of the "social-expression" industry was estimated at a modest but consistent 2 to 4 percent. But continued growth in revenue is deceptive. Even as new markets are being created, many of the old standbys fade away. In 1990, the *Wall Street Journal* celebrated the continuing success of the industry, saying: "The more society atomizes—the more divorces, the more latchkey kids, sky-diving grandmothers, and second careers—the more niches are created for greeting cards and greeting-card sales." A few years ago, a friend of mine received a card from her parents that directly addressed the growing complexity of postmodern life. A lesbian who had spent years working as a musician traveling with bands, my friend recently had settled down in the Boston area, developed a solid relationship with a solid girlfriend, and completed a professional degree at one of the area colleges. Her parents, who still lived in the midwestern metropolis in which she had grown up, expressed their joy at the new stability in her life by sending her a birthday card with a special "from-me-to-you" message. Absent any specific enunciating figure, the front colored with abstract pastel washes, the card said something like this:

Dear Daughter,
    I'm proud of the way you've grown up. I admit I still worry at times because the world has changed a lot since you were born.

Many of the choices you've had to make have been more difficult than those I faced when I was your age.

I haven't always agreed with your decisions but I hope you know that I respect your courage and independence in making them. You're doing all you can to be the person you want to be, and I admire that . . .

And remember—no matter what life brings, you will always be my daughter, and I will always love you. Happy birthday.

The card was signed, "Love, Mom & Dad," and a touching postscript was added: "please read all I's as We."[1]

This card does not use the strategies that I have identified as the keys to emotional eloquence in modern business culture. It does not posit an idealized world of feeling separate from the messiness of lived experience. The sentiment is not spoken out of the mouth of either an economically and socially disempowered figure or a displaced and idealized body. Its language is not the abstract, tightly condensed suggestion or the purposefully displaced announcement that the real feeling at the core of the message could never be articulated. Even though it never specifies the difficulties, the choices, the struggles that the daughter has lived through, the card seems extraordinarily precise in its depiction of reconciliation across generational change. This is an example of a "reconciliation" card using "universal specific" language, a type that Hallmark began to market at the beginning of the 1990s.[2] And the handwritten postscript—so perfectly inadequate to the task of demonstrating joint authorship, but so perfectly indicating the difficulty of two speaking as one—stands as clear evidence that the card was performing necessary work. There is no doubt that Mom bought, signed, and mailed the card. But the card's performance of real feeling should be thought of as coming from both of those whose names Mom wrote at the bottom of the card: Mom and Dad.

The conditions of greeting card production changed dramatically between the end of the 1950s and the beginning of the 1990s. The language of greeting cards changed as well, not in lockstep with the fundamental economic and social transformations, but in fluid response. This chapter will sketch the internal and external transformations of the greeting card industry that made it possible for cards like the one my friend received above to be produced and used. I cannot recount the larger story of the emotional history of the United States during the second half of the twentieth century. Instead, I will briefly contrast two styles of production: the fordist method, which was common to the top five greeting card companies at the end of World War II, and the postindustrial information management system, which organized production at Hallmark Cards by the mid-1980s. In juxtaposition to that story, I will also analyze two styles of cards that demarcate this period: the studio card, which originated in the 1950s, and the "from me-to-you" card, which came into mass production during the late 1980s and early 1990s. I hope that, read together, these stories of discursive and economic change will complete my argument about the imbrication of business culture and the soft language of greeting cards.

The Assembly Line of Feeling

In 1946, the Rust Craft Company celebrated forty years in the greeting card industry in part by publishing a pamphlet, *How Rust Craft Greeting Cards of Character Are Made*, and creating a photographic "Tour Through Rust Craft" (figure 6.1). Both items featured the company's thousand employees and twenty to twenty-five departments that contributed to the production of each card the company made. Part of a general public-relations trend that Roland Marchand has identified as "the good neighbor metaphor," these materials were obviously intended to give Rust Craft a common human face. None of the Rust family is shown. Instead, the ordinary working people—ranging from the illustrators and copywriters to the machine press operators, from the ladies applying glue and satin to the typists and file clerks—represent the company, making the point that those who work in the greeting card industry are just like those who buy the products.[3]

The photographic tour begins with a description of the statistical planning department: the place where "invaluable records . . . guide the planning and manufacturing departments." Across the industry, strict accounts were kept of which types of cards succeeded, and marketing

analyses of those successes broke the components of those cards into actuarial fragments. In this picture, one woman types while another rifles through file drawers. Three other employees work with pencil and paper at their neat desks. The next picture shows the stock control office. With its decisions guided by the statistical planning department and its records also maintained by pencil and paper, this office ensured that every retail outlet received the proper number of each season's cards in the right combination of styles. The general executive office employed twenty typists, all sitting at identical wooden desks. The billing and credit department was staffed by thirty-six more. Photographs of the editorial department, a separate "humorous" editorial department, and two branches of the art department fill out the picture of the creative side of the company. But the bulk of the photographs depict the repetitive mechanical processes of turning those creative ideas and painstakingly maintained records into millions of social-expression products.[4]

Twenty female employees in the dispatching department turned the artists' designs into reproducible copies. Eight more worked in the retouching department, ensuring that the reproductions had not lost any of the artists' technique. Only a few men and no women are shown in the offset-press department, as the space in the photograph is dominated by the gears, wheels, cylinders, and pistons of the large machines. Rust Craft owned three two-color presses. These machines could knock off about 4,500 impressions per hour; running full time, they were capable of printing the basic colors for the company's entire annual line. One of the offset-press operators appears to be African American; he is the only black person shown in any of the photographs. A troop of white male printers watches over the score of letterpress machines, while only one card-creasing machine is shown. The die-cutting machines, where the dies were shaped into the hearts and tops and dogs and flowers that would grace the fronts of the cards, were also staffed by men only. But once the machines were done with their noisy pressing of design and sentiment onto thin sheets of card, those sheets were inspected, cut into individual cards, folded, trimmed, glittered, ribboned, and boxed by hundreds of women working side by side in true fordist style. The caption describing one scene in the finishing department reads: "Cards move swiftly along an end-less belt as the ladies add first some glue, then cotton batting, sachet, and satin."[5]

Riding the rising tide of American economic growth and taking advantage of the efficiencies that mass production offered, the greeting card industry enjoyed two decades of expansion after World War II. In 1949, 3 billion greeting cards were sold in the United States. The marketing director for Rust Craft argued that each card shop in each small town across the country should be able to sell $1 worth of greeting cards per capita, with or without robust competition. In December 1956, the *New York Times* printed Rust Craft's suggestion that if a couple received fewer than twenty-seven Christmas cards, they "should seek a larger acquaintance." In February 1957, *Newsweek* named Rust Craft, Norcross, American Greetings, Gibson, and Hallmark as the five largest firms producing greeting cards in the United States. The magazine estimated that total sales for the industry topped 4 billion cards and $500 billion annually. The owner of Fifth Avenue Card Shop in New York boasted about the proliferation of card titles available, including those aimed directly at "great-grandmothers, brothers-in-law, and triplets." With this volume and variety of merchandise, detailed record keeping was essential. The trade magazine *Giftwares* emphasized the importance of taking regular, accurate inventories and entering into the "seasonal record book," the "seasonal work sheet," and the "everyday record book" the most significant details for each type of card: the title and subtitle (for example, "Mother" and "Our Mother"), number initially purchased, number sold, and price. Careful record keeping would enable each retail store to plan accurately for the growth in sales that the following year's social occasions would offer. But if this effort were too much for the store's personnel, each of the major greeting card firms offered special stock-control tickets that made reordering easier—as long as the store wanted another card of precisely that type from the same company. This system "eliminated nearly all the risk" from the business as it took "virtually every merchandising responsibility out of the buyers' and merchandisers' hands," as long as the "stock girl" remembered to send in the tickets at the right time. Throughout the late 1950s, those strategies worked.

Women's Wear Daily reported that greeting cards were the only division in the stationery industry experiencing regular growth, and this growth was phenomenal. For 1958, valentine sales increased 20 percent and Mother's Day sales increased 25 percent over the preceding year. In department stores across the country, greeting card sales rose at double the rate of the other departments. By 1959, Hallmark's sales alone were estimated at $80 million.[6]

Sparked by this growth and determined to maintain its reputation as the source for more sophisticated greeting cards, Norcross commissioned a series of trend reports in order to identify emerging themes, images, and issues that might affect the greeting card market. The report for June 1959 emphasized the impact of travel. Beginning with a claim that "over 30,000,000 people have moved each year since 1947," and reporting that "in the big corporations, men now expect to move every five years," the authors of the trend report suggested that Norcross use the image of the Gypsy in both design and sentiment, that the writers find a way to work the word "jet" into as many sentiments as possible, and that the artists use the image of the automobile to illustrate their cards. They also recommended the creation of a line of cards that could "poke fun at status-striving," which seemed to be on the rise. Considering the well-known fact that between 80 and 90 percent of all greeting cards were bought by women, the trend reports from 1958 and 1959 paid a surprising amount of attention to "things men like," as one of the reports put it. The report for April 1959 discussed foreign affairs, technology, economics, and leisure. It began with a brief description of the new showroom at IBM that compared the components of the new computers on display to flowers and jewels before cautioning its readers that these machines "may very well be the key to many of the troubles and the opportunities of our time." With the inflated yet vague language of public relations, the trend spotters worried that the combination of mobility, global political tensions, easily available consumer credit, and electronic computing added up to a potential "Super-Duper Revolution."[7]

This report, which seems to have described the coming of the postmodern world, went on to prescribe strategies that might enable Norcross greeting cards to "play an increasingly important role in our society." In a world where "more nations continue to threaten one another," where "science reaches out into space," and where technology continues to produce "greater marvels . . . with machines," human beings will feel greater "need to communicate with one another," the report claimed. "How *intuitively* and *sensitively* Norcross can express their anxieties, hopes, yearnings—the greater *service* Norcross will perform." The authors recommended putting beards on some of the men on the cards as a reflection of Fidel Castro's fame and "oriental eyes" on some of the women now that Hawaii was a state. But they also warned that the company had to pay attention to the obvious changes in distribution and production techniques that the new technologies and global conditions of business competition were sure to produce. Automation was the key, the report stated. Not only was automation important in "bookkeeping, production, shipping and distribution," but its significance would also affect the content and form of the cards themselves. Asserting that greeting cards were "a form of automation," the authors suggested that Norcross develop ways to increase the automatic qualities of its cards, perhaps by selling cards that included an extra tear-off sheet for the receiver's reply. One of the last of the surviving Norcross trend reports, issued in October 1959, predicted the coming dominance of "anti-sentimentality." This trend was already beginning to appear in greeting cards. But Norcross was not able to see that this creeping initial movement away from sentimentality among users of greeting cards was not simply a formal response to increasing automation, but marked the emergence of a new structure of feeling, brought into being by the rapid acceleration of the changes wrought by modern business. The era of the modern greeting card was peaking. As the economic forces that drove social change continued to increase in speed and complexity throughout the second half of the twentieth century, commercial tokens of affection would begin to show their effects.[8]

Studio Cards and the Turn to Irony

The Norcross trend report for October 1959 linked the emerging trend in "anti-sentimentality" to the "Upper Bohemian avant-garde trendsetters" in New York. Two years before this report, Bill Shane, vice president of Cincinnati-based Barker Greeting Cards, had acknowledged a growing taste for "sophistication" among greeting card buyers along the coasts, but he insisted that "cornball" remained the rule for "the Midwest and the South." In New York, a small company called the American Artists Group aimed at a more sophisticated market by loudly trumpeting that it had hired only "real artists" to design its Christmas cards from the moment of its inception in 1934. Hundreds of underemployed artists across the country had tried their hands at illustrating greeting cards for American Artists. While the president of the company, Samuel Golden, was quite proud of his company's innovations—he claimed credit (earned or not) for moving the Christmas card field away from a strict reliance on images of "the routine Santa Clauses, Doorways, Candles, etc. etc."—he also recognized the power of the inertial force of the mainstream card market. His correspondence with his artists reveals the tension between their desires to demonstrate their formal and cultural sophistication and the needs of established companies to service the still-dominant traditional card tastes. In one typical exchange from 1956, Golden insisted that he could not use the paintings submitted by one of his artists:

> I am very sorry to say that one of them—the one of the chorus girl—is absolutely out. It might be appropriate for a New Year's Eve ad, but I cannot imagine it being used for a Christmas card. I am returning the Madonna and Child to you because we have continuously been hounded by people who have taken exception to the representation of a "Madonna and Child" that looks more like a model for some cosmetics than the reverential thing religious people look for.[9]

Despite Golden's reasonable concerns about the limited range of designs that the traditional greeting card market could accept, many smaller companies were succeeding in selling what would soon be called studio cards. For the past several years, companies like Citation Cards, Fravessi-Lamont, and B-C Cynics Sanctum had been selling birthday cards illustrated with drawings of nearly naked "nature girls, " strategically covered by bits of fluff and glitter. William Box, working out of

Los Angeles, was drawing a raggedly dressed, sad-faced character who wondered morosely whether birthdays were always accompanied by parties.[10] Studio cards inherited the tart, earthy humor of the old comic or vinegar valentine, but they were not interested in policing the lower boundaries of the middle class. Instead, studio cards marked their antisentimental difference from the traditional lines of cards through the refusal of realistic forms of illustration and the addition of a heavy dose of irony in their sentiments. Indeed, the rise in popularity of studio cards represents a major shift in the discursive strategies available to greeting cards. While all greeting cards still had to enable both an identification with and a distancing from the sentiments enunciated on the cards, studio cards collapsed both processes into an ironic identification with the necessary failure of commercialized emotional expression. In the process, studio cards began to enunciate an emergent structure of feeling, one that would fit neatly, or as neatly as possible, with the social and economic transformations that we associate with postmodernity.

In 1957, American Greetings became the first of the major card companies to commit an entire production line, known as Hi Brow cards, to this style. The Hi Brow logo depicted a thin hand reaching straight up, the thumb and forefinger gripping a lorgnette in such a way that the hand looked almost like a martini glass. The implication that highbrow status derived from a combination of drink and learning was not serious. In fact, the logo and the name of the line itself parodied the pretensions of precisely those who felt they were above the use of greeting cards. Hi Brow cards were always jokes, and these jokes were often about the dream objects that signified class distinction. Commonly, the front of the card suggested an expensive gift: "How does a Jaguar sound?" or "How would you like a large check?" The inside would reveal a cheap pun: the jaguar sound would be a roar; the check would be a check mark. Hi Brow humor did not have to be sophisticated; the puns could be simple and silly. The attitude of the cards, their recognition of the impossibility of making good on the promise, effectively signaled their sophistication. The humor displayed in studio cards did not simply echo the feudal cynicism of Joseph P. McEvoy's *Slams of Life*. McEvoy's petulant insistence that he controlled the relationships with his maid, elevator man, and office boy through his ability to give or withhold presents would not have been possible without an assumption of the possibility of individual social agency, an agency capable of either maintaining or shifting the social positions of others. Studio card humor retained no such possibility. The emergent conditions of business were anchored in the systematic displacement of social agency and the accompanying decline of belief in autonomous individuality. The structure of feeling that engaged closely with these conditions recognized that the gift of a large check (one with plenty of zeros in its amount blank) would be made only under conditions in which it would make no effective social difference. A typical birthday card from 1967 read: "Because it's your Birthday, I've decided to give you my entire collection of famous artist prints." Inside the card were sets of fingerprints over names such as Picasso, Rembrandt, and Monet. The figure on the front of this card was a stylized caricature of an artist, with brushes in one hand and rolls of paper or canvas under an arm. In this card, the artist becomes both the author and the butt of the joke, as the card underlines the social functionality of art, its complicity with banal processes of individualization. When the promise of art is no different from the false promise of consumer capitalism, one might as well laugh.[11]

The identification that enabled these studio cards to be sendable, to represent something of the relationship between the sender and the receiver, was focused through the gap between what was promised on the front of the card and what was delivered inside. This was the "thing" of studio cards, the unrepresentable kernel of truth hidden in plain sight at the core of their humor. As they illustrated the impossibility of satisfaction, studio cards helped institutionalize the key emotional tone of the emergent structure of feeling: an ironic response to the failure of business culture to deliver emotional and material abundance even as the conditions of material production increased in speed and complexity. One successful studio card writer advised: "If you're going to write studio ideas, you have to assume, nitty-grittywise, that life is absurd. . . . It's all a game. . . . I'm telling you, sweet person, if this society of ours isn't a fountainhead of gag possibilities, I will personally, and without flinching, hand you my rubber duck for keepsies."[12]

Studio cards were not immediately accepted across the industry. In 1959, Henrietta Strong, founder of Brownie Cards, stated her firm belief that the "current rage" for studio cards would be "short-lived." "If you want to send a card to a friend, why send an insulting one?" she asked. "Cards with dignity and spiritual quality," she insisted, "will be an antidote for the 'beat' trend in greeting cards." But in 1968, H. Joseph Chadwick, a successful freelance card writer and the editor of *The Greeting Card Writer's Handbook*, claimed that while conventional cards remained the basic staple of the industry, studio cards had become a significant source of profits. By 1970, even staid Hallmark's studio line, Contemporary Cards, was generating 15 percent of its sales. Yet one Hallmark card seemed to announce the company's true stance on the trend. The figure on the front of this card sports the requisite beard, sandals, and striped sailor shirt that denominated beatnik fashion. But the sentiment earnestly disavows the tropes of the studio card. It loudly claims to contain no insults, no extreme language, and no far-out designing. Instead, it simply says Happy Birthday, "and means it!" Even in this card, the gap between promise—perhaps a promise of the ironic wit associated with beatnik figures of alienation— and the banalities of lived experience remains profound. One might as well be earnest.[13]

The Postmodern Context

Many works have been printed on the meaning of the postmodern condition, postmodernism, and postmodernity. Although much of this writing now seems of less significance than it might have at the time, I continue to find value in those discussions that foreground the set of material conditions that began to appear in dominance soon after the oil crisis of 1973 and the recession immediately following—the first major recession after World War II in the United States. At that point, what had been the strengths of fordist schemes of production and accumulation began to appear as weaknesses. First, the heavy investment in capital machinery and the resulting need to commit to large-scale production in advance of secure knowledge of market demand created rigidities in production that could not respond quickly enough to changing tastes

or material desires. As cheap energy disappeared, the costs of such production and marketing mismatches became unbearable. Second, im-
provements in communication and transportation technologies began to
exacerbate the "time-space compression" endemic to modernity. This
increased the global reach of capitalist endeavors, intensifying the competitive process and increasing the speed with which consumer tastes
changed both in response to product design and as a relatively independent motivator of new product innovation. The plasticity of international money markets increased both the sophistication and the volatility of financial institutions, resulting in an overheated competitive field of
banking, insurance, and investment firms, and increasing the fluidity of
capital. Finally, the apparent collapse of any grand narrative that could
challenge the dominance of market-based decision making focused cultural attention on the most immediate and marketlike forms of evaluating human interaction. The distinction between use value and exchange
value lost of much of its significance as symbolic products, in particular,
increasingly found their use in their exchange and their function in the
display of distinction.[14]

In response to these determinations, firms began to require and
generate new organizational forms and managerial skills. Whereas
fordist means of production and large corporate forms of organization
resulted in a specialized, educated, but mobile professional–managerial class that needed fungible expressions of emotional eloquence and
social connection, postfordist techniques of vertical disintegration,
flexible outsourcing, increased turnover speed, and global competition
for labor as well as goods have created an even more sensitive and less
secure managerial class. In his 1969 forecast of the transformation
from a goods economy to a knowledge economy, Peter F. Drucker
predicted the creation of an emergent business role he called "the new
entrepreneur." The role of this entrepreneur would not be that of an
autonomous individual, running his or her business mostly alone. Instead, this new role would take root in a large-scale business organization, and the new entrepreneur would have to learn how to innovate
within that structured environment. Following the theories of Joseph
Schumpeter, Drucker argued that innovation was the source of economic growth and, therefore, that large-scale business organizations

had to develop means to encourage the generation and effective implementation of new ideas. In effect, the focus on innovation shifted evaluations of the negative side of production away from considerations of cost to considerations of risk. The responsibility of the new entrepreneur was to calculate the risk of particular innovations and invent ways of realizing value from these innovations within an environment that had traditionally valued only the reproduction of its own familiar ways of doing things.[15]

Business practice did not quickly adapt to rationalizing entrepreneurship within the firm. A common introductory business textbook, in constant print and regularly updated from 1969 through 1986, describes the contradictions that the simultaneous desire for innovation and control produces in the business enterprise: "Some large corporations are now encouraging and rewarding . . . entrepreneurship within their company. They are giving employees more freedom and resources to pursue their own ideas. Though people in corporations often come up with new ideas, frequently those ideas never survive the many meetings required for analysis and final approval. . . . Control from the top, with much analysis and reporting, is deeply ingrained in many corporations." Drucker had described the existential anxiety that these young internal entrepreneurs would face as they took on the effective responsibilities of executives without the control to enforce those decisions: "The well-being of our entire society depends increasingly on the ability of these large numbers of knowledge workers to be effective in a true organization. . . . But the executive in organization is not informed by his environment. He has to decide for himself. If he does not decide, he cannot achieve results."[16]

The economic regime of flexible accumulation creates new economic niches as quickly as it destroys them. The most important skills in the postmodern middle class include, therefore, a high tolerance for risk and an ability to disassociate oneself from failure. Without such skills, newly downsized managers have found themselves unable to escape the irrational condition of having been fired for obeying the rules of the game. Intense competition at every level—producing new efficiencies within accepted business practices, suggesting innovative practices and products, struggling to increase profit in an atmosphere where profit is conceived of as the "objective" marker of all value—increases both the value of high-risk strategies and the costs that derive from their failures. Without high-risk decisions, a manager's rate of return on capital investment will not match that of the leaders in their field. With high-risk decision making, regular losses are inevitable. Only those managers who can endure the regular experience of loss while maintaining their enthusiastic embrace of and even celebration of the process that led to their defeat can reenter the game quickly enough to survive. In other words, the successful manager cannot afford to stand "in a tragic relation to commerce." The dominant form of selfhood constructed in postmodern capitalism recognizes that its most significant communities are "work communities" and that these communities are "created through disjunctures and problems and are unstable, prone to entropy and dismantling."[17]

Katherine Newman's important analysis of downward mobility in the 1980s begins with a description of one of those who was not able to bounce back quickly or to disassociate himself from the failure over which he had no control. David Patterson was a computer executive whose family recently had moved to the New York area following his latest promotion. They had bought a new house, new cars, and the country-club membership appropriate to their standing. Soon afterward, a consolidation in the computer industry forced Patterson's company to close his division, and he lost his job. After Patterson was laid off, the country-club membership went, the house went, and the circle of friends that had welcomed them to their new suburban community went. Newman's description of Patterson's state of mind after months of unemployment captures the feeling of loss for one unable to bounce back quickly: "All David could think about was what was wrong with me? Why doesn't anyone call me? What have I done wrong? . . . Could people tell that he was anxious? Were people avoiding him on the street because they couldn't stand to come face to face with desperation? Was he offending potential employers, coming on too strong? With failure closing in from all directions the answer came back 'It must be me.'" David Patterson's response represents the intensely felt personal responsibility for a structural failure and the social penalties that accrue to personal experiences of desperation and anxiety. Business within the condition of postmodernity is characterized by swift intensities of feeling alternating unpredictably with slow stretches of despair. It has engaged and rewarded a structure of feeling that can, if not integrate, at least tolerate the coexistence of these unpredictable extremes in a pleasurable and meaningful way.[18]

The Hallmark of Postmodernity

In 1970, Hallmark's market dominance of the industry was secure, maintained in large part through intensive advertising, particularly the brilliantly targeted vehicle of the *Hallmark Hall of Fame*, and the extensive computer capabilities at the heart of its marketing research. During the previous ten years, the number of firms in the greeting card industry had shrunk by almost 30 percent. Most of the companies that went out of business during this time were small, with fewer than fifty employees. Large firms had held a powerful competitive advantage in the production of modern greeting cards because they could more easily manage the very large fixed costs associated with the machines of mass production. In turn, reliance on these machines created long lead times. This meant that successful designs could not be quickly rerun. One of the crucial decisions about a card, therefore, was an estimation of its future marketplace success. A more accurate estimate would ensure that the press run would be large enough to service demand, but not so large as to tie up materials and storage in excess inventory and, consequently, deprive an alternative, more successful card of those resources. Effective gauging of the market was crucial for any firm's success.[19]

According to company claims, Hallmark was the first major greeting card company to computerize any of its large-scale operations. Its first computer application was order processing, implemented in 1961. John Collins, vice president of Hallmark's Management Information Systems in 1986, said that order processing was automated "when it became apparent that we could not maintain quality displays in card shops, control our inventory well enough, or grow quickly enough with the old labor-intensive order filling process." According to Collins, this single step in automation gave Hallmark an incredible competitive advantage in its "ability to select and deliver products to the marketplace." By 1970,

Hallmark's market research was being processed by three IBM system 360s and one IBM 7074, which together dealt with "some 70,000 decisions" per card, a stark contrast to the pencil-and-paper–driven "statistical planning department" that Rust Craft had touted in 1946. Hallmark's Management Information Systems division soon became very powerful, employing more than two hundred people in the mid-1980s. At this point, its biggest system was the "pre-production planning system," which made decisions about all the "processes needed to get a product ready for manufacturing." In 1981, this system evaluated the potential success of "eighty-five coded characteristics from price to paper stock to size and subject and sentiment" before approving the production of each card. An expanded version of Hallmark's first computerized system, order processing, was also quite large. By 1986, order processing was able to select the proper product to replace a sold-out 90-cent father's birthday card by considering not only how well the card had done at the store where it had sold out, but how well it had done at other stores, and exactly how well all other 90-cent father's birthday cards were doing in precisely the same type of retail store across the country.[20]

The ability to maintain and access this highly detailed level of information reinforced the intensely competitive quality of the greeting card industry. Greeting cards that cost approximately 7 cents to make and sold at retail for 50 cents represented a potential profit margin greater than 200 percent for the manufacturer. Irvine Hockaday, Jr., who was named president of Hallmark in 1986, admitted, "It is hard to find any business with the profitability of greeting cards." Despite the clear dominance of the major companies, this high-profit potential continued to lure new firms into the industry. To some, greeting cards seemed like "the archetypal product for the post-industrial age." As computerized techniques increased the flexibility of design and decreased some of the manufacturing costs, small firms that specialized in particular occasions for sending cards or that worked to excavate newer and smaller niches for social expression could flourish—at least until one of the majors bought them out or drove them out of business. The Metropolitan Museum of Art placed copies of its more famous paintings on Christmas cards. Recycled Paper Products expanded the appeal of everyday, nonoccasion cards as it developed a niche of educated female customers who appreciated the company's environmentalist gesture and "whimsical animal" images, particularly the cat drawings of artist Sandra Boynton. Companies such as Freedom Greetings and Orphan Productions targeted the growing black middle class. The Sunshine Line produced cards with explicit Christian themes. Other companies recognized the demand for valentines unrestricted by heteronormative constraints. During the 1980s, as it had been in the 1950s, innovation in design and sentiment was more likely to be found among smaller firms, struggling to exploit previously ignored relationships and occasions for social expression. These companies created the field of "alternative cards," the name of which suggested that the cards were different from those produced by the majors—different in their forms of production, their content, and the social needs they claimed to address. But just as they had in the 1950s, the major firms quickly recognized profitable niches and developed new lines to exploit them.[21]

By 1990, the number of very small greeting card companies was estimated to be more than seven hundred. Among the major firms, however, only those, like Hallmark, that had developed and implemented huge sophisticated database management and information systems found themselves able to adapt and grow. By the early 1980s, the big-five greeting card companies had been reduced to the big three: Hallmark, American Greetings, and Gibson. Rust Craft and Norcross had been driven out of business, largely because they were unable to develop the computerized record-keeping systems that could coordinate the machines of mass production with the growing variety of sentiments. By 1986, Hallmark boasted of 32,000 different *types* of cards (not simply different content, but different categories— that is, a "from me-to-you" Dear Daughter reconciliation birthday card). Robert Stark, Hallmark's executive vice president during this time, explained the fundamental importance of computerized information management to the greeting card industry: "When you do several billion dollars, and do it 50 cents at a time, you're running a very complex business." Computerized record keeping enabled the company to retain the fordist capacity to reproduce any one of its cards by the millions, if the card reached that level of marketplace success. Such machines also encouraged the application of postfordist techniques. By the end of the 1980s, American Greetings was championing CAESAR (Computer Assisted Editorial Sentiment Analysis and Retrieval), its extensive database of greeting card copy, and its recent application of "just in time manufacturing methods to the creative process." In order to speed up the delivery of new card ideas to the marketplace, the company had replaced the linear movement of a card idea from a writer to the head of editorial to the art department to an individual artist back to editorial, with new "concept development" teams that included both artists and writers and that competed with one another to get their ideas accepted for production. By the mid-1990s, Hallmark was attempting to spark innovative collaboration by picking artists' and writers' names out of a hat and assigning to these random pairings project ideas to develop.[22]

Postfordism does not imply the abandonment of the mechanical advantages of mass production. Hallmark's massive production facilities in Lawrence, Kansas, and Liberty, Missouri, still produce the dies that raise the letters and form the hearts, and continue to apply the foil, special inks, and glitter to almost 20,000 cards an hour. But postfordism does require the development of new forms of organization and record keeping. These forms of human interaction and knowledge production reward and reinforce the sensitivities and skills of a "distributed individuality within a complex environment," one precisely capable of avoiding a tragic relationship with business processes and organizations while maintaining a belief in and commitment to constant increases in productivity even in the face of failure. This is the structure of feeling constructed in Hallmark's intensely competitive writing sessions, where ideas for new cards are forced out at a rate of one dozen or so per person per hour. When the results are read out loud, the winners are acclaimed, with the losers outnumbering the winners by about twenty to one.[23]

With Love, from Me to You

The complexity of the greeting card business derives from its peculiar placement at the heart of the densely layered structures of feeling produced in business. No other cultural product represents a more evident concatenation of the contradictions at the core of the life of business,

ranging from corporate consolidation of fordist processes to postindustrial global capitalism, whether at the beginning or the end of the
twentieth century. In the 1910s, the founders of the modern greeting
card industry fought against the chaotic business practices favored
among post card jobbers by establishing professional trade organizations to limit the risks of intense competition. The current conditions
of greeting card production filter creative high-risk behavior through
flexible systems of organization and knowledge production in order to
most efficiently and profitably operate the machines of mass production. Yet even in this high-risk, high-pressure, competitive environment, Hallmark has long been recognized as one of the better corporations to work for in the United States. Mainstream journalism
articles written about the company regularly tout paid research trips to
Las Vegas and London as well as on-the-clock movie viewing. As of
1990, employees owned one-third of the company. One card-writing
workshop came up with this slogan to describe the experience of working at Hallmark: "Happy people saying happy things." The company
apparently has devised a means of combining the structural need for
high-risk behavior with the ability of employees to disassociate themselves from the personal responsibility for loss in a pleasurable and
meaningful way.[24]

This system of production has been able to develop cards like the
one with which this chapter began: the "universal specific" card, which
captures an apparently unique moment of emotional communication
shared by thousands. The marketplace success of these cards has been
explained by longtime Hallmark writer Barbara Loots: "People want
their card to be exactly their own—from me to you." From-me-to-you
cards must, therefore, be specific and exact, yet general. How is this accomplished? The texts of these cards convey both the intimacy of the
emotion and the generality of such feelings through their heavy use of
shifter pronouns such as "I" and "you"—hence their name. The crucial
feeling of intimacy is created through the acknowledgment of conflict.
This strategy works in greeting cards only because conflict had been
purged from greeting card discourse for so long. The discursive intimacy of the cards creates the feeling of specificity, even though the
conditions described in the text are explicitly recognized as common

experiences. In fact, one of the tasks of this line of cards is to acknowledge the commonality of difficult moments. A very recent card seemingly designed to express a feeling of commitment to a relationship despite current conflicts illustrates this phenomenon:

> No one ever said that love was easy. I know we've had some dif-
> ficult moments lately, and sometimes I wonder if we'll ever see
> eye to eye or if our actions will ever reflect what we really feel in-
> side. But I want you to know my heart still belongs to you.[25]

As the card announces, everyone experiences the difficulty of love.
Everyone knows there are times when lovers have to be apart. And almost everyone wonders if the actions of lovers ever reflect what they
really feel. By announcing these simple truths, this card reassures both
the sender and the receiver that their experience of conflict is not really their fault; it does not accurately express their personal ability to feel
love in their hearts. The commitment to and the responsibility for the
relationship are both present and absent in this card, both acknowledged and deflected. If this relationship fails, it will not be the personal responsibility of either of the partners. However risky love might be
for them, at least they tried. And they can try again. The earnest sincerity of their love should not be doubted. The senders and receivers
of this card (along with "everyone") can continue to conduct the high-
risk behavior of love as long as they retain the ability to bounce back
after repeated failures.

From-me-to-you cards eschew the ironic distancing common to
studio cards, even as they share a central focus on the gap between
promise and actuality. Whereas studio cards humorously announce
the disjuncture between feeling and action that characterizes emotional communication after the decline of the modern, from-me-to-
you cards recognize the complex and conflicted experience of feeling
in a world structured by this gap. Both genres have moved beyond the
modern greeting card's insistence that feeling cannot be spoken, in
order to speak simply and clearly the apparently necessary and inevitable loss of the modern ideals of material and emotional abundance. These ideals need no longer survive through the strategies of

displacement and condensation that enabled the mute authenticity of mass feeling. Greeting cards need no longer acknowledge a residual longing for individually composed emotional eloquence. "Everyone" can now acknowledge the inescapable structural factors that belie the dear old modern belief in the autonomy of personal feeling. No longer are greeting cards used by "those inclined to disguise their feelings," but by those inclined to articulate universally and specifically the feelings that are produced within us. In a claim marvelously general but also intimately accurate, David Harvey states that "the greater the ephemerality, the more pressing the need to discover or manufacture some kind of eternal truth that might lie therein." Perhaps the ephemerality of feeling in the postmodern condition has produced its own eternal truth: feeling is structured by forces beyond the heart. Eight billion cards a year testify to the contemporary empirical validity of this eternal truth.[26]

Notes

Introduction

1. Raymond Williams, *Marxism and Literature* (Oxford: Oxford University Press, 1977), p. 87.

2. Ibid., pp. 132–33.

3. Ibid., p. 131.

4. Quoted in Richard Todd, "We Have Several Tons of Excess Sequins," *Audience*, March–April 1971, p. 10.

5. Stephen Papson, "From Symbolic Exchange to Bureaucratic Discourse: The Hallmark Greeting Card," *Theory, Culture and Society* 3 (1986): 100; Leigh Eric Schmidt, *Consumer Rites: The Buying and Selling of American Holidays* (Princeton, N.J.: Princeton University Press, 1995); Luna Lambert, "The Seasonal Trade: Gift Cards and Chromolithography in America, 1874–1910" (Ph.D. diss., George Washington University, 1980); Melissa Schrift, "Icons of Femininity in Studio Cards: Women, Communication and Identity," *Journal of Popular Culture* 27 (1994): 111–22; Micaela Di Leonardo, "The Female World of Cards and Holidays: Women, Families, and the Work of Kinship," *Signs* 12 (1987): 440–53; Eva Ilouz, *Consuming the Romantic Utopia: Love and the Cultural Contradictions of Capitalism* (Berkeley: University of California Press, 1997), pp. 247–87.

6. Arlie Hochschild, *The Commercialization of Intimate Life: Notes from Home and Work* (Berkeley: University of California Press, 2003); Christopher Lasch, *Haven in a Heartless World: The Family Besieged* (New York: Norton, 1977). The separate-spheres debate is long and involved. For a review of the relevant literature up to the mid-1980s, see Linda Kerber, "Separate Spheres, Female Worlds, Woman's Place: The Rhetoric of Women's History," *Journal of American History* 75 (1988): 9–39. Laura Romero also gives an important critique of the figure of the domestic woman in *Home Fronts: Domesticity and Its Critics in the Antebellum United States* (Durham, N.C.: Duke University Press, 1997). For a final attempt to cast this division into the historiographic past, see Cathy Davidson, ed., "No More Separate Spheres" [special issue], *American Literature* 70 (1998), and Walter Benjamin, *The Arcades Project*, trans. Howard

Eiland and Kevin McLaughlin (Cambridge, Mass.: Harvard University Press, 1999), p. 460.

7. The trend report for June 1959 is in the Norcross Greeting Card Collection, series 1, box X, Archives Center, National Museum of American History, Behringer Center, Smithsonian Institution, Washington, D.C.

1. Vicious Sentiments

1. David Berdan's lecture notes, class notes, and pamphlets are in the Berdan Family Papers, Joseph Downs Collection of Manuscripts and Printed Ephemera, Winterthur Museum, Garden, and Library, Winterthur, Del.

2. Drafts of Berdan's valentines as well as the valentines he received from others can be seen in the Berdan Family Papers, Joseph Downs Collection.

3. Leigh Eric Schmidt, *Consumer Rites: The Buying and Selling of American Holidays* (Princeton, N.J.: Princeton University Press, 1995), p. 39; Charles Sellers, *The Market Revolution: Jacksonian America, 1815–1846* (New York: Oxford University Press, 1991).

4. June Howard, *Publishing the Family* (Durham, N.C.: Duke University Press, 2001), pp. 222–41; Ann Douglas, *The Feminization of American Culture* (New York: Anchor Books, 1988); Jane Tompkins, *Sensational Designs: The Cultural Work of American Fiction, 1790–1860* (New York: Oxford University Press, 1985). I adapt the phrase "culture of sentimentalism" from Shirley Samuels, ed., *The Culture of Sentiment: Race, Gender, and Sentimentality in Nineteenth-Century America* (New York: Oxford University Press, 1992), in which appear many important contributions to the classic debate. In *Home Fronts: Domesticity and Its Critics in the Antebellum United States* (Durham, N.C.: Duke University Press, 1997), Lora Romero recognized that both sides of the Douglas–Tompkins debate required a stabilizing figure of the domestic woman who worked to orient both dominant ideology and resistance. On the figure of the sentimental male, see Mary Chapman and Glenn Hendler, eds., *Sentimental Men: Masculinity and the Politics of Affect in American Culture* (Berkeley: University of California Press, 1999); Glenn Hendler, *Public Sentiments: Structures of Feeling in Nineteenth-Century American Literature* (Chapel Hill: University of North Carolina Press, 2001); and Bruce Burgett, *Sentimental Bodies: Sex, Gender, and Citizenship in the Early Republic* (Princeton, N.J.: Princeton University Press, 1998).

5. Sellers, *Market Revolution*, pp. 372, 391; Raymond Williams, *Marxism and Literature* (New York: Oxford University Press, 1977), pp. 83–89. I use Williams's concept of structure of feeling because of its conceptual flexibility combined with its rigorous insistence on the material structuring of emotional life.

6. Colin Campbell, *The Romantic Ethic and the Spirit of Modern Consumerism* (Cambridge, Mass.: Blackwell, 1987), pp. 72–73. The classic discussion of commodities brought to the marketplace is, of course, Adam Smith, *The Wealth*

of Nations (1776; reprint, Amherst, N.Y.: Prometheus Books, 1991). For Smith's discussion of the role that "effectual demand" plays in the distinction between natural and market price, see pp. 58–67. For a discussion of the role of feeling in the performance of elite status in the eighteenth century, see Jay Fliegelman, *Declaring Independence: Jefferson, Natural Language and the Culture of Performance* (Stanford, Calif.: Stanford University Press, 1993).

7. Nancy Armstrong, *Desire and Domestic Fiction* (New York: Oxford University Press, 1987), pp. 8, 23–24, 94–95.

8. Gillian Brown, *Domestic Individualism: Imagining Self in Nineteenth Century America* (Berkeley: University of California Press, 1990), pp. 3, 59.

9. Lori Merish, *Sentimental Materialism: Gender, Commodity Culture and Nineteenth-Century American Literature* (Durham, N.C.: Duke University Press, 2000), pp. 4, 116, 117; Adam Smith, *The Theory of Moral Sentiments* (1759; reprint, Indianapolis: Liberty Fund Press, 1969), and *Wealth of Nations*. Many commentators have noted that the term "sympathy" does not appear in Smith's *Wealth of Nations*, and self-interest is specifically eliminated as a basis for moral action in his *Theory of Moral Sentiments*. See, for example, the entry on Smith in *The Encyclopedia of Philosophy* (New York: Macmillan, 1967), vol. 7, pp. 461–63. My point is that the two philosophical concepts are coproductions of market societies. Both concepts rely on the construct of an interior self that anchors and situates both self-interest and sympathy.

10. Mary Louise Kete, *Sentimental Collaborations: Mourning and Middle-Class Identity in Nineteenth-Century America* (Durham, N.C.: Duke University Press, 2000), pp. xv, 2, 6, 17, 53.

11. Karen Halttunen, *Confidence Men and Painted Women: A Study of Middle-Class Culture in America, 1830–1870* (New Haven, Conn.: Yale University Press, 1982), pp. 194–95; Stuart Blumin, *The Emergence of the Middle Class: Social Experience in the American City, 1760–1900* (New York: Cambridge University Press, 1989), pp. 68, 191. John Kasson, Kenneth Ames, and Katherine C. Grier have agreed with Halttunen on the importance of the public demonstration and mutual recognition of sincerity, gentility, refinement, and domesticity for the populations that were gathering in the cities of the Northeast and were struggling to distinguish themselves and their families from the families of ironworkers, carpenters, and other artisans and mechanics. They have reinforced Halttunen's linkage of the performance of sincerity to a "sentimental code of conduct," a set of public behaviors that were intended to filter through the language of sentimentalism the state of an individual's character. See John Kasson, *Rudeness and Civility: Manners in Nineteenth-Century America* (New York: Noonday Press, 1990); Kenneth Ames, *Death in the Dining Room and Other Tales of Victorian Culture* (Philadelphia: Temple University Press, 1992); and Katherine C. Grier, *Culture and Comfort: Parlor Making and Middle-Class Identity, 1850–1930* (Washington, D.C.: Smithsonian Institution Press, 1988).

12. Karen Lystra, *Searching the Heart: Women, Men, and Romantic Love in Nineteenth-Century America* (New York: Oxford University Press, 1989), pp. 7, 28–53.

13. Etiquette books that described hard-and-fast rules connecting interior character to public behavior proliferated throughout the nineteenth century. Despite the evident problems of inferring actual behavior from prescriptive literature, not only Armstrong's and Halttunen's studies, but also the work of Kasson, Ames, and Grier, rely heavily on these commercially produced packages of social knowledge, for they seem to illustrate explicitly the ideological terms within which economic relations and structures were translated into and lived in noneconomic realms, in the arenas of consumption, social networks, and private life. Several arguments have been put forth about why these etiquette books were so widely distributed during this period; they all turn on this issue of the anxieties of a class in formation. Halttunen argues that "by the 1830s . . . to be middle-class was to be, in theory, without fixed social status" (*Confidence Men*, p. 29). The popularity of etiquette books derived from the profound fluidity of a society in transformation, wrenching itself to fit entirely new material forms of production and commercial forms of exchange. Clearly, etiquette books were both a form of anxiety management regarding the instability of status and a means of commercially exploiting the social tensions that developed as industrialization produced new forms of wealth and as commercial and managerial developments created new forms of occupation. They were a response to the rising awareness of class born out of tremendous social upheaval, and they neatly expressed the contradictions of sentimentalism.

As explicit conveyors of dominant ideology, etiquette books of the nineteenth century simply could not state directly the economic grounding of their knowledge. As Kasson states, "if the crucial role of money were starkly revealed, 'the best people' would both forfeit their moral authority and the emulation and respect it brought and join in the free-for-all of the market on an equal footing with the rawest newcomer" (*Rudeness and Civility*, p. 67). The direct acknowledgment of the decisive role of fortune would short-circuit the flow of sympathy that was the emotional key to the ideological and emotional formation of the new middle classes. But it was not simply the role of money that had to be hidden or erased in the discourse of etiquette books. In addition, the books had to deny their conditions of production and consumption, their very existence as objects of mass culture.

The authors of etiquette books were often self-conscious about their contradictory status as public sources of exactly the social knowledge that was believed to provide the ultimate proof of one's character—the most common nineteenth-century word for the authentic interior self. Those who wrote etiquette books and other guides to public behavior—such as letter writers, guides to business conduct, and valentine writers—often mediated this contradiction in an introduction. Establishing a pact between the reader and the author, the introduction might declare, for example, that the material included refers simply to the rules of society in New York, for which the person of good character from, let us say, Baltimore might need some guidance. By 1878, Mrs. H. O. Ward could insist: "The compiler of this volume is well aware that it is customary upon introducing any work to the public, professedly treating upon an improvement in manners, to apologize for so doing, but she does not consider any such apology necessary. Society has its grammar as language has, and the rules of that grammar must be learned" (*Sensible Etiquette of the Best Society, Customs, Manners, Morals and Homeculture* [Philadelphia: Porter & Coates, 1878]). Such a bold affirmation of the artificial and conventional character of manners was probably a marker of the decline of etiquette books as transparent conveyors of sentimentalism as an active social philosophy capable of guiding and informing the mutual communication of authentic interior selves.

Sentimentalism survived as a coherent social philosophy as long as its methods of discernment, refinement, and grace were believed to be the direct and accurate reflection of status that could, therefore, guarantee a certain class standing. But after the middle of the century, changing historical conditions rendered its own internal contradictions—which turned on the manner by which authentic interior selves could make themselves known to each other—too evident and too debilitating for the original form of sentimentalism to continue. In the very act of revealing the terms of the sentimental code of conduct, etiquette books undercut the basic association between public behavior and private character. Even as they articulated the basic ideology of sentimental business, they stimulated the potential for class-passing. They rendered explicit the cultural aspects of class, status, and prestige, and inspired the search for innovative means of achieving them. When mass culture demonstrated its capacity to reveal not simply the momentary content, but the very existence, of a social code that linked authentic interiority to class position, also revealing that the denial of such a code was necessary to its proper functioning, then the procedures and processes of sentimentalism could no longer discriminate successfully between class fragments. It was only at this point that the word "sentimental" began to take on the meanings of weakness and superficiality that we now associate with it. According to the *Oxford English Dictionary*, the earliest appearances of "sentimental" carry a favorable connotation: "Everything clever and agreeable is comprehended in that word." By 1862, it connoted foolishness and vacuity: "You have no sentimental nonsense . . . to fear from me" (compact ed. [Oxford: Clarendon Press, 1971], vol. 2, p. 471).

14. Lystra, *Searching the Heart*, pp. 7, 18; Blumin, *Emergence of the Middle Class*.

15. Berdan Family Papers, Joseph Downs Collection. For a discussion of overt class consciousness during the antebellum period, see Blumin, *Emergence of the Middle Class*, pp. 285–90. For a conflicting opinion, see Sean Wilentz, *Chants Democratic: New York City and the Rise of the American Working Class, 1788–1850* (New York: Oxford University Press, 1984).

16. James Oliver Horton and Lois E. Horton, *In Hope of Liberty: Culture, Community, and Protest Among Northern Free Blacks, 1700–1860* (New York: Oxford University Press, 1997); *Strong's Annual Valentine Advertiser for St. Valentine's Day, Feb. 14, 1847* (New York: Strong, 1847). One of Strong's "Gem Writers" was given to a young David G. Goddard by "his teacher, M. J. E. Libby," and is currently at the American Antiquarian Society, Worcester, Mass. See *Gem Valentine Writer* (New York: Strong, n.d.), and *Love Points Inscribed to the Valentine Writer by a Green-un* (New York: Strong, 1849). Copies are in the Norcross Greeting Card Collection, Archives Center, National Museum of American History, Behringer Center, Smithsonian Institution, Washington, D.C. The Norcross *Love Points* is dated 1850.

17. I have now referred to the "Green-un" and will soon refer to the "Master of Hearts" as the authors of the works their prefaces introduce. At the same time, I have asserted that many of these verses were copied in part or in whole from other writers, and that even many of the verses that appear for the first time in either of these works were compilations of common phrases and similes. Originality is a problematic concept. Our concepts of artistic creativity and originality do not fit the conditions of production within which these commercial packages of emotional eloquence were created. Each valentine writer contains enough variation to distinguish it from the others with which it competed. Each package, therefore, was an original work—if by original we mean that there was no previous version that was exactly like it. Variation within repetition describes the originality of works of mass culture. Whoever composed the verses and however many individuals were involved in putting together the verses in the booklet, it does no disservice to the legitimacy of those processes of composing, compiling, and ordering involved in the production of each booklet to subsume the totality of their functions under the single title of author. Nor does including the Green-un or the Master of Hearts in the pantheon of authors of nineteenth-century mass culture damage the author function. Any body of work—including a valentine writer—is stabilized and concretized by reference to its author. The author's name serves to mark the boundaries of this body of work, and Green-un or Master of Hearts will suffice as well as any other name for the authors of these writers.

18. *A Collection of New and Original Valentines, Serious & Satirical, Sublime & Ridiculous, on all the ordinary names, professions, trades, etc.; With an Introductory Treatise on the Composition of a valentine by a Master of Hearts* (London: Ward & Lock, 1857).

19. For another brief discussion of the dangers of writing one's own valentine, see "St. Valentine and Valentines," *Harper's Weekly*, 13 February 1869, pp. 104–5.

20. *Hymen's Revenge, against Old, Bachelors, and Impertenent Coxcombs; or, a New Valentine Writer for the Present Year, Being a Choice Collection of Valentines, Humorous, and Satirical, Chiefly Original Written expressly for this work* (London: Kidwell, 1805). A copy is in the Norcross Collection, series 2, box 41.

21. Norcross Collection, series 2, box 32.

22. Frances Crocker's valentines are in the Valentine Collection, box 3, folder 1, American Antiquarian Society. Isaiah Thomas was a successful book publisher and the founder of the American Antiquarian Society.

23. Harry Sunderland, "Kate's Valentine," *Godey's Lady's Book*, February 1850.

24. Norcross Collection, series 2, box 41.

25. Schmidt, *Consumer Rites*, p. 71.

26. *Comic Valentine Writer. Comprising the best pieces suitable for the purpose to be found in the whole range of Poetical Literature, besides many appropriate originals* (New York: Strong, n.d.).

27. These comics are in a loose-leaf binder entitled "Early Valentines, Lace," in the Graphic Arts Division, American Antiquarian Society.

28. "Miss Gray Hairs and Wrinkles," series 2, box 29, folder 7; "Nasty Old Bachelor," series 2, box 29, folder 4; "To a Clerk," series 2, box 29, folder 6; "The Swell Clerk," series 2, box 29, folder 4; "The True Billingsgate Fishmonger," series 2, box 29, folder 1; "My Lovely Blacksmith," series 2, box 29, folder 3; "Mortar-Spreading Knave," series 2, box 29, folder 3; "Tin-Smith," series 2, box 29, folder 3, all in the Norcross Collection.

29. "Nursery Maid," series 2, box 29, folder 5; "My Pretty Milliner," series 2, box 29, folder 4, both in the Norcross Collection.

30. "Early Valentines, Lace"; *Comic Valentine Writer*; "Dingy Dear," Norcross Collection, series 2, box 18, folder 3; Eric Lott, *Love and Theft: Blackface Minstrelsy and the American Working Class* (New York: Oxford University Press, 1993).

31. *Strong's Annual Valentine Advertiser*, p. 5; "Thy Name Is Now the Magic Spell," series 2, box 14, folder 3; "I Cannot Long These Pangs Endure," series 2, box 1, both in the Norcross Collection.

32. Jonathan King, quoted in Carroll Alton Means, "Embossed and 'Laced' Paper" (manuscript, American Antiquarian Society), p. 4; Charles Dickens, "Cupid's Manufactory," *All the Year Round: A Weekly Journal*, 20 February 1864, pp. 26–30.

33. "St. Valentine's Day," *Harpers Weekly*, 21 February 1880, p. 113.

34. Marion Winslow Emerson, "Pioneer Career Woman and Her Valentines," *Hobbies: The Magazine for Collectors*, February 1948; "Made First Valentine

in United States," *Boston Globe*, 14 February 1901; Ruth Webb Lee, *A History of Valentines* (London: Batsford, 1953); Schmidt, *Consumer Rites*, p. 360. See also Elizabeth White, "Sentimental Enterprise: Sentiment and Profit in American Market Culture, 1830–1880" (Ph.D. diss., Yale University, 1995). Receipts from the 1850s for the Howland family business, signed by C. A. Howland, are in the Warshaw Collection, Archives Center, National Museum of American History, Behringer Center, Smithsonian Institution, Washington, D.C.

35. The oldest version is the article "Made First Valentine," which was based on an interview held with Esther Howland near the end of her life. This story was reprinted almost exactly in the *Ladies' Home Journal*, February 1903. Emerson worked for the Antiquarian Society in the 1940s and seems to have dedicated quite a bit of her time to expanding Howland's story, including, apparently, inventing the existence of diaries supposed to have been kept by the women who worked for her. In *History of Valentines*, Lee relies heavily on Emerson's version of the story. Gloria Christensen has focused Esther's family's connection to the Pilgrim John Howland Society ("Esther Howland," *New England Quarterly* 33 [1969]).

36. Howland was not the first person to understand the ability of folded bits of paper to represent complex feelings. Handmade puzzle purses, intricately folded sheets of paper with different messages on each revealed side, were exchanged both as valentines and as general love tokens. Howland found a way to convey complexity and layering using colors and textures that could be assembled by relatively unskilled manual laborers, almost all of whom were women. For discussions of puzzle purses and other early handmade valentines, see Lee, *History of Valentines*, and Schmidt, *Consumer Rites. Strong's Annual Valentine Advertiser*, p. 3; Norcross Collection, series 2, box 21A.

37. Esther Howland white valentine, "Absent but Ever Dear, " and gold valentine, "First Love," Norcross Collection, series 2, box 13, folder 16.

38. Emerson, "Pioneer Career Woman"; Christensen, "Esther Howland"; "Made First Valentine." Lee describes it in this way: "Each girl was assigned a special task. One cut out pictures and kept them assorted in boxes. Another, with models to work from, made the backgrounds, passing them to still another who gave them further embellishment. So the sentimental valentines went on and on, from hand to hand, until finally the last one called for in the orders had been completed. . . . Instead of crediting Henry Ford with 'mass production' innovations, it appears the honor should go to Miss Howland as the first with progressive assembly" (*History of Valentines*, p. 54).

39. *The Heart of the Commonwealth: or, Worcester as it is: being A correct Guide to the Public Buildings and Institutions and to Some of the Principal Manufactories and Shops and Wholesale and Retail Stores in Worcester and Vicinity* (Worcester, Mass.: Howland, 1856), p. 74.

40. Dickens, "Cupid's Manufactory," p. 28.

2. The Nineteenth-Century Christmas Card

1. Janet Huntington McKelvey, "The Christmas Card," Louis Prang Files, vol. 9, New York Public Library, New York, N.Y.

2. Ernest Dudley Chase, *The Romance of Greeting Cards: An Historical Account of the Origin, Evolution and Development of Christmas Cards, Valentines and Other Forms of Greeting Cards from the Earliest Days to the Present Time. In Commemoration of the Fiftieth Anniversary of Rust Craft Greeting Cards, 1906–1956*, ed. James D. Chamberlain, with an introduction by Stephen Q. Shannon (Dedham, Mass.: Rust Craft, 1956).

3. George Buday, *The History of the Christmas Card* (London: Rockliff, 1954), pp. 6–15.

4. Ibid. A copy of the Horsley–Cole card is in Chase, *Romance of Greeting Cards*, p. IV.

5. Buday, *History of the Christmas Card*, pp. 12–15; Chase, *Romance of Greeting Cards*, p. 196. For more on the imagery of nature in the depiction of abundance, see T. J. Jackson Lears, *Fables of Abundance: A Cultural History of Advertising in America* (New York: Basic Books, 1994).

6. "The Autobiography of Louis Prang," in Mary Margaret Sittig, "L. Prang and Company, Fine Art Publishers" (Master's thesis, George Washington University, 1970), pp. 123–56.

7. Schenck business card, Louis Prang Files, vol. 1. For a valuable discussion of the function of images in processes of bourgeois naturalization, see Norman Bryson, *Vision and Painting: The Logic of the Gaze* (London: Macmillan, 1983).

8. McKelvey, "Christmas Card," p. 7.

9. Ibid.

10. Ibid., p. 8.

11. Peter Marzio, *The Democratic Art: Pictures for a Nineteenth Century America* (Boston: Godine, 1979), p. 116; Louis Prang, in "How Chromos Are Made," *Prang's Chromo: A Journal of Popular Art* 1, no. 1 (1868): 1–2. Original copies of *Prang's Chromo* are in the Boston Public Library, Boston, Mass.

12. Neil Harris, "Color and Media: Some Comparisons and Speculations," in *Cultural Excursions: Marketing Appetites and Cultural Tastes in Modern America* (Chicago: University of Chicago Press, 1990), pp. 318–36; Ellen Gruber Garvey, *Adman in the Parlor: Magazines and the Gendering of Consumer Culture, 1880s to 1910s* (New York: Oxford University Press, 1996), pp. 16–50.

13. "Autobiography of Louis Prang," p. 50.

14. Louis Prang to *New York Tribune*, 26 November 1866, in "Controversy with an Art Critic," *Prang's Chromo: A Journal of Popular Art* 1, no. 2 (1868): 2–3.

15. The relevant editorials in the *Nation* have been ascribed to two authors: in *Democratic Art*, Marzio credits the journal's editor, E. L. Godkin; in *Cultural*

Excursions, Harris follows *Poole's Index to Periodical Literature*, which cites Russell Sturgis as the author of "Color Printing from Wood and Stone," *Nation*, 10 January 1867, p. 36. In *Fables of Abundance*, Lears discusses Godkin's editorial of 1874, in which he coined the term "chromo-civilization" (p. 269). Prang and Tait disagreed about the placement of the chromolithographer's signature on the print. Tait felt that only his name should appear on a copy of his painting, while Prang argued that the chromolithographer was also an artist who had contributed aesthetically to the production of the print. William Harring's name appears on Tait's *Ducklings* and *Chickens*. See A. F. Tait to Louis Prang, 4 and 6 December 1866, A. F. Tait Papers, Joseph Downs Collection of Manuscripts and Printed Ephemera, Winterthur Museum, Garden, and Library, Winterthur, Del.

16. Prang to *New York Tribune*, 26 November 1866.

17. Sturgis, "Color Printing from Wood and Stone."

18. Russell Sturgis, "Chromo-lithographs, American, English, and French," *Nation*, 31 October 1867, p. 352.

19. Prang chromolithograph of *Barefoot Boy*, Prints Division, Boston Public Library; John Greenleaf Whittier, "Barefoot Boy," in *Whittier's Complete Poems* (Boston: Houghton Mifflin, 1892), pp. 521–22. For another discussion of the nostalgia for boyhood in the works of postbellum white writers, see Richard Lowry, "Domestic Interiors: Boyhood Nostalgia and Affective Labor in the Gilded Age," in Joel Pfister and Nancy Schnog, eds., *Inventing the Psychological: Toward a Cultural History of Emotional Life in America* (New Haven, Conn.: Yale University Press, 1997), pp. 110–30.

20. *Hartford Evening Post*, quoted in *Prang's Chromo: A Journal of Popular Art* 1, no. 3 (1868): 4.

21. Frederick Douglass to Louis Prang, 14 June 1870, in Katharine Morrison McClinton, *The Chromolithographs of Louis Prang* (New York: Potter, 1973), p. 37; Prang chromolithograph of *Portrait of Senator Revels*, Prints Division, Library of Congress, Washington, D.C.

22. Douglass to Prang, 14 June 1870.

23. Stuart Blumin, *The Emergence of the Middle Class: Social Experience in the American City, 1760–1900* (New York: Cambridge University Press, 1989), pp. 263–65.

24. Catharine Esther Beecher and Harriet Beecher Stowe, *The American Woman's Home or, Principles of Domestic Science; Being a Guide to the Formation and Maintenance of Economical, Healthful, Beautiful and Christian Homes* (1869; reprint, Watkins Glen, N.Y.: American Life Foundation, Library of Victorian Culture, 1979), p. 84.

25. Quoted in *Prang's Chromo: A Journal of Popular Art* 1, no. 4 (1868): 6.

26. Russell Sturgis, "Testimonials in Art and Literature," *Nation*, 19 December 1867, pp. 506–7; E. L. Godkin, "Chromo-civilization," *Nation*, 24

September 1874, pp. 201–2; *Buffalo Courier*, quoted in *Prang's Chromo: A Journal of Popular Art* 1, no. 3 (1868): 6.

27. Walter Benjamin, *The Arcades Project*, trans. Howard Eiland and Kevin McLaughlin (Cambridge, Mass.: Harvard University Press, 1999). See, in particular, section N, "On the Theory of Knowledge, Theory of Progress," pp. 456–88.

28. Max Weber, *The Protestant Ethic and the Spirit of Modern Capitalism*, trans. Talcott Parsons (New York: Scribner, 1958); Colin Campbell, *The Romantic Ethic and the Spirit of Modern Consumerism* (Cambridge, Mass.: Blackwell, 1987), pp. 58–95.

29. For discussions of the modern Christmas, see Steven Nissenbaum, *The Battle for Christmas: A Cultural History of America's Most Cherished Holiday* (New York: Vintage Books, 1996); Penne L. Restad, *Christmas in America, a History* (New York: Oxford University Press, 1995); Leigh Eric Schmidt, *Consumer Rites: The Buying and Selling of American Holidays* (Princeton, N.J.: Princeton University Press, 1995); William B. Waits, *The Modern Christmas in America* (New York: New York University Press, 1993); Karal Ann Marling, *Merry Christmas! Celebrating America's Greatest Holiday* (Cambridge, Mass.: Harvard University Press, 2000); and Daniel Miller, ed., *Unwrapping Christmas* (Oxford: Clarendon Press, 1993).

30. In addition to the sources listed in the previous note, see Marcel Mauss, *The Gift: The Form and Reason for Exchange in Archaic Societies*, trans. Ian Cunnison (New York: Norton, 1967), and Lewis Hyde, *The Gift: Imagination and the Erotic Life of Property* (New York: Vintage Books, 1983). For an intriguing expansion of these ideas, see Jean Baudrillard, *Symbolic Exchange and Death*, trans. Ian Hamilton Grant (London: Sage, 1993).

31. Kenneth Ames, *Death in the Dining Room and Other Tales of Victorian Culture* (Philadelphia: Temple University Press, 1992), pp. 35–43; Thorstein Veblen, *The Theory of the Leisure Class* (1899; reprint, New York: Dover, 1994), pp. 48–53.

32. Ames, *Death in the Dining Room*; Veblen, *Theory of the Leisure Class*; Maude Cook, *20th Century Hand book of Etiquette, or Key to Social and Business Success* (Philadelphia: Co-Operative Publishing, 1899), pp. 51–52.

33. For examples of colorful business and visiting cards beyond the market established by Prang, see the catalogs of the Atlantic Card Company and the Ohio Card Company in the Norcross Greeting Card Collection, Archives Center, National Museum of American History, Behringer Center, Smithsonian Institution, Washington, D.C., and the Joseph Downs Collection; illustrated visiting cards, Mensden Scrapbook Collection, book 1, p. 44; illustrated hidden name cards, document 354, both in the Joseph Downs Collection.

34. Wilhelm Von Bezold, *The Theory of Color in Its Relation to Art and Art-Industry* (Boston: Prang, 1876), p. 175.

35. Louis Prang, in *Prang's Chromo: A Journal of Popular Art* 1, no. 4 (1868): 5.

36. "Autobiography of Louis Prang," pp. 152–54; for a list of Prang's merchandise from this period, see *Catalog of Louis Prang and Co. for the Season, 1873*, Joseph Downs Collection.

37. Lydia Maria Child, "Illustrations of Progress," *New York Independent*, reprinted in *Prang's Chromo: A Journal of Popular Art* 1, no. 2 (1868): 1.

38. According to Luna Lambert, Prang's promotional competitions were the first of their kind ("The Seasonal Trade: Gift Cards and Chromolithography in America, 1874–1910" [Ph.D. diss., George Washington University, 1980]). Competitions sponsored by European firms began after Prang's first award was announced. Her extensive discussion of the gift-card industry provides helpful background against which the specific contributions of Prang can be measured.

39. Prang duly noted Rosina Emmet's teacher in his circular announcing the prize. A copy of the circular is in the Norcross Collection, series 2, box 42.

40. William Merritt Chase, quoted in Ronald G. Pisano, *A Leading Spirit in American Art: William Merritt Chase, 1849–1918* (Seattle: Henry Art Gallery, 1983), p. 87. This book celebrates Chase's teaching style.

41. Sarah Burns, *Inventing the Modern Artist: Art and Culture in Gilded Age America* (New Haven, Conn.: Yale University Press, 1996), p. 151. This book has taught me a tremendous amount about Chase, whose association with bohemianism is discussed on pp. 254, 261, and 266.

42. *Boston Advertiser*, 25 November 1880, quoted in a Louis Prang & Company circular, 26 November 1880, Norcross Collection, series 2, box 44. William Dean Howells mentions the *Boston Advertiser* in *The Rise of Silas Lapham* (1885; reprint, New York: Library of America, 1982). Bromfield Corey reads it, and the narrator describes it as "the only daily there is in the old-fashioned Bostonian sense" (p. 992).

43. Decorative Art, "Defense of the Judges," *New York Tribune*, 27 February 1881, Norcross Collection, series 2, box 44.

44. *Prang's Third Competition in Christmas Card Designs* [circular signed by R. E. Moore of the American Art Gallery], 11 July 1881, Norcross Collection, series 2, box 42.

45. Ibid.

46. *Prang's Prize Christmas Cards* [circular], 1882, Norcross Collection, series 2, box 42; Dora Wheeler Christmas card, "Good Tidings of Great Joy," Hallmark Archive, Hallmark Cards, Inc., Kansas City, Mo.

47. "Christmas Scatter Many Joys About You," Norcross Collection, series 2, box 3, folder 3.

48. "A Hearty Christmas Greeting," series 2, box 3, folder 4; "A Merry Christmas," series 2, box 3, folder 3, both in the Norcross Collection.

49. Prang, in *Prang's Chromo* 1, no. 4, p. 5; "Our New Publishing House," *Paper World* 1 (1880): 3–4.

50. Thorstein Veblen, *The Instinct for Workmanship, and the State of the Industrial Arts* (1914; reprint, New York: Huebsch,1922), pp. 30, 33, 199, and passim.

51. "Full of Mirth and Fun," Norcross Collection, series 2, box 42, folder 5.

52. Louis Prang, speech, 1897, Louis Prang Collection, box 1, Archives of American Art, Washington, D.C.

53. "Just over from Japan," Norcross Collection, series 2, box 43.

54. "A Modern Santa Claus," Louis Prang Files, vol. 3, p. 36; Paul Mullins, "The Contradictions of Consumption: An Archaeology of African America and Consumer Culture, 1850–1930" (Ph.D. diss., University of Massachusetts, 1996), pp. 435–38.

55. W. E. B. Du Bois, *The Souls of Black Folk*, in *Writings*, ed. Nathan Huggins (1902; reprint, New York: Library of America, 1986), pp. 363–64.

56. Howells, *Rise of Silas Lapham*, p. 905.

57. Amy Kaplan, *The Social Construction of American Realism* (Chicago: University of Chicago Press, 1988), p. 43.

58. Howells, *Rise of Silas Lapham*, p. 874.

59. Ibid.

60. Ibid., p. 923.

61. Ibid.

62. Ibid., p. 921.

63. Ibid., p. 922.

64. Ibid., p. 822.

65. Ibid., p. 887.

66. Ibid., p. 1021.

67. Quoted in C. Wright Mills, *White Collar: The American Middle Classes* (New York: Oxford University Press, 1956), p. xiv.

3. Corporate Sentiment

1. Olivier Zunz, *Making America Corporate, 1870–1920* (Chicago: University of Chicago Press, 1990); Roland Marchand, *Creating the Corporate Soul: The Rise of Public Relations and Corporate Imagery in American Big Business* (Berkeley: University of California Press, 1998); Naomi R. Lamoreaux, *The Great Merger Movement in American Business, 1895–1904* (New York: Cambridge University Press, 1985).

2. On the dominance of comics, see "St. Valentine's Day," *Harper's Weekly*, 21 February 1880, p. 113, and "Old Saint Valentine," *American Stationer*, 19 January 1901, p. 1; Visiting and Fancy Card Manufactory circular, Warshaw Collection, box 3, Archives Center, National Museum of American History, Behringer Center, Smithsonian Institution, Washington, D.C.; the valentines carried by the American News Company are discussed in "New Valentines," *American Stationer*, 19 January 1901, p. 4; William J. Burkhardt's

firm is mentioned in "Christmas Envelopes and Cards," *American Stationer*, 4 November 1905, p. 16; the history of McLoughlin Brothers is presented in Earl Reeves, "Malice in the Mail Box," *Collier's*, 13 February 1926, p. 19; Dutton's imported Ernst Nister's Easter and Christmas cards are advertised in *American Stationer*, 6 January 1900, p. 27; Raphael Tuck's valentines are advertised in *American Stationer*, 10 November 1900, p. 31.

3. On George C. Whitney's early career, see "Peaceful Death for George C. Whitney," *Worcester Daily Gazette*, 7 November 1915; a scrapbook containing several of Whitney's nineteenth-century valentines, along with a circular advertising his wares and announcing his branch offices for 1886, are in the Whitney Sample Book, 1886–87, document 24, Joseph Downs Collection of Manuscripts and Printed Ephemera, Winterthur Museum, Garden, and Library, Winterthur, Del. See also Elizabeth White, "Sentimental Enterprise: Sentiment and Profit in American Market Culture, 1830–1880" (Ph.D. diss., Yale University, 1995). Richard Ohmann describes the 1880s as a period in which manufacturers were still discovering the idea of a name brand and of national marketing (*Selling Culture: Magazines, Markets and Class at the Turn of the Century* [London: Verso, 1996]), pp. 82–91). Whitney was ahead of the curve among not only valentine and Christmas card publishers, but most manufacturers in the country. Ohmann discusses classic examples in which crises over production led to efforts to promote a national brand name through national advertising—Duke's cigarettes, Quaker oatmeal, Uneeda biscuits. Ohmann's main argument runs against the dominant interpretation of mass culture, which sees crises of mass production as driving innovations in marketing and advertising. He suggests that national advertising developed instead as a marketing technique for new kinds of goods that could be categorized as "convenience products," commodities that signified the quick, the modern, the new. To a certain degree, greeting cards fit into this category; they saved the labor of writing a letter. To the extent that the use of greeting cards merged with the practice of sending post cards, they clearly participated in the promotion of the modern.

4. "Peaceful Death"; "George C. Whitney Company Will Be Liquidated," *Worcester Daily Gazette*, 12 February 1942, p. 12.

5. George C. Whitney Company versions of Esther Howland–style valentines: "May Love Brighten Your Life" and "Fond Remembrance," Joseph Downs Collection, Whitney Sample Book, 1886–87, document 24; "I Can Sing and I Can Sew," Norcross Greeting Card Collection, series 2, box 7, folder 6, Archives Center, National Museum of American History, Behringer Center, Smithsonian Institution, Washington, D.C. Whitney's line of cheaper valentines is praised in "Whitney's Valentines," *American Stationer*, 4 November 1905, p. 5. For a discussion of organizational trends in business at the turn of the twentieth century, see Thomas Cochran, *American Business in the Twen-*

tieth Century (Cambridge, Mass.: Harvard University Press, 1972). Whitney's success in this area also kept his firm on the margins of the industry that would be created. Whitney's valentines and Christmas cards continued to appeal to children until the company closed during World War II. But his firm never competed with the major companies that arose in the first two decades of the twentieth century to build the modern greeting card.

6. Ernest Dudley Chase, *The Romance of Greeting Cards: An Historical Account of the Origin, Evolution and Development of Christmas Cards, Valentines and Other Forms of Greeting Cards from the Earliest Days to the Present Time. In Commemoration of the Fiftieth Anniversary of Rust Craft Greeting Cards, 1906–1956*, ed. James D. Chamberlain, with an introduction by Stephen Q. Shannon (Dedham, Mass.: Rust Craft, 1956), p. 33. Whitney's line is praised for its "many original and striking designs" in "Novel Art Goods," *American Stationer*, 29 December 1900, p. 4. By 1905, the same journal was happy to announce: "A specially good feature of the [Whitney] line is that the most striking things have not been confined to the expensive numbers, but they are scattered with fine discretion throughout the whole line, so that many of the good new things may be obtained at the popular prices. Whereas in former years, the shapes in the cheaper numbers have been confined pretty much to hearts, squares, etc., these numbers are shown this year in all the new and odd shapes" ("Whitney's Valentines," p. 4).

7. Here I mean to suggest some of the argument developed by Lewis Mumford in *Technics and Civilization* (1934; reprint, New York: Harcourt, Brace & World, 1963). Mumford sees the machine as a neutral technological development, an enlargement upon the tool but not a different ontological category. According to Mumford, machine-made cultural items are not necessarily inferior in quality. The issue of cultural quality is more complicated, necessarily including consideration of the human issues the item is intended to address and the human problems that it is supposed to consider or even help solve. Mumford lays the responsibility for the decline in quality that typically accompanies machine production not on the machine itself, but on those who share a philosophy of quantity, a philosophy supported by the economics of industrial capitalism.

8. "Post Card Sales," *American Stationer*, 2 September 1905, p. 6.

9. Gerald Cullinan, *The United States Postal Service* (New York: Praeger, 1973); Frank Staff, *The Picture Post Card and Its Origins* (New York: Praeger, 1966), pp. 54–62.

10. Cochran, *American Business*, p. 41; "Post Card Sales."

11. Alfred Holzman advertisement, *American Stationer*, 16 January 1906, p. 16; Edward Stern Company advertisement, *American Stationer*, 5 September 1905; the lines of holiday post cards carried by the American News Company were promoted in a series of stories in the same journal; "Holiday Post Cards,"

American Stationer, 23 September 1905, p. 18; "New Post Cards," *American Stationer*, 14 October 1905, p. 14; Souvenir Post Card Company advertisement, *American Stationer*, 24 September 1909; "The Post Card World" discusses the year's Thanksgiving cards in *American Stationer*, 9 October 1909, p. 24. The historical shift from a production-oriented society to a consumer-oriented society has a large literature, among the highlights of which are Leo Lowenthal, *Literature, Popular Culture and Society* (Palo Alto, Calif.: Pacific Books, 1961); Warren Susman, *Culture as History* (New York: Pantheon Books, 1984); and Richard Wightman Fox and T. J. Jackson Lears, eds., *The Culture of Consumption: Critical Essays in American History, 1880–1980* (New York: Pantheon Books, 1983).

12. Compare the Dutton advertisements in *American Stationer*, August 28, 1909, p. 13, and *American Stationer*, January 22, 1910, p. 7; Auburn Post Card Manufacturing Company, Auburn, Indiana, flyer, Warshaw Collection, box 1, folder 2. The P. F. Volland Company began to publish holiday post cards in Chicago in 1908 (Chase, *Romance of Greeting Cards*, p. 204). Joyce Hall began to sell post cards in Norfolk, Nebraska, in 1905 and in Kansas City, Missouri, in 1910 (Joyce Hall, with Curtiss Anderson, *When You Care Enough* [Kansas City, Mo.: Hallmark, 1979]). Also in 1910, the Elite Post Card Company began to produce its own cards in Kansas City ("The Post Card World," *American Stationer*, 22 January 1910, p. 22).

13. The crisis in the post card industry was addressed in many "Post Card World" columns throughout the spring, summer, and fall of 1910—for example, "Post Cards," *American Stationer*, 26 March 26 1910, pp. 42–44; "Cards and Books," *American Stationer*, 1 October 1910, p. 8; and "Does the Tariff Protect?" *American Stationer*, 5 November 1910, p. 28.

14. Hall and Anderson, *When You Care Enough*, pp. 25–38.

15. "Does the Tariff Protect?"; "The Call to Arms in the Post Card Trade," *American Stationer*, 29 November 1910, p. 28. Flyers for many small post card companies are in the Norcross Collection and the Warshaw Collection. The autonomy of traveling salesmen during this period is discussed in Zunz, *Making America Corporate*, and Timothy B. Spears, *100 Years on the Road: The Traveling Salesman in American Culture* (New Haven, Conn.: Yale University Press, 1995).

16. Dutton advertisement, *American Stationer*, 28 August 1909, p. 13.

17. "The Christmas Trade," *American Stationer*, 1 January 1910, p. 26; Chase, *Romance of Greeting Cards*, pp. 192, 195, 199, 200, 203–5; Wolfgang Saxon, "Irving Stone, 90, an Innovator in the Greeting Card Industry," *New York Times*, 19 January 2000, p. C27; Morry Weiss, *American Greetings Corporation* (New York: Newcomen Society, 1982).

18. Thomas Cochran, *Social Change in America* (New York: Harper & Row, 1971), p. 100. W. Lloyd Warner, Marchia Meeker, and Kenneth Eells claim

that a significant amount of Sinclair Lewis's abiding popularity derives from his "accurate knowledge" of the operations of class and social structure in the United States. They go on to say: "The general conclusions from scientific field studies of social status in the several regions of American society correspond very closely with what novelists, such as Edith Wharton, Theodore Dreiser, John Marquand, and others [including Lewis], report about status in America" (*Social Class in America: A Manual of Procedure for the Measurement of Social Status* [Chicago: Science Research Associates, 1949], pp. v, 6, 232–41). Olivier Zunz follows C. Wright Mills in dismissing Warner and his associates as the sociologists whom businessmen loved to read (*Why the American Century?* [Chicago: University of Chicago Press, 1998], pp. 98–103). His theorization of status as opposed to class conflict implied a rather benign, if still stratified, social system.

19. Elsie Clews Parsons, "Friendship, a Social Category," *American Journal of Sociology* 21 (1915): 230–33. For a suggestive and highly influential discussion of the cultural changes associated with the coming to dominance of the concept of personality, see Warren Susman, "'Personality' and the Making of Twentieth Century Culture," in *Culture as History*, pp. 271–85.

20. Mary A. Jordan, "On College Friendships," *Harper's Bazar*, December 1901, p. 726; "My Friendships: What They Have Taught and Brought Me," *Harper's Bazar*, November 1912, p. 548.

21. Tom Pendergast, *Creating the Modern Man: American Magazines and Consumer Culture, 1900–1950* (Columbia: University of Missouri Press, 2000), p. 150; Edgar A. Guest, "The Art of Making Friends," *American Magazine*, November 1928, pp. 7–9, 141–43; "The Kind of Friends Who Have Helped Me Most in Business," *American Magazine*, May 1928, pp. 143–45; Courtney Ryley Cooper, "Who Are Your Friends?" *American Magazine*, March 1933, pp. 36–37, 133–36. See also Fred C. Kelly, "Salesmanship and Courtship," *American Magazine*, February 1927, pp. 10–11, 64–65, and Joseph Cummings and J. C. Chase, "How Many Friends Have You?" *American Magazine*, August 1932, pp. 44–45, 100–101. The full development of the business theory of friendship came in 1936 when Dale Carnegie published *How to Win Friends and Influence People*. By this point, the mutual entanglements of business and friendship were so widely recognized as to be both common sense and a source of widespread anxieties, resulting in the massive sales of this book.

22. Sinclair Lewis, *Babbitt* in *Lewis at Zenith: Main Street, Babbitt, Arrowsmith* (1922; reprint, New York: Harcourt, Brace & World, 1961), pp. 377–80. This novel has no well-drawn female characters. The women are foils for the actions of the men. They also function as representations of the social contradictions pulling at the men. The business world that Lewis describes is also relentlessly white. Lewis is less sanguine about the exclusion of racialized minorities than he is about the misogynist aspects of this world, clearly pointing

out his characters' racial hostilities while letting their masculine anxieties go unmarked. Perhaps his un–self-conscious depiction of this homosocial business world renders the picture all that more useful.

23. Ibid., p. 543.

24. Ibid., p. 563.

25. Ibid., p. 550.

26. Ibid., p. 391.

27. Ibid., p. 455.

28. Ibid., p. 576.

29. Neil Harris regards *Babbitt* not so much as a novel but as a series of set pieces designed to demonstrate consumption and leisure as arenas for status competition ("The Drama of Consumer Desire," in *Cultural Excursions: Marketing Appetites and Cultural Tastes in Modern America* [Chicago: University of Chicago Press, 1990], pp. 174–97). Such an interpretation underestimates the element of identification between Lewis and Babbitt that lifts the character of George Babbitt out of the one-dimensional. Babbitt's world is a world of consumer goods, but it is also a world of business associates. Affect and power articulate both sets of objects into networks of meaning.

30. Abbe Ernest Dimnet, "Let's Speak of Friendship," *Rotarian*, December 1936, pp. 8–11; Robert F. Salade, "The Modern Master Printer," *American Printer*, 5 October 1923, p. 41; Cochran, *American Business*, pp. 57, 70, 188.

31. Chase, *Romance of Greeting Cards*, pp. 214–15.

32. Sydney J. Burgoyne to F. J. Clampitt, 9 August 1918, box 7, folder 7; advertising costs from March 1917, in bill from J. Rowland Mix Advertising Agency, box 5, folders 7 and 17; advertising costs in 1919, in bill from William H. Rankin Advertising Agency, box 17, folder 7, all in the P. F. Volland Company Archives, Chicago Public Library, Chicago, Ill.

33. P. F. Volland Company, special advertising insert, *American Stationer*, 26 March 1910; "Raise Two Lips for Me," Norcross Collection, series 2, box 7.

34. M. J. Turner & Company, bill for designing, engraving, mechanical-illustrating, and catalog-building, box 5, folder 19; Marquette Lithography Company, box 5, folder 7; Card Beveling and Gilding Company, box 5, folder 3; Barnes-Crosby Company, for photoengraving, box 3, folder 12; Nu-Art Engraving Company, for stamping and amending, box 3, folder 7, all in the Volland Archives.

35. Among the numerous examples that can be cited are Mrs. C. L. Kohler, bill, October 1917, box 1, folder 3; Maginal Wright Enright, bills, box 6, folder 11, box 11, folder 12, and box 13, folder 8; Edward Poucher to Paul Volland, 1 July 1918 and 8 August 1918, box 7, folder 8; and Poucher to Volland, telegram, 15 August 1918, box 7, folder 8, all in the Volland Archives; "The Law and the Lady," *Chicago Tribune*, 7 May 1919, p. 8.

36. "Miniature of Washington Made Her Kill," *Chicago Tribune*, 6 May 1919, p. 1; "Woman Kills Publisher," *New York Times*, 6 May 1919, p. 10; "Law and the Lady." I want to compare directly Paul Volland's manner of appropriating Vera Trepagnier's heirloom with Louis Prang's strategy of reproducing historically significant images. Among Prang's commercial failures was his reproduction of Theodore Kauffman's *Portrait of Senator Revels*. In line with his general policy, Prang had purchased the painting outright from the artist. Under the laws then in force, once Prang owned the painting, he had the right to make copies of it. As the first African-American senator, elected during Reconstruction, Hiram Revels could be seen as an image of African-American achievement or national unity, or as a symbol of northern domination over its defeated enemy. Prang's reproductions of the realistic and dignified portrait of Revels had the potential to act as a cultural force, countering the stereotyped blackface images prevalent in nineteenth-century mass culture.

Volland, on the contrary, was primarily interested in the market value of his reproductions of George Washington, not in any potential social meaning. He did not care why the portrait of Washington would be popular, nor was he concerned with any effects that the circulation of the image might produce. In fact, within business ideology, the transaction could be considered as an economic exchange purified of social meaning. Theoretically, contracts are engaged in by autonomous and putatively equal parties. As Brook Thomas has argued, to the extent that contractual relations promise an egalitarian approach to economic exchange (theoretically any two subjects can enter into an economic relationship), that promise is violated by the contract's refusal to consider the specific differences that individuate the two partners in the exchange (*American Literary Realism and the Failed Promise of Contract* [Berkeley: University of California Press, 1997], esp. pp. 4–5). Status differences and power relations that obtain in the social world do exert pressures and enforce limits on the values produced in and exchanged through business transactions.

37. In "Woman Kills Publisher," the *New York Times* published the company's version of the murder of Volland, quoting clerks in the office to the effect that "the woman had a hallucination that the publishing company owed her $5,000 in royalties." See also Jackson Lears's discussion of Sherwood Anderson in "Sherwood Anderson: Looking for the White Spot," in Richard Wightman Fox and T. J. Jackson Lears, eds., *The Power of Culture: Critical Essays in American History* (Chicago: University of Chicago Press, 1993), pp. 13–37.

38. J. P. McEvoy, *Slams of Life: With Malice for All, and Charity Toward None* (Chicago: Volland, 1919), p. 121.

39. J. P. McEvoy, *Show Girl* (New York: Simon and Schuster, 1928).

40. Ibid., p. 411.

41. Ibid., pp. 3–4.

42. Ibid., p. 68.

43. Ibid., pp. 68–69.

44. "From One 'Specialist' to Another," Norcross Collection, series 2, box 2, folder 1.

45. John Dewey, "Individualism, Old and New," in Jo Ann Boydston, ed., *The Later Works, 1925–1953*, vol. 5, *1929–1930* (Carbondale: Southern Illinois University Press, 1988), p. 80.

46. Ibid., p. 58.

47. Raymond Williams, *Marxism and Literature* (New York: Oxford University Press, 1977), pp. 83–89; Dewey, "Individualism," p. 59.

48. Cochran, *American Business*, p. 83. For a contemporary vision of the advantages of large-scale organizations, see Enoch Burton Gowin, *The Selection and Training of the Business Executive* (New York: Macmillan, 1918), esp. pp. 1–11.

49. Cochran, *American Business*, p. 57.

50. Erwin Schell, "Analyzing the Executive's Job," in Henry Metcalf, ed., *Business Management as a Profession* (Chicago: Shaw, 1927), p. 309.

51. Dewey, "Individualism," p. 70.

52. The list of qualities of managers and executives is in Gowin, *Selection and Training*, pp. 40–41. Absolutely indispensable for understanding the close relationships between business and domestic life is Angel Kwolek-Folland, *Engendering Business: Men and Women in the Corporate Office, 1870–1930* (Baltimore: Johns Hopkins University Press, 1994). This section of this chapter is deeply indebted to Kwolek-Folland's work. For a discussion of literary representations of the effort to produce loyalty to the firm, see Christopher Wilson, *White Collar Fictions: Class and Social Representation in American Literature, 1885–1925* (Athens: University of Georgia Press, 1992). In 1924, *American Printer* thanked all the businesses that had sent it Christmas cards the past season, recognizing the role that this domestic practice was playing in business relations ("How they Greeted Us—With Cards, broadsides, and books, our friends wished us well," *American Printer*, 5 February 1924, p. 25). Marchand discusses the efforts of corporate public-relations departments to create the "corporate soul" in *Creating the Corporate Soul*, esp. pp. 7–47.

53. Karl D. Fernstrom, Robert F. Elder, Wyman P. Fiske, Albert A. Schaeffer, and B. Alden Thresher, *Organization and Management of a Business Enterprise* (New York: Harper, 1935), pp. 212–13, 10; H. Sticker, "Character Reading—In one easy lesson for the printing salesman," *American Printer*, 19 March 1928, pp. 66–68; Thorstein Veblen, *The Theory of Business Enterprise* (New York: Scribner, 1904), pp. 84–85. See also Schell, "Analyzing the Executive's Job."

54. Hall and Anderson, *When You Care Enough*, p. 71. The language of displacement and condensation is drawn from psychoanalysis. I will elaborate my use of these terms in chapter 4, but here the basic meanings are sufficient. In-

tense affects are often displaced—that is, attached to objects outside of their original aim. Objects are equally often the locus of highly condensed—that is, multiple and layered—sets of affects and meanings. Sigmund Freud works through these terms initially in *Interpretation of Dreams*, trans. James Strachey (New York: Avon Books, 1965), pp. 311–44. A more concise discussion can be found in Freud's *New Introductory Lectures on Psychoanalysis*, trans. James Strachey (New York: Norton, 1965), p. 19.

55. Sample book of Ernest Chase's cards, 1912, Norcross Collection, series 3, box 9; "Gets More Per Word than Kipling," *American Magazine*, January 1916, pp. 50–52; Chase, *Romance of Greeting Cards*, p. 195.

56. "Gets More Per Word," pp. 51–52. Just for fun, let's work out the math on this single card. Let's say that the card cost 10 cents. We don't know for sure, but that price point would be typical for a relatively new card with minimal decoration. Total retail sales thus equaled $35,000 in the first year. Let's say that Davis gave a 40 percent discount to his retailers. That means that he grossed $21,000. If we assume that cost figures for his products were not very different from the costs incurred by Volland (for whom we have detailed records), then we can estimate the costs of production for those 350,000 cards. Volland paid Eaton, Crane, and Pike $14.58 for 1,600 cut cards of Dresden White vellum. If the same costs hold, then Davis paid $3,178.16 for the basic cards. If he beveled the edges of these cards, it cost $1 per thousand cards, or $350. The lettering cost $5 per line, or $20. The engraving cost $1 for the zinc plate to be cut. Volland had 75,000 cards printed for $181.50. That works out to $847.60 for printing 350,000 cards. The total cost of production for these cards would have equaled $4,796.76, leaving a net return on these cards of $16,203.24. This accounts for only production costs. It does not include costs for shipping or overhead or costs of promotion. Still, the profit potential in this business is evident.

57. Chase, *Romance of Greeting Cards*, pp. 218–19; "Off the Record," *Fortune*, November 1931, p. 10.

58. Hall and Anderson discuss the controversy in *When You Care Enough*, pp. 68–69, and Chase details the signing of Joseph McEvoy and Edgar Guest to the George Buzza Company in *Romance of Greeting Cards*, pp. 205–6. Magazines as varied as *Fortune* and *Literary Digest* commented on the market success of cards written by McEvoy and Guest ("Off the Record"; "Greetings: 1936 Sales of Christmas and New Year's Cards Expected to Break All Records," *Literary Digest*, 7 November 1936, p. 42).

59. Olive Percival, "Individual Christmas Cards, the Drawings of George Wolfe Plank," *House Beautiful*, December 1914, pp. 20–21.

60. "Christmas Thoughts of You" and "The Season's Greetings," series 5, box 455; "A Merry Christmas," series 5, box 455; "With Love for Mother," series 5, box 1304, all in the Norcross Collection.

61. Elizabeth Sprague and Curtiss Sprague, *How to Design Greeting Cards* (Pelham, N.Y.: Bridgman, 1926), pp. 9–10; Edward C. Bridgman, "Greetings as a Business," *American Printer*, 20 October 1923, pp. 32–35; Florence Lemmon, "Let's Have a Real Christmas Card This Year," *House Beautiful*, December 1925, pp. 628, 657, 684, 686.

62. Walter Frame, "Christmas Cards for You to Make," *Better Homes and Gardens*, November 1933, p. 28; Sprague and Sprague, *How to Design Greeting Cards*, pp. 50, 61.

63. G. Bishop Pulsifer, "If You Are Not in the Christmas Card Business, You're Missing Something Big," *American Photography*, December 1932, pp. 698–704; Arthur Norcross to Mr. Chaffee, 16 August 1927, Norcross Collection, series 1, box 11.

64. Bridgman, "Greetings as a Business"; Chase, *Romance of Greeting Cards*; Leigh Eric Schmidt, *Consumer Rites: The Buying and Selling of American Holidays* (Princeton, N.J.: Princeton University Press, 1995).

4. Condensation, Displacement, and Masquerade

1. For contemporary information on the percentages of Christmas card to other greeting card sales, see "Off the Record," *Fortune*, November 1931, pp. 10, 16, and "Greetings: 1936 Sales of Christmas and New Year's Cards Expected to Break All Records," *Literary Digest*, 7 November 1936, p. 42. Although Paul Volland was hiring most of his production work done throughout the 1910s, Hall Brothers first invested in its own production facilities in 1915. Many companies followed along soon after. "Norcross Almanac," Norcross Greeting Card Collection, series 1, box 30, Archives Center, National Museum of American History, Behringer Center, Smithsonian Institution, Washington, D.C.

2. On Norcross's image, see Ernest Dudley Chase, *The Romance of Greeting Cards: An Historical Account of the Origin, Evolution and Development of Christmas Cards, Valentines and Other Forms of Greeting Cards from the Earliest Days to the Present Time. In Commemoration of the Fiftieth Anniversary of Rust Craft Greeting Cards, 1906–1956*, ed. James D. Chamberlain, with an introduction by Stephen Q. Shannon (Dedham, Mass.: Rust Craft, 1956), pp. 208–9. In 1957 Bill Shane, executive vice president of the Barker Greeting Card Company, said: "Sophistication is for the coasts. Cornball is for the Midwest and the South" (quoted in "Industry: Hearts and Profits," *Newsweek*, 18 February 1957, pp. 88–89). The Norcross Collection contains many examples of the company's early promotional materials, including the "Norcross Almanac," series 1, box 30. For the list of holidays for which cards were being produced in 1956, see Chase, *Romance of Greeting Cards*, p. vii. Birthday cards were available throughout the year as part of the "everyday" line. For a nicely detailed and even-handed discussion of the roles played by greeting card manufacturers,

florists, and candy makers in the promotion and development of consumer-oriented holidays, see Leigh Eric Schmidt, *Consumer Rites: The Buying and Selling of American Holidays* (Princeton, N.J.: Princeton University Press, 1995).

3. For discussions of sendability, see Joyce Hall, with Curtiss Anderson, *When You Care Enough* (Kansas City, Mo.: Hallmark, 1979); Chase, *Romance of Greeting Cards*, pp. 216–26 and passim; and *Rust Craft Writers' Manual*, p. 24, Norcross Collection, series 1, box X-2.

4. "To My Valentine," series 5, box 1503; "Hello Pop," series 5, box 1107, both in the Norcross Collection.

5. "My Mother," series 5, box 1305; "Valentine Greetings to My Mother," series 5, box 1500; "To My Mother," series 5, box 1304; "I'm So Proud of You, Mother," series 5, box 1305; "Love to a Very Dear Mother," series 5, box 1305; "An Old Time Christmas," series 5, box 454; "Christmas Greetings," series 5, box 454; "Wishing You a Very Merry Christmas," series 2, box 2; "I'm in a Fog," series 5, box 1507; "To My Daddy," series 5, box 1107, all in the Norcross Collection.

6. Wendy Morris, "The Researcher's Guide to Ethnic Imagery in the Rustcraft Greeting Card Collection Occasion Cards, 1927–1959" (manuscript, Norcross Collection); Matthew Frye Jacobson, *Whiteness of a Different Color: European Immigrants and the Alchemy of Race* (Cambridge, Mass.: Harvard University Press, 1998); Michael Rogin, *Blackface, White Noise: Jewish Immigrants in the Hollywood Melting Pot* (Berkeley: University of California Press, 1996). Prompted by complaints from its members, the NAACP wrote several letters to Hallmark in the early 1950s requesting that the company cease the publication of blackface cards (NAACP Papers, Part 15: Segregation and Discrimination, Complaints and Responses, 1940–1955, series B, microfilm reel 13, Manuscripts Division, Library of Congress, Washington, D.C.). Hallmark responded by requesting the input of the Publicity Department, headed by Henry Lee Moon, in the design of future lines of cards. However, Hallmark continued to produce blackface cards well into the 1960s. Stereotypes of other ethnic groups appeared on such cards as "Confucius Say—Hell," series 5, box 1292; "It's Just the Gypsy in My Soul" series 5, box 1508; and "I'm on Warpath," series 5, box 1170, all in the NAACP Papers.

7. "Black in the Face," Norcross Collection, series 6, box 2014.

8. For discussions of blackface minstrelsy, see Constance Rourke, *American Humor* (1931; reprint, New York: Doubleday, 1953); Alexander Saxton, *The Rise and Fall of the White Republic* (New York: Verso, 1990); Robert Toll, *Blacking Up: The Minstrel Show in Nineteenth-Century America* (New York: Oxford University Press, 1974); Eric Lott, *Love and Theft: Blackface Minstrelsy and the American Working Class* (New York: Oxford University Press, 1993); Dale Cockrell, *Demons of Disorder: Early Blackface Minstrels and Their World* (New York: Cambridge University Press, 1997); William T. Lhamon, *Raising Cain: Blackface Performance from Jim Crow to Hip Hop* (Cambridge, Mass.: Harvard University

Press, 1998); Rogin, *Blackface, White Noise*; and Hans Nathan, *Dan Emmett and the Rise of Early Negro Minstrelsy* (Norman, Okla.: Oklahoma University Press, 1977). For discussions of the proliferation of these images in material culture, see Fath Davis Ruffins, "Ethnic Imagery in the Landscape of Commerce," in Susan Strasser, Charles McGovern, and Matthias Judt, eds., *Getting and Spending: European and American Consumer Societies in the Twentieth Century* (Washington, D.C., and New York: German Historical Institute and Cambridge University Press, 1998), pp. 379–405; Kenneth Goings, *Mammy and Uncle Mose: Black Collectibles and American Stereotyping* (Bloomington: Indiana University Press, 1994); and Patricia A. Turner, *Ceramic Uncles and Celluloid Mammies: Black Images and Their Influence on Culture* (New York: Anchor Books, 1994).

9. Linda Williamson, *Playing the Race Card: Melodramas of Black and White from Uncle Tom to O. J. Simpson* (Princeton, N.J.: Princeton University Press, 2001), p. 15 and passim.

10. Ian Gordon, *Comic Strips and Consumer Culture, 1890–1945* (Washington, D.C.: Smithsonian Institution Press, 1998), pp. 24–26, 62–67. On the use of these images and other collectibles to maintain negative concepts of African Americans, see Goings, *Mammy and Uncle Mose*. "Clinging Melon Vine," Domestic Life Collection of Greeting Cards, box 9, National Museum of American History, Behringer Center, Smithsonian Institution, Washington, D.C.; "Ah's a Neckin' Nigga," series 6, box 2024; "Ah Ain't No Loafa on a Sofa," series 5, box 1505, both in the Norcross Collection.

11. Ralph Ellison, *Invisible Man* (1952; reprint, New York: Vintage Books, 1995), pp. 272–73.

12. Red Star Drug Store advertisement, *Chicago Defender*, 22 December 1928, pt. 1, p. 7; "Remember to Send Greeting Cards," *Chicago Defender*, December 25, 1926, pt. 2, p. 3; Kevin Gaines, *Uplifting the Race: Black Leadership, Politics, and Culture in the Twentieth Century* (Chapel Hill: University of North Carolina Press, 1996), pp. 75, 207; E. Franklin Frazier, *Black Bourgeoisie* (New York: Free Press, 1957), pp. 38–42, 71–85. The persistence of a "strong work orientation," a "strong achievement orientation," and "strong kinship bonds" among black families in corporate America is documented in Susan D. Toliver, *Black Families in Corporate America* (Thousand Oaks, Calif.: Sage, 1998), pp. 58–63.

13. For a discussion of the fund-raising activities of Alpha Kappa Alpha, see Deborah Whaley, "By Culture, by Merit" (Ph.D. diss., University of Kansas, 2001). Cards sent by Langston Hughes, Aaron Douglas, and W. C. Handy are in the Greeting Card Collection, Art and Artifacts Division, Schomburg Center for Research in Black Culture, New York, N.Y.; card sent by W. E. B. Du Bois is in the Florence Luscomb Papers, Schlesinger Library, Cambridge, Mass.; Jeanette Temple Daindridge Papers, Kansas Collection, Kenneth Spencer Research Library, University of Kansas, Lawrence, Kans.; cards saved

by Leigh Walton and Hosea Hudson are in the Greeting Card Collection, Schomburg Center; "Negro Characters in Current Valentines: Mah Love Am Deeper than the Ocean, Lemme Pour It in Yah Ear," *Philadelphia Tribune*, 5 February 1931, p. 1.

14. "De Days of Slavery's Gone," P. F. Volland Company Archives, box 44, Chicago Public Library, Chicago, Ill.; "Hello, Honey Chile," series 5, box 1530; "You's the Nicest Kind of Friend," series 5, box 1282; "Wish ah Could Lay Eyes on You," series 5, box 1171, all in the Norcross Collection; Color-Tone, Bronze Craft, and Tawny Tints cards are in the Greeting Card Collection, boxes 3 and 4, Schomburg Center.

15. "Even Santa's Scotch This Year," Norcross Collection, series 5, box 459.

16. "Need a Pin-Up Gal?" Norcross Collection, series, 5, box 1520. For a discussion of the interlocking of heterosexual desire and wartime political demands, see Robert B. Westbrook, "'I Want a Girl, Just Like the Girl that Married Harry James': American Women and the Problem of Political Obligation in World War II," *American Quarterly* 42 (1990): 587–614. For an extension of this link into the cold war period, see Elaine Tyler May, *Homeward Bound: American Families in the Cold War Era* (New York: Basic Books, 1988).

17. "I May Not Be an Angel—But—," series 5, box 1520; "Just a Line on the Boss' Time," series 5, box 1169; "Hello Gorgeous," series 5, box 1507, all in the Norcross Collection. George Chauncey has written that "gay" was a code word, referring to "absolutely everything in any way pleasant or desirable," but not meaning exclusively homosexual. Literary representations of men "with a camp sensibility and an intimate knowledge of the homosexual scene" used the word frequently (*Gay New York: Gender, Urban Culture, and the Making of the Gay Male World, 1890–1940* [New York: Basic Books, 1994], pp. 14–21).

18. Joan Riviere, "Womanliness as Masquerade," *International Journal of Psychoanalysis* 10 (1929): 306. Another aspect of this article is quite interesting. Riviere's chief case study is a white woman who has regular fantasies of being assaulted by black men. She successfully deflects the assault in each case by encouraging the black man to engage with her sexually. Riviere fails to comment on whether or not this is also an essential aspect of womanliness.

19. "A Big 'Hello' for My Wife on Valentine's Day," Norcross Collection, series 5, box 1516.

20. As Catherine Belsey has written: "Modern Western culture privileges private life and personal experience over every other kind of satisfaction. . . . Social stability thus depends in more ways than one on the profoundly anti-social couple, cultivating their relationship, tending it, agonizing over its moments of crisis, anxiously watching it grow" (*Desire: Love Stories in Western Culture* [Cambridge, Mass.: Blackwell], pp. 5–6).

21. "To My Best Pal—Dad," series 5, box 1107; "To the Best Father in the World," series 5, box 1107; "To Dad on His Day," series 5, box 1107; "Here's

a Very Special Greeting," series 5, box 1107; "Well—Guess Who," series 5, box 1107; "Christmas Greetings to My Husband," series 5, box 488, all in the Norcross Collection.

22. Evan S. Connell, *Mrs. Bridge* (1959; reprint, San Francisco: North Point Press (1981).

23. Evan S. Connell, *Mr. Bridge* (San Francisco: North Point Press, 1969), p. 1.

24. "To the Dearest Wife in All the World," Norcross Collection, series 5, box 1519.

25. *Rust Craft Writer's Manual*, p. 26, Norcross Collection, series 1, box X-2.

26. Ibid., p. 18; H. Joseph Chadwick, *The Greeting Card Writer's Handbook* (New York: Writer's Digest, Funk & Wagnalls, 1968), p. 14.

27. "Tidy Little Rows," series 5, box 1502; "All My Love's Behind It," series 5, box 1513; "A New Slant," series 5, box 1518; "Bashful Type," series 5, box 1520, all in the Norcross Collection.

28. Candace Clark discusses the continuation of this tradition of the inarticulable nature of sympathy in "Sympathy Biography and Sympathy Margin," *American Journal of Sociology* 93 (1987): 290–321; sympathy cards, Norcross Collection, series 5, box 864.

29. "An Angel," Domestic Life Collection, box 6.

5. Knitting the Social Lace

1. Meggers Collection, boxes 3, 12, and 14, Domestic Life Collection of Greeting Cards, National Museum of American History, Behringer Center, Smithsonian Institution, Washington, D.C. Information about William Meggers can be found at http://www.cstl.nist.gov/nist839/839.01/meggers.html. William and Edith's first daughter, Betty Jean, became an important archaeologist. Information about her is available at http://emuseum.mnsu.edu/information/biography/kimno/meggers_betty.html.

2. Micaela Di Leonardo, "The Female World of Cards and Holidays: Women, Families, and the Work of Kinship," *Signs* 12 (1987): 443. Di Leonardo suggests that the status-mediating function of kinwork might be limited to the middle class.

3. Alfred Chandler, Jr., *The Visible Hand: The Managerial Revolution in American Business* (Cambridge, Mass.: Harvard University Press, 1979), pp. 8–9.

4. Talcott Parsons, "The Kinship System of the Contemporary United States," *American Anthropologist* 45 (1943): 22–38.

5. Ruth Cavan and Katherine Ranck, *The Family and the Depression: A Study of One Hundred Chicago Families* (Chicago: University of Chicago Press, 1938), p. 3; quoted in Paula Fass, *The Damned and the Beautiful: American Youth in the 1920s* (New York: Oxford University Press, 1977), pp. 97–98. See also Ernest

Burgess, *The Family, from Institution to Companionship* (New York: American Book, 1945); M. C. Elmer, *The Sociology of the Family* (Boston: Ginn, 1945); and Robert Angell, *The Family Encounters the Depression* (New York: Scribner, 1936). Historians examining the transformations in family structure include Christopher Lasch, *Haven in a Heartless World: The Family Besieged* (New York: Basic Books, 1977); Steven Mintz and Susan Kellogg, D*omestic Revolutions: A Social History of American Family Life* (New York: Free Press, 1988); and Stephanie Coontz, *The Way We Never Were: American Families and the Nostalgia Trap* (New York: Basic Books, 1992).

6. Cavan and Ranck, *Family and the Depression*, pp. 2–9.

7. Meggers Collection, box 14. The translation of Ch. Fabry's card from the French is by the author.

8. W. Lloyd Warner, *The Corporation in the Emergent American Society* (New York: Harper, 1962), pp. 16–17.

9. The valentine that Ben sent to his mother and the cards inherited from Mrs. J. Reid are in box 1, and the scrapbooks and lists are in box 3, of the Benjamin Platt Forbes Collection, Ohio Historical Society, Columbus, Ohio.

10. Biographical information is from the finding aid for the Helen Sioussat Collection, National Association of Broadcasters Archives, University of Maryland, College Park, Md.

11. Anne Rittenhouse, *Greeting Cards: When and How to Use Them* (New York: Greeting Card Association, 1926), pp. 5, 8.

12. Hope and Johnnie Hanes card, series 3, box 1; all other cards, series 3, boxes 2 and 3, all in the Helen Sioussat Collection.

13. Florence Luscomb Papers, box 6, folders 129, 130, 131, 142, and 145, Schlesinger Library, Radcliffe Institute, Cambridge, Mass. For information on Luscomb's life, see Sharon Hartman Storm, *Political Woman: Florence Luscomb and the Legacy of Radical Reform* (Philadelphia: Temple University Press, 2001).

14. Warner, *Corporation*, p. 5.

15. Collections of nineteenth-century valentines and Christmas cards held at the American Antiquarian Society, the National Museum of American History, the Society for the Preservation of New England Antiquities, and the Winterthur Museum, Garden, and Library show that writing on cards with printed messages was quite rare. See the mailed holiday post cards in the Norcross Greeting Card Collection, series 2, box 3, Archives Center, National Museum of American History, Behringer Center, Smithsonian Institution, Washington, D.C. Gertrude Maurer Post Card Collection courtesy of Cathy Lynn Gosser.

16. Criticism of the "impersonal" greeting card is ubiquitous in popular periodicals of the first half of the twentieth century. For one early example, see Carlyle Ellis, "Put Your Self in Your Gift Cards—A Loving Touch Banishes Formality, and Is Easy," *Delineator*, December 1915, p. 29; Norcross

promotional material, Norcross Collection, series 1, box 11, folder 6; Joyce Hall, with Curtiss Anderson, *When You Care Enough* (Kansas City, Mo.: Hallmark, 1979), p. 71.

17. Examples of Service Notes are in the Norcross Collection, series 1, box 27, folder 1. The bricoleur makes do with what is given to her, transforming the detritus of mass culture into the personalized tools of a creative individual. For a lengthy discussion, see Michel DeCerteau, *The Practice of Everyday Life*, trans. Steven Rendall (Berkeley: University of California Press, 1984). The concept of the punctum, the aspect of an image that captures the eye of the individual observer and renders that image forever personalized, is elaborated by Roland Barthes in *Camera Lucida: Reflections on Photography*, trans. Richard Howard (New York: Hill and Wang, 1981). "People Who Make Noise," Florence Luscomb Papers, box 6, folder 142.

18. All examples are drawn from the Collection of Greeting Cards, boxes 1, 3, 4, 6, 7, and 8, Popular Culture Library, Bowling Green State University, Bowling Green, Ohio.

19. "Poetry Ain't Hot Stuff," Helen Sioussat Collection, box 1.

20. All examples are drawn from the Collection of Greeting Cards, boxes, 4, 7, and 8.

21. All examples are drawn from the Domestic Life Collection, box 17.

6. All This Senseless Rationality

1. Dennis Farney, "Inside Hallmark's Love Machine," *Wall Street Journal*, 14 February 1990, pp. B1, B10; Gerri Hirshey, "Happy [ ] Day to You," *New York Times Magazine*, 2 July 1995, pp. 20–27, 34, 43–45; "Dear Daughter," collection of the author.

2. Reconciliation cards are discussed in Farney, "Inside Hallmark's Love Machine," p. B10, and the development of "universal specific" language is traced in Hirshey, "Happy [ ] Day to You," p. 25.

3. Unpaginated print version of "A Tour Through Rust Craft," series 1, box X-1; *How Rust Craft Greeting Cards of Character Are Made*, series 1, box X-1, both in the Norcross Greeting Card Collection, Archives Center, National Museum of American History, Behringer Center, Smithsonian Institution, Washington, D.C. Since the photographs for the tour provide a more detailed view of the production process than does the pamphlet, my discussion is based primarily on it. Roland Marchand, *Creating the Corporate Soul: The Rise of Public Relations and Corporate Imagery in American Big Business* (Berkeley: University of California Press, 1998), pp. 357–63.

4. "Tour Through Rust Craft."

5. *How Rust Craft Greeting Cards of Character Are Made*, p. 16; "Tour Through Rust Craft."

6. Frank Shaw, "Your Greeting Card Market," *Modern Stationer*, May 1950; "Just How Many Greeting Cards Should a Person Receive This Christmas?" *New York Times*, 5 December 1956; "Industry: Hearts and Profits," *Newsweek*, 18 February 1957, pp. 88–89; "Record Keeping for Greeting Card Sales," *Giftwares*, August 1958; Fred Eichelbaum, "Greeting Cards Lead in Stationery Field," *Women's Wear Daily*, 9 May 1958; "Hallmark Puts Bards to Work Selling Cards," *Advertising Age*, 6 July 1959, all in scrapbooks in the Norcross Collection, series 3.

7. An incomplete set of the anonymous and unpaginated trend reports is in the Norcross Collection, series 1, box X. The reports seem to be organized as a set of talking points or outlines for oral presentation, since they include references to visual aids that are not included in the written versions. Consumer credit not only was easily available, but was easily and increasingly exploited. In 1958, the total amount of consumer debt was calculated to be $45 billion. In 1965, it reached $94.8 billion. By 1988, it had exploded to $666 billion. For a careful analysis of the development of consumer credit and its impact on consumer culture, see Lendol Calder, *Financing the American Dream: A Cultural History of Consumer Credit* (Princeton, N.J.: Princeton University Press, 1999), which presents these figures on pp. 9–10.

8. Trend report for April 1959 [italics in the original], Norcross Collection, series 1, box X.

9. Bill Shane, quoted in "Industry: Hearts and Profits," p. 88; Samuel Golden to Edward Costikyan, 10 March 1953, microfilm reel 2; Samuel Golden to Ken Barker, 25 June 1956, microfilm reel 2, both in American Artists Group Collection, Archives of American Art, Washington, D.C. For more on the marketing strategies used by the American Artists Group, see Barry Shank, "Subject, Commodity, Marketplace: The American Artists Group and the Mass Production of Distinction," *Radical History Review* 76 (2000): 25–52.

10. Examples of Citation, Fravessi-Lamont, B-C Cynics Sanctum, and William Box cards are in the Collection of Greeting Cards, boxes 7 and 8, Popular Culture Library, Bowling Green State University, Bowling Green, Ohio.

11. These Hi Brow cards are in the Collection of Greeting Cards, box 8; J. P. McEvoy, *Slams of Life: With Malice for All, and Charity Toward None* (Chicago: Volland, 1919). Pierre Bourdieu covers the social function of art in *Distinction: A Social Critique of the Judgement of Taste*, trans. Richard Nice (Cambridge, Mass.: Harvard University Press, 1984), and *The Rules of Art: Genesis and Structure of the Literary Field*, trans. Susan Emanuel (Stanford, Calif.: Stanford University Press, 1992).

12. Bob Hammerquist, "How to Write Studio Cards and Still Have Time Left for Sex," in H. Joseph Chadwick, ed., *The Greeting Card Writer's Handbook* (New York: Writer's Digest, Funk & Wagnalls, 1968), pp. 101–21. For a discussion of the "thing"—that unrepresentable kernel of truth at the heart of

every ideological representation—see Slavoj Zizek, *The Sublime Object of Ideology* (New York: Verso, 1989). Melissa Schrift discusses the images of women's bodies in studio cards in "Icons of Femininity in Studio Cards: Women, Communication and Identity," *Journal of Popular Culture* 27 (1994): 111–22.

13. Henrietta Strong, quoted in Dorothy Roe, "Sentiment Never Goes Out of Style," *Dover (Ohio) Reporter*, 26 July 1959, Rust Craft Scrapbook, Norcross Collection, series 3; Chadwick, *Greeting Card Writer's Handbook*, p. 5; Richard Todd, "We Have Several Tons of Excess Sequins," *Audience*, March–April 1971, pp. 4–11; "And Means It," Collection of Greeting Cards, box 8.

14. My discussion of the condition of postmodernity is drawn most heavily from David Harvey, *The Condition of Postmodernity: An Inquiry into the Origins of Cultural Change* (Oxford: Blackwell, 1989). I have found other useful discussions of the postmodern to include François Lyotard, *The Postmodern Condition: A Report on Knowledge*, trans. Geoff Bennington and Brian Massumi (Minneapolis: University of Minnesota Press, 1984); Fredric Jameson, *Postmodernism, or the Cultural Logic of Late Capitalism* (Durham, N.C.: Duke University Press, 1991); Jean Baudrillard, *For a Critique of the Political Economy of the Sign*, trans. Charles Levin (St. Louis: Telos Press, 1981); and Zygmunt Bauman, *Intimations of Postmodernity* (London: Routledge, 1992).

15. Peter F. Drucker, *The Age of Discontinuity: Guidelines to Our Changing Society* (New York: Harper & Row, 1969), pp. 42–57, 145–46.

16. Jerry B. Poe, *An Introduction to the American Business Enterprise*, 6th ed. (Homewood, Ill.: Irwin, 1986), p. 17; Drucker, *Age of Discontinuity*, pp. 199–200. In the same passage, Drucker explains that "in the knowledge organization," by which he means industries operating in the knowledge economy, "every knowledge worker is an 'executive.'" By 1990, the importance of innovation lay at the center of Peter Senge's influential *The Fifth Discipline: The Art and Planning of the Learning Organization* (New York: Doubleday Currency, 1990). For Senge, regular innovation requires constant learning, and the difference between an effective business organization and one that fails lies in the organization's ability to learn. Senge is, in effect, a structuralist, arguing for the importance of "systems thinking" as the key to understanding the problems that businesses face. For further evidence of the dissemination of these ideas into the mainstream of management literature, see John E. Tropman, *The Management of Ideas in the Creating Organization* (Westport, Conn.: Quorum Books, 1998); Ralph Stacey, *Complexity and Creativity in Organizations* (San Francisco: Berrett-Koehler, 1996); and any of Tom Peters's many popular books, especially *Liberation Management: Necessary Disorganization for the Nanosecond Nineties* (New York: Knopf, 1992).

17. Mary Britton King, "Make Love, Not Work: New Management Theory and the Social Self," *Radical History Review* 76 (2000): 20. The belief that

profit is the sole objective marker of all value is endemic in business publications, but for one example among many see Senge, *Fifth Discipline*, p. 15.

18. Katherine S. Newman, *Falling from Grace: Downward Mobility in the Age of Affluence* (Berkeley: University of California Press, 1988), pp. 1–7. In *Methodology of the Oppressed* (Minneapolis: University of Minnesota Press, 2000), Chela Sandoval argues that this structure of feeling, while seemingly new in the overdeveloped countries, is actually quite similar to one common in the less developed world.

19. Todd, "We Have Several Tons," p. 4; Harvard Business School, *Holiday Greetings, Inc., (Abridged)*, report of the Harvard Business School (Boston: Harvard Business School Publications, 1988), pp. 1–2. Hallmark's history of successful advertising, particularly the popularity of *Hallmark Hall of Fame*, is discussed in "Hallmark Puts Bards to Work." Todd discusses the continued success of the show in "We Have Several Tons," p. 5. See also Jeff Kisseloff, "A Half-Century of Quality, Paid for by Greeting Cards," *New York Times*, 31 January 1999, p. 31.

20. John Collins, quoted in Harvard Business School, *Hallmark Cards*, report of the Harvard Business School (Boston: Harvard Business School Publications, 1986), pp. 3–5; Todd, "We Have Several Tons," p. 4; "Tour Through Rust Craft"; James McKinley, "If You've Got an Ounce of Feeling, Hallmark Has a Ton of Sentiment," *American Heritage* 34 (1982): 75; Harvard Business School, *Hallmark Cards*, p. 9.

21. Irvine Hockaday, Jr., quoted in Robert McGough, "Pansies Are Green," *Forbes*, 10 February 1986, p. 89; Metropolitan Museum of Art, Recycled Paper Products, and Black Santa Christmas cards, collection of the author; Freedom Greetings Kwanzaa card, Susie Page Collection of Afro-American Greeting Cards, folder 9, National Museum of American History, Behringer Center, Smithsonian Institution, Washington, D.C.; Orphan Productions cards, Art and Artifacts Division, Schomburg Center for Research in Black Culture, New York, N.Y.; Sunshine Lines cards, Collection of Greeting Cards, box 1. Mention of Recycled Paper's success with its "whimsical animal" images is in McGough, "Pansies Are Green," p. 90, while Schrift discusses Recycled Paper's appeal to educated women in "Icons of Femininity," pp. 118–19. By the early 1990s, Gibson was marketing Black Santa cards to the black middle class. Hallmark was aggressively pursuing this group as well with its Mahogany division, and producing cards drawn by B. Kliban to compete with Sandra Boynton's cat cards. The significance of "alternative cards" and the late movement of the major greeting card companies to latch onto this development are discussed in Hirshey, "Happy [ ] Day to You," p. 23. Blue Mountain Arts's successful suit forcing Hallmark to destroy thousands of its blatantly copied cards is discussed in Farney, "Inside Hallmark's Love Machine," p. B1.

22. "Concept Development: Marrying the Words and the Pictures," *Expressions*, November 1989, p. 4; Robert Stark, quoted in McGough, "Pansies Are Green," p. 90; "CAESAR Rules the Sentiments," *Expressions*, November 1989, p. 5; John Grossman, "The Kiss," *Sky*, January 1998, pp. 62–67.

23. King, "Make Love, Not Work," p. 20. Hallmark's mechanical production methods are described in Grossman, "Kiss," pp. 62–67, and its writing sessions in Hirshey, "Happy [ ] Day to You," pp. 21–22, and Farney, "Inside Hallmark's Love Machine," p. B1.

24. Hallmark is a privately owned corporation and is not required to publicize many aspects of its financial operations. Apparently, the company is quite proud of its profit-sharing plan, as this figure of one-third employee ownership shows up in many journalistic pieces about the company. Other company benefits, such as trips and movie tickets, are also widely publicized. See, for example, Farney, "Inside Hallmark's Love Machine," p. B1; Hirshey, "Happy [ ] Day to You," p. 22; and John Grossman, "Life as a Hallmarker," *Sky*, January 1998, p. 65.

25. Barbara Loots, quoted in Farney, "Inside Hallmark's Love Machine," p. B10; "No One Ever Said," collection of the author.

26. Joyce Hall, with Curtiss Anderson, *When You Care Enough* (Kansas City, Mo.: Hallmark, 1979), p. 71; Harvey, *Condition of Postmodernity*, p. 292. The figure of 8 billion cards a year is cited in Hirshey, "Happy [ ] Day to You," p. 21, while that of 7.5 billion is given in Grossman, "Kiss," p. 62.

Bibliography

Archival Collections

American Antiquarian Society. Graphic Arts Division. Worcester, Mass.

American Artists Group Collection. Archives of American Art, Washington, D.C.

Boston Public Library. Prints Division. Boston, Mass.

Daindridge, Jeanette Temple. Papers. Kansas Collection, Kenneth Spencer Research Library, University of Kansas, Lawrence, Kans.

Domestic Life Collection of Greeting Cards. National Museum of American History, Behringer Center, Smithsonian Institution, Washington, D.C.

Downs, Joseph. Collection of Manuscripts and Printed Ephemera. Winterthur Museum, Garden, and Library, Winterthur, Del.

Forbes, Benjamin Platt. Collection. Ohio Historical Society, Columbus, Ohio.

Greeting Cards, Collection of. Popular Culture Library, Bowling Green State University, Bowling Green, Ohio.

Library of Congress. Prints Division. Washington, D.C.

Luscomb, Florence. Papers. Schlesinger Library, Radcliffe Institute, Cambridge, Mass.

Mendsden Scrapbook Collection. Joseph Downs Collection of Manuscripts and Printed Ephemera. Winterthur Museum, Garden, and Library, Winterthur, Del.

NAACP. Papers. Manuscript Division. Library of Congress, Washington, D.C.

Norcross Greeting Card Collection. Archives Center, National Museum of American History, Behringer Center, Smithsonian Institution, Washington, D.C.

Page, Susie. Collection of Afro-American Greeting Cards. National Museum of American History, Behringer Center, Smithsonian Institution, Washington, D.C.

P. F. Volland Company. Archives. Chicago Public Library, Chicago, Ill.

Prang, Louis. Collection. Archives of American Art, Washington, D.C.

——. Files. New York Public Library, New York, N.Y.

Schomburg Center for Research in Black Culture. Greeting Card Collection. Art and Artifacts Division. New York, N.Y.

Sioussat, Helen. Collection. National Association of Broadcasters Archives, University of Maryland, College Park, Md.

Society for the Preservation of New England Antiquities. Boston, Mass.

Valentine Collection. American Antiquarian Society. Worcester, Mass.

Warshaw Collection. Archives Center, National Museum of American History, Behringer Center, Smithsonian Institution, Washington, D.C.

Secondary Sources

Ames, Kenneth. *Death in the Dining Room and Other Tales of Victorian Culture*. Philadelphia: Temple University Press, 1992.

Angell, Robert. *The Family Encounters the Depression*. New York: Scribner, 1936.

Armstrong, Nancy. *Desire and Domestic Fiction*. New York: Oxford University Press, 1987.

Barthes, Roland. *Camera Lucida: Reflections on Photography*. Translated by Richard Howard. New York: Hill & Wang, 1981.

Bauman, Zygmunt. *Intimations of Postmodernity*. London: Routledge, 1992.

Baudrillard, Jean. *For a Critique of the Political Economy of the Sign*. Translated by Charles Levin. St. Louis: Telos Press, 1981.

——. *Symbolic Exchange and Death*. Translated by Ian Hamilton Grant. London: Sage, 1993.

Beecher, Catharine Esther, and Harriet Beecher Stowe. *The American Woman's Home or, Principles of Domestic Science; Being a Guide to the Formation and Maintenance of Economical, Healthful, Beautiful and Christian Homes*. 1869. Reprint. Watkins Glen, N.Y.: American Life Foundation, Library of Victorian Culture, 1979.

Belsey, Catherine. *Desire: Love Stories in Western Culture*. Cambridge, Mass.: Blackwell, 1994.

Benjamin, Walter. *The Arcades Project*. Translated by Howard Eiland and Kevin McLaughlin. Cambridge, Mass.: Harvard University Press, 1999.

Bezold, Wilhelm Von. *The Theory of Color in Its Relation to Art and Art-Industry*. Boston: Prang, 1876.

Blumin, Stuart. *The Emergence of the Middle Class: Social Experience in the American City, 1760–1900*. New York: Cambridge University Press, 1989.

Bourdieu, Pierre. *Distinction: A Social Critique of the Judgement of Taste*. Translated by Richard Nice. Cambridge, Mass.: Harvard University Press, 1984.

——. *The Rules of Art: Genesis and Structure of the Literary Field*. Translated by Susan Emanuel. Stanford, Calif.: Stanford University Press, 1992.

Bridgman, Edward C. "Greetings as a Business." *American Printer*, 20 October 1923, pp. 32–35.

Brown, Gillian. *Domestic Individualism: Imagining Self in Nineteenth Century America*. Berkeley: University of California Press, 1990.

Bryson, Norman. *Vision and Painting: The Logic of the Gaze*. London: Macmillan, 1983.

Buday, George. *The History of the Christmas Card*. London: Rockliff, 1954.

Burgess, Ernest. *The Family, from Institution to Companionship*. New York: American Book, 1945.

Burgett, Bruce. *Sentimental Bodies: Sex, Gender, and Citizenship in the Early Republic*. Princeton, N.J.: Princeton University Press, 1998.

Burns, Sarah. *Inventing the Modern Artist: Art and Culture in Gilded Age America*. New Haven, Conn.: Yale University Press, 1996.

Calder, Lendol. *Financing the American Dream: A Cultural History of Consumer Credit*. Princeton, N.J.: Princeton University Press, 1999.

"CAESAR Rules the Sentiments." *Expressions*, November 1989, p. 5.

"The Call to Arms in the Post Card Trade." *American Stationer*, 29 November 1910, p. 28.

Campbell, Colin. *The Romantic Ethic and the Spirit of Modern Consumerism*. Cambridge, Mass.: Blackwell, 1987.

"Cards and Books." *American Stationer*, 1 October 1910, p. 8.

Cavan, Ruth, and Katherine Ranck. *The Family and the Depression: A Study of One Hundred Chicago Families*. Chicago: University of Chicago Press, 1938.

Chadwick, H. Joseph, ed. *The Greeting Card Writer's Handbook*. New York: Writer's Digest, Funk & Wagnalls, 1968.

Chandler, Alfred, Jr. *The Visible Hand: The Managerial Revolution in American Business*. Cambridge, Mass.: Harvard University Press, 1979.

Chapman, Mary, and Glenn Hendler, eds. *Sentimental Men: Masculinity and the Politics of Affect in American Culture*. Berkeley: University of California Press, 1999.

Chase, Ernest Dudley. *The Romance of Greeting Cards: An Historical Account of the Origin, Evolution and Development of Christmas Cards, Valentines and Other Forms of Greeting Cards from the Earliest Days to the Present Time. In Commemoration of the Fiftieth Anniversary of Rust Craft Greeting Cards, 1906–1956*. Edited by James D. Chamberlain, with an introduction by Stephen Q. Shannon. Dedham, Mass.: Rust Craft, 1956.

Chase, Joseph Cummings. "How Many Friends Have You?" *American Magazine*, August 1932, pp. 44–45, 100–101.

Chauncey, George. *Gay New York: Gender, Urban Culture, and the Making of the Gay Male World, 1890–1940*. New York: Basic Books, 1994.

Child, Lydia Maria. "Illustrations of Progress." *New York Independent*. Reprinted in *Prang's Chromo: A Journal of Popular Art* 1, no. 2 (1868): 1.

Christensen, Gloria. "Esther Howland." *New England Quarterly* 33 (1969).

"Christmas Envelopes and Cards." *American Stationer*, 4 November 1905, p. 16.

"The Christmas Trade." *American Stationer*, 1 January 1910, p. 26.

Clark, Candace. "Sympathy Biography and Sympathy Margin." *American Journal of Sociology* 93 (1987): 290–321.

Cochran, Thomas. *American Business in the Twentieth Century*. Cambridge, Mass.: Harvard University Press, 1972.

——. *Social Change in America*. New York: Harper & Row, 1971.

Cockrell, Dale. *Demons of Disorder: Early Blackface Minstrels and Their World*. New York: Cambridge University Press, 1997.

A Collection of New and Original Valentines, Serious & Satirical, Sublime & Ridiculous, on all the ordinary names, professions, trades, etc.; With an Introductory Treatise on the Composition of a valentine by a Master of Hearts. London: Ward & Lock, 1857.

Comic Valentine Writer. Comprising the best pieces suitable for the purpose to be found in the whole range of Poetical Literature, besides many appropriate originals. New York: Strong, n.d.

"Concept Development: Marrying the Words and the Pictures." *Expressions*, November 1989, p. 4.

Connell, Evan S. *Mr. Bridge*. San Francisco: North Point Press, 1969.

——. *Mrs. Bridge*. 1959. Reprint. San Francisco: North Point Press, 1981.

"Controversy with an Art Critic." *Prang's Chromo: A Journal of Popular Art* 1, no. 2 (1868): 2–3.

Cook, Maude. *20th Century Hand Book of Etiquette, or Key to Social and Business Success*. Philadelphia: Co-Operative Publishing, 1899.

Coontz, Stephanie. *The Way We Never Were: American Families and the Nostalgia Trap*. New York: Basic Books, 1992.

Cooper, Courtney Ryley. "Who Are Your Friends?" *American Magazine*, March 1933, pp. 36–37, 133–36.

Cullinan, Gerald. *The United States Postal Service*. New York: Praeger, 1973.

Davidson, Cathy, ed. "No More Separate Spheres" [special issue]. *American Literature* 70 (1998).

DeCerteau, Michel. *The Practice of Everyday Life*. Translated by Steven Rendall. Berkeley: University of California Press, 1984.

Dewey, John. "Individualism, Old and New." In Jo Ann Boydston, ed., *The Later Works, 1925–1953*. Volume 5, *1929–1930*, pp. 41–123. Carbondale: Southern Illinois University Press, 1988.

Dickens, Charles. "Cupid's Manufactory." *All the Year Round: A Weekly Journal*, 20 February 1864, pp. 26–30.

Di Leonardo, Micaela. "The Female World of Cards and Holidays: Women, Families, and the Work of Kinship." *Signs* 12 (1987): 440–53.

Dimnet, Abbe Ernest. "Let's Speak of Friendship." *Rotarian*, December 1936, pp. 8–11.

"Does the Tariff Protect?" *American Stationer*, 5 November 1910, p. 28.

Douglas, Ann. *The Feminization of American Culture*. New York: Anchor Books, 1988.

Drucker, Peter F. *The Age of Discontinuity: Guidelines to Our Changing Society*. New York: Harper & Row, 1969.

Du Bois, W. E. B. *The Souls of Black Folk*. In *Writings*. Edited by Nathan Huggins. 1902. Reprint. New York: Library of America, 1986.

Eichelbaum, Fred. "Greeting Cards Lead in Stationery Field." *Women's Wear Daily*, 9 May 1958.

Ellis, Carlyle. "Put Your Self in Your Gift Cards—A Loving Touch Banishes Formality, and Is Easy." *Delineator*, December 1915, p. 29.

Ellison, Ralph. *Invisible Man*. 1952. Reprint. New York: Vintage Books, 1995.

Elmer, M. C. *The Sociology of the Family*. Boston: Ginn, 1945.

Emerson, Marion Winslow. "Pioneer Career Woman and Her Valentines." *Hobbies: The Magazine for Collectors*, February 1948, n.p.

Farney, Dennis. "Inside Hallmark's Love Machine." *Wall Street Journal*, 14 February 1990, pp. B1, B10.

Fass, Paula. *The Damned and the Beautiful: American Youth in the 1920s*. New York: Oxford University Press, 1977.

Fernstrom, Karl D., Robert F. Elder, Wyman P. Fiske, Albert A. Schaeffer, and B. Alden Thresher. *Organization and Management of a Business Enterprise*. New York: Harper, 1935.

Fliegelman, Jay. *Declaring Independence: Jefferson, Natural Language and the Culture of Performance*. Stanford, Calif.: Stanford University Press, 1993.

Fox, Richard Wightman, and T. J. Jackson Lears, eds. *The Culture of Consumption: Critical Essays in American History, 1880–1980*. New York: Pantheon Books, 1983.

Frame, Walter. "Christmas Cards for You to Make." *Better Homes and Gardens*, November 1933, pp. 28, 38.

Frazier, E. Franklin. *Black Bourgeoisie*. New York: Free Press, 1957.

Freud, Sigmund. *Interpretation of Dreams*. Translated by James Strachey. New York: Avon Books, 1965.

——. *New Introductory Lectures on Psychoanalysis*. Translated by James Strachey. New York: Norton, 1965.

Gaines, Kevin. *Uplifting the Race: Black Leadership, Politics, and Culture in the Twentieth Century*. Chapel Hill: University of North Carolina Press, 1996.

Garvey, Ellen Gruber. *Adman in the Parlor: Magazines and the Gendering of Consumer Culture, 1880s to 1910s*. New York: Oxford University Press, 1996.

Gem Valentine Writer. New York: Strong, n.d.

"George C. Whitney Company Will Be Liquidated." *Worcester Daily Gazette*, 12 February 1942, p. 12.

"Gets More per Word than Kipling." *American Magazine*, January 1916, pp. 50–52.

Godkin, E. L. "Chromo-civilization." *Nation*, September 1874, pp. 201–202.

Goings, Kenneth. *Mammy and Uncle Mose: Black Collectibles and American Stereotyping*. Bloomington: Indiana University Press, 1994.

Gordon, Ian. *Comic Strips and Consumer Culture, 1890–1945*. Washington, D.C.: Smithsonian Institution Press, 1998.

Gowin, Enoch Burton. *The Selection and Training of the Business Executive*. New York: Macmillan, 1918.

"Greetings: 1936 Sales of Christmas and New Year's Cards Expected to Break All Records." *Literary Digest*, 7 November 1936, p. 42.

Grier, Katherine C. *Culture and Comfort: Parlor Making and Middle-Class Identity, 1850–1930*. Washington, D.C.: Smithsonian Institution Press, 1988.

Grossman, John. "The Kiss." *Sky*, January 1998, pp. 62–67.

——. "Life as a Hallmarker." *Sky*, January 1998, p. 65.

Guest, Edgar A. "The Art of Making Friends." *American Magazine*, November 1928, pp. 7–9, 141–43.

Hall, Joyce, with Curtiss Anderson. *When You Care Enough*. Kansas City, Mo: Hallmark, 1979.

"Hallmark Puts Bards to Work Selling Cards." *Advertising Age*, 6 July 1959.

Halttunen, Karen. *Confidence Men and Painted Women: A Study of Middle-Class Culture in America, 1830–1870*. New Haven, Conn.: Yale University Press, 1982.

Harris, Neil. *Cultural Excursions: Marketing Appetites and Cultural Tastes in Modern America*. Chicago: University of Chicago Press, 1990.

Harvard Business School. *Hallmark Cards*. Report of the Harvard Business School. Boston: Harvard Business School Publications, 1986.

——. *Holiday Greetings, Inc. (Abridged)*. Report of the Harvard Business School. Boston: Harvard Business School Publications, 1988.

Harvey, David. *The Condition of Postmodernity: An Inquiry into the Origins of Cultural Change*. Oxford: Blackwell, 1989.

The Heart of the Commonwealth: or, Worcester as it is: being A correct Guide to the Public Buildings and Institutions and to Some of the Principal Manufactories and Shops and Wholesale and Retail Stores in Worcester and Vicinity. Worcester, Mass.: Howland, 1856.

Hendler, Glenn. *Public Sentiments: Structures of Feeling in Nineteenth-Century American Literature*. Chapel Hill: University of North Carolina Press, 2001.

Hirshey, Gerri. "Happy [ ] Day to You." *New York Times Magazine*, 2 July 1995, pp. 20–27, 34, 43–45.

Hochschild, Arlie. *The Commercialization of Intimate Life: Notes from Home and Work*. Berkeley: University of California Press, 2003.

"Holiday Post Cards." *American Stationer*, 23 September 1905, p. 18.

Horton, James Oliver, and Lois E. Horton. *In Hope of Liberty: Culture, Community and Protest Among Northern Free Blacks, 1700–1860*. New York: Oxford University Press, 1997.

"How Chromos Are Made." *Prang's Chromo: A Journal of Popular Art* 1, no. 1 (1868): 1–2.

"How They Greeted Us—With Cards, broadsides, and books, our friends wished us well." *American Printer*, 5 February 1924, p. 25.

Howard, June. *Publishing the Family*. Durham, N.C.: Duke University Press, 2001.

Howells, William Dean. *The Rise of Silas Lapham*. 1885. Reprint. New York: Library of America, 1982.

Hyde, Lewis. *The Gift: Imagination and the Erotic Life of Property*. New York: Vintage Books, 1983.

Hymen's Revenge against Old Maids, Old Bachelors, and Impertenent Coxcombs; or, a New Valentine Writer for the Present Year, Being a Choice Collection of Valentines, Humorous, and Satirical, Chiefly Original Written expressly for this work. London: Kidwell, 1805.

Ilouz, Eva. *Consuming the Romantic Utopia: Love and the Cultural Contradictions of Capitalism*. Berkeley: University of California Press, 1997.

"Industry: Hearts and Profits." *Newsweek*, 18 February 1957, pp. 88–89.

Jacobson, Matthew Frye. *Whiteness of a Different Color: European Immigrants and the Alchemy of Race*. Cambridge, Mass.: Harvard University Press, 1998.

Jameson, Fredric. *Postmodernism, or the Cultural Logic of Late Capitalism*. Durham, N.C.: Duke University Press, 1991.

Jordan, Mary A. "On College Friendships." *Harper's Bazar*, December 1901, pp. 722–27.

"Just How Many Greeting Cards Should a Person Receive This Christmas?" *New York Times*, 5 December 1956.

Kaplan, Amy. *The Social Construction of American Realism*. Chicago: University of Chicago Press, 1988.

Kasson, John. *Rudeness and Civility: Manners in Nineteenth-Century America*. New York: Noonday Press, 1990.

Kelly, Fred C. "Salesmanship and Courtship." *American Magazine*, February 1927, pp. 10–11, 64–65.

Kerber, Linda. "Separate Spheres, Female Worlds, Woman's Place: The Rhetoric of Women's History." *Journal of American History* 75 (1988): 9–39.

Kete, Mary Louise. *Sentimental Collaborations: Mourning and Middle-Class Identity in Nineteenth-Century America*. Durham, N.C.: Duke University Press, 2000.

"The Kind of Friends Who Have Helped Me Most in Business." *American Magazine*, May 1928, pp. 143–45.

King, Mary Britton. "Make Love, Not Work: New Management Theory and the Social Self." *Radical History Review* 76 (2000): 15–24.

Kisseloff, Jeff. "A Half-Century of Quality, Paid for by Greeting Cards." *New York Times*, 31 January 1999, p. 31.

Kwolek-Folland, Angel. *Engendering Business: Men and Women in the Corporate Office, 1870–1930*. Baltimore: Johns Hopkins University Press, 1994.

Lambert, Luna. "The Seasonal Trade: Gift Cards and Chromolithography in America, 1874–1910." Ph.D. diss., George Washington University, 1980.

Lamoreaux, Naomi R. *The Great Merger Movement in American Business, 1895–1904*. New York: Cambridge University Press, 1985.

Lasch, Christopher. *Haven in a Heartless World: The Family Besieged*. New York: Norton, 1977.

"The Law and the Lady." *Chicago Tribune*, 7 May 1919, p. 8.

Lears, T. J. Jackson. *Fables of Abundance: A Cultural History of Advertising in America*. New York: Basic Books, 1994.

——. "Sherwood Anderson: Looking for the White Spot." In Richard Wightman Fox and T. J. Jackson Lears, eds., *The Power of Culture: Critical Essays in American History*, pp.13–37. Chicago: University of Chicago Press, 1993.

Lee, Ruth Webb. *A History of Valentines*. London: Batsford, 1953.

Lemmon, Florence. "Let's Have a Real Christmas Card This Year." *House Beautiful*, December 1925, p. 628.

Lewis, Sinclair. *Lewis at Zenith: Main Street, Babbitt, Arrowsmith*. 1922. Reprint. New York: Harcourt, Brace & World, 1961.

Lhamon, William T. *Raising Cain: Blackface Performance from Jim Crow to Hip Hop*. Cambridge, Mass.: Harvard University Press, 1998.

Lott, Eric. *Love and Theft: Blackface Minstrelsy and the American Working Class*. New York: Oxford University Press, 1993.

Love Points Inscribed to the Valentine Writer by a Green-un. New York: Strong, 1849.

Lowenthal, Leo. *Literature, Popular Culture and Society*. Palo Alto, Calif.: Pacific Books, 1961.

Lowry, Richard. "Domestic Interiors: Boyhood Nostalgia and Affective Labor in the Gilded Age." In Joel Pfister and Nancy Schnog, eds., *Inventing the Psychological: Toward a Cultural History of Emotional Life in America*, pp.110–30. New Haven, Conn.: Yale University Press, 1997.

Lyotard, François. *The Postmodern Condition: A Report on Knowledge*. Translated by Geoff Bennington and Brian Massumi. Minneapolis: University of Minnesota Press, 1984.

Lystra, Karen. *Searching the Heart: Women, Men, and Romantic Love in Nineteenth-Century America*. New York: Oxford University Press, 1989.

"Made First Valentine in United States." *Boston Globe*, 14 February 1901.

Marchand, Roland. *Creating the Corporate Soul: The Rise of Public Relations and Corporate Imagery in American Big Business*. Berkeley: University of California Press, 1998.

Marling, Karal Ann. *Merry Christmas! Celebrating America's Greatest Holiday*. Cambridge, Mass.: Harvard University Press, 2000.

Marzio, Peter. *The Democratic Art: Pictures for a Nineteenth Century America.* Boston: Godine, 1979.

Mauss, Marcel. *The Gift: The Form and Reason for Exchange in Archaic Societies.* Translated by Ian Cunnison. New York: Norton, 1967.

May, Elaine Tyler. *Homeward Bound: American Families in the Cold War Era.* New York: Basic Books, 1988.

McClinton, Katharine Morrison. *The Chromolithographs of Louis Prang.* New York: Potter, 1973.

McEvoy, J. P. *Show Girl.* New York: Simon and Schuster, 1928.

——. *Slams of Life: With Malice for All, and Charity Toward None.* Chicago: Volland, 1919.

McGough, Robert. "Pansies Are Green." *Forbes,* 10 February 1986, pp. 89–92.

McKinley, James. "If You've Got an Ounce of Feeling, Hallmark Has a Ton of Sentiment." *American Heritage* 34 (1982): 71–79.

Means, Carroll Alton. "Embossed and 'Laced' Paper." American Antiquarian Society, Worcester, Mass. Manuscript, n.d.

Merish, Lori. *Sentimental Materialism: Gender, Commodity Culture and Nineteenth-Century American Literature.* Durham, N.C.: Duke University Press, 2000.

Miller, Daniel, ed. *Unwrapping Christmas.* Oxford: Clarendon Press, 1993.

Mills, C. Wright. *White Collar: The American Middle Classes.* New York: Oxford University Press, 1956.

"Miniature of Washington Made Her Kill." *Chicago Tribune,* 6 May 1919, p. 1.

Mintz, Steven, and Susan Kellogg. *Domestic Revolutions: A Social History of American Family Life.* New York: Free Press, 1988.

Mullins, Paul. "The Contradictions of Consumption: An Archaeology of African America and Consumer Culture, 1850–1930." Ph.D. diss, University of Massachusetts, 1996.

Mumford, Lewis. *Technics and Civilization.* 1934. Reprint. New York: Harcourt, Brace & World, 1963.

"My Friendships: What They Have Taught and Brought Me." *Harper's Bazar,* November 1912, p. 548.

Nathan, Hans. *Dan Emmett and the Rise of Early Negro Minstrelsy.* Norman: University of Oklahoma Press, 1977.

"Negro Characters in Current Valentines: Mah Love Am Deeper than the Ocean, Lemme Pour It in Yah Ear." *Philadelphia Tribune,* 5 February 1931, p. 1.

"New Post Cards." *American Stationer,* 14 October 1905, p. 14.

"New Valentines." *American Stationer,* 19 January 1901, p. 4.

Newman, Katherine S. *Falling from Grace: Downward Mobility in the Age of Affluence.* Berkeley: University of California Press, 1988.

Nissenbaum, Steven. *The Battle for Christmas: A Cultural History of America's Most Cherished Holiday.* New York: Vintage Books, 1996.

"Novel Art Goods." *American Stationer*, 29 December 1900, p. 4.

"Off the Record." *Fortune*, November 1931, pp. 10, 16.

Ohmann, Richard. *Selling Culture: Magazines, Markets and Class at the Turn of the Century*. London: Verso, 1996.

"Old Saint Valentine." *American Stationer*, 19 January 1901, p. 1.

"Our New Publishing House." *Paper World* 1 (1880): 3–5.

Papson, Stephen. "From Symbolic Exchange to Bureaucratic Discourse: The Hallmark Greeting Card." *Theory, Culture and Society* 3 (1986): 99–111.

Parsons, Elsie Clews. "Friendship, a Social Category." *American Journal of Sociology* 21 (1915): 230–33.

Parsons, Talcott. "The Kinship System of the Contemporary United States." *American Anthropologist* 45 (1943): 22–38.

"Peaceful Death for George C. Whitney." *Worcester Daily Gazette*, 7 November 1915.

Pendergast, Tom. *Creating the Modern Man: American Magazines and Consumer Culture, 1900–1950*. Columbia: University of Missouri Press, 2000.

Percival, Olive. "Individual Christmas Cards, the Drawings of George Wolfe Plank." *House Beautiful*, December 1914, pp. 20–21.

Peters, Tom. *Liberation Management: Necessary Disorganization for the Nanosecond Nineties*. New York: Knopf, 1992.

Pisano, Ronald G. *A Leading Spirit in American Art: William Merritt Chase, 1849–1918*. Seattle: Henry Art Gallery, 1983.

Poe, Jerry B. *An Introduction to the American Business Enterprise*. 6th ed. Homewood, Ill: Irwin, 1986.

"Post Card Sales." *American Stationer*, 2 September 1905, p. 6.

"The Post Card World." *American Stationer*, 22 January 1910, p. 22.

"Post Cards." *American Stationer*, 26 March 1910, pp. 42–44.

Pulsifer, G. Bishop. "If You Are Not in the Christmas Card Business, You're Missing Something Big." *American Photography*, December 1932, pp. 698–704.

"Record Keeping for Greeting Card Sales." *Giftwares*, August 1958.

Reeves, Earl. "Malice in the Mail Box." *Collier's*, 13 February 1926, p. 19.

"Remember to Send Greeting Cards." *Chicago Defender*, 25 December 1926, pt. 2, p. 3.

Restad, Penne L. *Christmas in America: A History*. New York: Oxford University Press, 1995.

Rittenhouse, Anne. *Greeting Cards: When and How to Use Them*. New York: Greeting Card Association, 1926.

Riviere, Joan. "Womanliness as Masquerade." *International Journal of Psychoanalysis* 10 (1929): 303–12.

Roe, Dorothy. "Sentiment Never Goes Out of Style." *Dover (Ohio) Reporter*, 26 July 1959.

Rogin, Michael. *Blackface, White Noise: Jewish Immigrants in the Hollywood Melting Pot*. Berkeley: University of California Press, 1996.

Romero, Lora. *Home Fronts: Domesticity and Its Critics in the Antebellum United States*. Durham, N.C.: Duke University Press, 1997.

Rourke, Constance. *American Humor*. 1931. Reprint. New York: Doubleday, 1953.

Ruffins, Fath Davis. "Ethnic Imagery in the Landscape of Commerce." In Susan Strasser, Charles McGovern, and Matthias Judt, eds., *Getting and Spending: European and American Consumer Societies in the Twentieth Century*, pp. 379–405. Washington, D.C., and New York: German Historical Institute and Cambridge University Press, 1998.

"St. Valentine and Valentines." *Harper's Weekly*, 13 February 1869, pp. 104–5.

"St. Valentine's Day." *Harper's Weekly*, 21 February 1880, p. 113.

Salade, Robert F. "The Modern Master Printer." *American Printer*, 5 October 1923, p. 41.

Samuels, Shirley, ed. *The Culture of Sentiment: Race, Gender, and Sentimentality in Nineteenth-Century America*. New York: Oxford University Press, 1992.

Sandoval, Chela. *Methodology of the Oppressed*. Minneapolis: University of Minnesota Press, 2000.

Saxon, Wolfgang. "Irving Stone, 90, an Innovator in the Greeting Card Industry." *New York Times*, 19 January 2000, p. C27.

Saxton, Alexander. *The Rise and Fall of the White Republic*. New York: Verso, 1990.

Schell, Erwin. "Analyzing the Executive's Job." In Henry Metcalf, ed., *Business Management as a Profession*, pp. 306–17. Chicago: Shaw, 1927.

Schmidt, Leigh Eric. *Consumer Rites: The Buying and Selling of American Holidays*. Princeton, N.J.: Princeton University Press, 1995.

Schrift, Melissa. "Icons of Femininity in Studio Cards: Women, Communication and Identity." *Journal of Popular Culture* 27 (1994): 111–22.

Sellers, Charles. *The Market Revolution: Jacksonian America, 1815–1846*. New York: Oxford University Press, 1991.

Senge, Peter M. *The Fifth Discipline: The Art and Planning of the Learning Organization*. New York: Doubleday Currency, 1990.

Shank, Barry. "Subject, Commodity, Marketplace: The American Artists Group and the Mass Production of Distinction." *Radical History Review* 76 (2000): 25–52.

Shaw, Frank. "Your Greeting Card Market." *Modern Stationer*, May 1950.

Sittig, Mary Margaret. "L. Prang and Company, Fine Art Publishers." Master's thesis, George Washington University, 1970.

Smith, Adam. *The Theory of Moral Sentiments*. 1759. Reprint. Indianapolis: Liberty Fund Press, 1967.

——. *The Wealth of Nations*. 1776. Reprint. Amherst, N.Y.: Prometheus Books, 1991.

Spears, Timothy B. *100 Years on the Road: The Traveling Salesman in American Culture*. New Haven, Conn.: Yale University Press, 1995.

Sprague, Elizabeth, and Curtiss Sprague. *How to Design Greeting Cards*. Pelham, N.Y.: Bridgman, 1926.

Stacey, Ralph. *Complexity and Creativity in Organizations*. San Francisco: Berrett-Koehler, 1996.

Staff, Frank. *The Picture Postcard and Its Origins*. New York: Praeger, 1966.

Sticker, H. "Character Reading—In one easy lesson for the printing salesman." *American Printer*, March 1928, pp. 66–68.

Storm, Sharon Hartman. *Political Woman: Florence Luscomb and the Legacy of Radical Reform*. Philadelphia: Temple University Press, 2001.

Strong's Annual Valentine Advertiser for St. Valentine's Day, Feb. 14, 1847. New York: Strong, 1847.

Sturgis, Russell. "Chromo-lithographs, American, English, and French." *Nation*, 31 October 1867, p. 352.

——. "Color Printing from Wood and Stone." *Nation*, 10 January 1867, p. 36.

——. "Testimonials in Art and Literature." *Nation*, 19 December 1867, pp. 506–7.

Sunderland, Harry. "Kate's Valentine." *Godey's Lady's Book*, February 1850.

Susman, Warren. *Culture as History*. New York: Pantheon Books, 1984.

Thomas, Brook. *American Literary Realism and the Failed Promise of Contract*. Berkeley: University of California Press, 1997.

Todd, Richard. "We Have Several Tons of Excess Sequins." *Audience*, March–April 1971, pp. 4–11.

Toliver, Susan D. *Black Families in Corporate America*. Thousand Oaks, Calif.: Sage, 1998.

Toll, Robert. *Blacking Up: The Minstrel Show in Nineteenth-Century America*. New York: Oxford University Press, 1974.

Tompkins, Jane. *Sensational Designs: The Cultural Work of American Fiction, 1790–1860*. New York: Oxford University Press, 1985.

Tropman, John E. *The Management of Ideas in the Creating Organization*. Westport, Conn.: Quorum Books, 1998.

Turner, Patricia A. *Ceramic Uncles and Celluloid Mammies: Black Images and Their Influence on Culture*. New York: Anchor Books, 1994.

Veblen, Thorstein. *The Instinct for Workmanship and the State of the Industrial Arts*. 1914. Reprint. New York: Huebsch, 1922.

——. *The Theory of Business Enterprise*. New York: Scribner, 1904.

——. *The Theory of the Leisure Class*. 1899. Reprint. New York: Dover, 1994.

Waits, William B. *The Modern Christmas in America*. New York: New York University Press, 1993.

Ward, Mrs. H. O. *Sensible Etiquette of the Best Society, Customs, Manners, Morals and Homeculture*. Philadelphia: Porter & Coates, 1878.

Warner, W. Lloyd. *The Corporation in the Emergent American Society*. New York: Harper, 1962.

Warner, W. Lloyd, Marchia Meeker, and Kenneth Eells. *Social Class in America: A Manual of Procedure for the Measurement of Social Status*. Chicago: Science Research Associates, 1949.

Weber, Max. *The Protestant Ethic and the Spirit of Modern Capitalism*. Translated by Talcott Parsons. New York: Scribner, 1958.

Weiss, Morry. *American Greetings Corporation*. New York: Newcomen Society, 1982.

Westbrook, Robert B. "'I Want a Girl, Just Like the Girl that Married Harry James': American Women and the Problem of Political Obligation in World War II." *American Quarterly* 42 (1990): 587–614.

Whaley, Deborah. "By Culture, by Merit." Ph.D. diss., University of Kansas, 2001.

White, Elizabeth. "Sentimental Enterprise: Sentiment and Profit in American Market Culture, 1830–1880." Ph.D. diss., Yale University, 1995.

"Whitney's Valentines." *American Stationer*, 4 November 1905, p. 5.

Whittier, John Greenleaf. "Barefoot Boy." In *Whittier's Complete Poems*, pp. 521–22. Boston: Houghton Mifflin, 1892.

Wilentz, Sean. *Chants Democratic: New York City and the Rise of the American Working Class, 1788–1850*. New York: Oxford University Press, 1984.

Williams, Raymond. *Marxism and Literature*. Oxford: Oxford University Press, 1977.

Williamson, Linda. *Playing the Race Card: Melodramas of Black and White from Uncle Tom to O. J. Simpson*. Princeton, N.J.: Princeton University Press, 2001.

Wilson, Christopher. *White Collar Fictions: Class and Social Representation in American Literature, 1885–1925*. Athens: University of Georgia Press, 1992.

"Woman Kills Publisher." *New York Times*, 6 May 1919, p. 10.

Zizek, Slavoj. *The Sublime Object of Ideology*. New York: Verso, 1989.

Zunz, Olivier. *Making America Corporate, 1870–1920*. Chicago: University of Chicago Press, 1990.

——. *Why the American Century?* Chicago: University of Chicago Press, 1998.

Index

Numbers in italics refer to pages on which illustrations appear.